THE VALUE OF MONEY
CONTROVERSIAL ECONOMIC CULTURES IN EUROPE: ITALY AND GERMANY

Preface by
Jean-Claude Trichet

Edited by
C. Liermann Traniello, T. Mayer, F. Papadia, M. Scotto

Bibliographische Information der Deutschen Nationalbibliothek:
Die Deutsche Nationalbibliothek verzeichnet diese Publikation in der Deutschen Nationalbibliographie; detaillierte bibliographische Daten sind im Internet über http://dnb.d-nb.de abrufbar.
© Villa Vigoni Editore | Verlag, Loveno di Menaggio 2021
Tutti i diritti riservati. – Alle Rechte vorbehalten.
www.villavigoni.eu

Assistenza editoriale – Redaktionsarbeit: Manuele Veggi
Impaginazione – Satz: Studio Logos
Stampa – Druck: Grafiche Boffi, Giussano (MB)
Printed in Italy.
ISBN (ITA): 978-88-944986-2-2
ISBN (DE): 978-3-96966-480-3

"With that bequest I intend to pay homage and give new life to the tradition dating back to Enrico Mylius[1] and to Goethe". It was with these words in his will that Ignazio Vigoni (1905-1983) clarified how the memory of the past should constitute the founding element of that "centre of high Italian-German culture", which would be established as a result of his wish to leave his property in Loveno, on Lake Como, to the German Federal Republic. It was precisely from the intuition of Ignazio Vigoni that Villa Vigoni was born, along with the long-lasting commitment by Italy and Germany to create a unique institution for the promotion of the German-Italian relations in a European context. But what was that "tradition" Ignazio Vigoni referred to? This is an obligation that we at Villa Vigoni never stop questioning ourselves about. Above all, we strive to understand how this tradition can guide us in our times and reveal something of today's Europe. A topic that has always fascinated and engaged us in long debates is precisely the one proposed by this book: the controversial economic cultures between Italy and Germany. In fact, we have always wondered why in recent years two countries like Italy and Germany, historically so inclined to the art of market, which presupposes a profound knowledge of the "other", have too often experienced reciprocal misunderstandings when it comes to economics. What disturbs us about these misunderstandings is not the difference between our cultures, which is legitimate and even precious, but rather the lack of profound mutual knowledge that leads to rifts in our relationship. Sadly, we almost had the impression that the cultural and economic spheres, so intrinsically linked, were inextricably moving away from each other, something unnatural in our eyes. In the history of our continent, was not the market one of the primary means to establish solid cultural relations both among European peoples and vis-à-vis the rest of the World? This has certainly been the case from the Mediterranean to the great mercantile routes of northern Europe, and the European Union as we know it today was not by chance born out of an economic community.

Furthermore, we cannot forget that Enrico Mylius, the spiritual founder of Villa Vigoni, who contributed so much to the cultural relations between Italy and Germany in the XIX century, was above all a merchant. For these reasons, we have strongly committed to the creation of this book, with the extreme joy and satisfaction of seeing so many prestiogious scholars believe in our project. In particular, we would like here to extend our heartfelt thanks to the other two editors of the volume, Thomas Mayer and Francesco Papadia, who in months of intense work have built precious bridges between Italy and Germany in the field of cultural economics and economic cultures.

Christiane Liermann Traniello and Matteo Scotto

---

1   Frankfurt am Main 1769, Milan 1854.

Table of Contents

Preface   11
    Jean-Claude Trichet

Introduction   19
    Thomas Mayer, Francesco Papadia

Chapter I
After Bretton Woods: German-Italian Monetary Policy Divergence

Pride and Prejudice in Italy   31
    Fabio Colasanti

The Bundesbank between Bretton Woods and Economic and
Monetary Union — a German Perspective   47
    Ludger Schuknecht

The Banca d'Italia-Tesoro Divorce and the Fascist Legacy   55
    Federico Fubini

Are the Germans Obsessed with Inflation and Central Bank
Independence?   63
    Tobias Piller

Chapter II
Exploring the Reasons of the Alpine Divide

On the Origins of the German and Italian Policy Paradigms
towards European Monetary Integration   75
    Ivo Maes

Exploring the Reasons of the Alpine Divide: Italian and German
Monetary Histories since Unification   83
    Francesco Papadia

The Influence of Economic Schools. The Case of Italy   91
    Pierluigi Ciocca

The Influence of Economic Schools. The Case of Germany   99
    Thomas Mayer

Alpine Divide – Is it Mostly Fiscal?   107
    Hans-Helmut Kotz

Differences between Italian and German Public Finances: a
Long-Term Economic Perspective   121
    Lucio Pench

Chapter III
Approaches to Economic and Monetary Union

The Legacy of the Bundesbank   137
    Otmar Issing

The Legacy of the Banca d'Italia   145
    Lorenzo Codogno

Wrestling with Maastricht in France, Germany and Italy.
The Role of the Intellectual Framework   155
    Daniel Gros

The Turbulent Period around the Time of Maastricht 163
André Sapir

Beyond the Clash of Cultures 171
Gertrude Tumpel-Gugerell

The Euro Crisis: Clash of Cultures? 177
Harold James

Chapter IV
The Way Forward

Monetary, Fiscal and Financial Policy Interactions – Conceptual and
Policy Considerations 187
Klaus Masuch

"Haus, Casa or Maison". The Perfect Opening for Talking about
EMU Architecture 205
Giulio Tremonti

Is the ECB Ready for the Next 20 Years of Monetary Union? 211
Pier Carlo Padoan

The ECB is not Ready for the Next 20 Years of Monetary Union 219
Gunther Schnabl

An International Role for the Euro? 229
Stefano Micossi

The Necessity for a New International Role of the Euro 241
Sabine Seeger

Preface

Jean-Claude Trichet

The Value of Money. Controversial Economic Cultures in Europe: Italy and Germany is a remarkable collective book. It permits to understand better the unique historic euro monetary endeavour for three reasons. First, it integrates the multiple angles of vision on monetary union offered by eminent academics and remarkable personalities having been active in making it. Second, it explores with great pertinence the layers of the historic project, whether monetary, economic, cultural or political. Last, but not least, in organizing a dialogue between Germany and Italy, it explores two major components in the fabric of the Euro area.

In many simplified visions, Germany and Italy are presented respectively as the North and South Poles of the single currency area. The emblematic protestant sanctuary of monetary stability and sound ordoliberalism management on the one hand, the catholic chapel where monetary laxism, fiscal and macroeconomic "laissez-faire" would find refuge on the other hand. From that bipolar presentation, it is frequently argued that such oppositions are deeply rooted in the history of the two countries, in their underlying values, in their cultural DNA.

A great value of the book is to show that such narratives make no justice to many facts that are known but forgotten, little known or not known at all. For instance, that the lira was more stable than the German currency during some long periods of times. That the lira never experienced hyperinflation. That Italy invented the double entry system of accounting and largely created financial capitalism. Also, that the independence of the Bundesbank was designed by the Allies after World War II and that Chancellor Konrad Adenauer was profoundly irritated by this independence.

Equally, that the success of Germany and the Deutschemark after World War II was not only remarkable but a powerful emblematic symbol of political turnaround. That the successive leaders of the Bundesbank proved from the inception of the Institution a great degree of lucidity and political courage. Or that a high degree of frankness in the German public debate, with pros and cons being exposed openly, should not be confused with unilateral aggressivity vis-à-vis countries in need: after all the heated debates, when help was needed, successive governments and the German Bundestag were always on board to participate.

Let me mention personal memories: I had the privilege to negotiate the Maastricht Treaty with Horst Köhler and Mario Draghi. The three of us were "Staatssekretäre" and director generals of our respective Treasuries. The three of us were representing our governments and bringing our ways of thinking, our values. The three of us were profoundly dedicated Europeans.

Another great privilege when I came to the European central bank was to work with Otmar Issing and Tommaso Padoa-Schioppa, eminent members of the Executive Board of the ECB, responsible respectively for economics and international affairs. They were eminent professionals, deeply cultivated, bringing Goethe and Dante in the conversation and as dedicated as courageous Europeans.

And it is a pleasure to have yet another occasion of a professional interaction with Francesco Papadia, one of the editors of the book, who carried out standard and non-standard monetary policy measures during my tenure as ECB President.

In the heat of the great financial crisis, when I had to explain and defend the new unseen (at the time) non-standard measures, I referred several times to Max Weber's famous distinction between ethic of conviction and ethic of responsibility. I am quoting what I said in August 2010 at Jackson Hole: "The ethic of conviction makes the decision-maker find his essence in the constancy of his inner relation to certain ultimate value. There must be therefore a full integrity between intention and action. [...] According to the ethic of responsibility, actions have to be analysed in terms of their consequences, taking account of their causal relationship to the empirical world. The stress is put therefore on the integrity between action and consequences".[1] At the time, I presented standard policy measures as associated with ethic of conviction and non-standard measures with ethic of responsibility. From that standpoint, Max Weber is luminous in my eyes when he says: "The ethic of conviction and the ethic of responsibility are no absolute opposites. They are complementary to one another".

Needless to say, in this extraordinary demanding period of crisis, the German intuition was inclining more to the ethic of conviction and the Italian preference was more on the side of the ethic of responsibility. We needed both: they were clearly complementary.

This is not to deny that in the great financial crisis, Germany proved a superior degree of resilience and Italy a particular vulnerability. But in this respect, I would like to stress a peculiar cultural difference, which has in my opinion, very little to do with

---

1   "Central banking in uncertain times: conviction and responsibility", speech by Jean-Claude Trichet at the symposium on *Macroeconomic challenges: the decade ahead* (Jackson Hole, Wyoming, 27 August 2010).

protestant ordoliberalism on the German side and of catholic laxism on the Italian side. It relates to the present dominant culture of social partners in the two countries.

In Italy, the social partners playing a kind of role model are often enterprises that are in the public sector – or were in the public sector – and unions used to negotiations in the public sector, including the civil service. In such an environment, isolated from considerations relating to competition issues in the domestic and foreign markets, negotiations appear very much as a zero-sum game. It is perfectly legitimate for the unions and employees to get the maximum level of wages and salary increases. It is not for them to internalize the consequences of the negotiation for the overall competitiveness of the entity concerned. Any additional gains appear good not only for the employees but also for society as a whole. To the eyes of the employees, in a simplified approach, these additional gains will activate demand, foster growth and contribute to economic prosperity. It goes without saying that there are also many remarkable corporate businesses in Italy that are plunged in tough competition in their domestic markets and abroad. In such firms, entrepreneurs and employees are fully aware of the necessity to maintain appropriate cost competitiveness in order to preserve market share, consolidate jobs and create new jobs. But it does not seem that the influence of these social partners is able to challenge the dominant culture of social negotiations in the country as a whole.

In Germany, two factors contribute to a different culture: First, the size of the competitive part of the economy, more particularly of the manufacturing sector in comparison with the rest of the economy; Second, the fact that the German economy is massively exporting and that a very large proportion of businesses have a direct experience of the fierce competition in foreign markets. As a consequence, it is not surprising that the culture of social partners in exporting private firms is the dominant culture of social partners in the society as a whole. This is not to say that there is no public sector in Germany or that there are no businesses that are protected from the heat of competition. But their culture is in a minority position. The dominant culture of social partners considers natural that a common goal of entrepreneurs, unions and employees is the competitiveness of the firm. In this culture, it is appropriate to accept cost moderation, including wage moderation, if it appears necessary to preserve and reinforce the market share of the firm and, therefore, to preserve today's jobs and pave the way to create new jobs.

If this analysis carries part of the truth, it explains why the dominant culture in Italy would push for more cost increases than would be required in terms of optimal cost competitiveness. In Germany, we observe the reverse. The influence of the dominant culture contributes to preserving and reinforcing cost competitiveness of corporate businesses and of the economy as a whole.

Such a persistent structural difference between Italy and Germany helps explaining what has been observed both before the euro and in the time of the single currency.

First, before the euro inception. We have part of the explanation why the lira had to depreciate or devalue (when in the exchange rate mechanism) frequently vis-à-vis the Deutschemark. Feeling the persistent push upward of its costs in lira, Italy would have to re-establish an appropriate level of cost competitiveness through successive downward realignments. By the virtue of its social partners culture, Germany was in a permanent excellent competitive position calling for periodic appreciation (or re-evaluation when in an exchange rate mechanism) of the Deutschemark.

To sum up in a simplified but economically pertinent mode: the Deutschemark was nominally strong but competitive, i.e. weak, in real terms, most of the time; the lira was nominally weak but uncompetitive, i.e. strong in real terms, most of the time. These two paradoxes were often difficult to understand by public opinion. How can a strong currency give a high level of competitiveness to its economy despite frequent re-evaluation? How can a weak currency never fully catch up its previous losses of cost competitiveness despite devaluations? The key is to examine the evolution of all nominal costs in the economy: wages and salaries, unit labour costs, nominal costs, national inflation. If nominal costs are increasing slowly with a significant degree of moderation, we have the response to the first question. If they have a permanent tendency to increase rapidly, one has the response to the second question.

Second, after the euro introduction. There can be no more realignments between Italy and Germany. But there are still different national nominal costs and prices evolutions, expressed in euro, in the two member countries. As was the case with different currencies without realignment, a relative moderation or a relative acceleration of nominal costs signal, respectively, reinforcement or deterioration of the cost competitiveness of the economy concerned.

As previously noted, the overall competitiveness of an economy does not depend only on its cost competitiveness. Many important elements are of a non-cost nature. The reinforcement of the competitive position of an economy in the medium and long run depends in particular on its capacity to improve total factor and labour productivity. All things being equal, the more productivity augments, the more room there is for an increase of nominal wages. To the extent that productivity levels and productivity gains are low and have been low in Italy for a long period, there is an important space for improvement in the future. That being said, if unit labour costs (incorporating both nominal wages and salaries increases, and labour productivity progress) augment too rapidly the deterioration of the cost competitive position is unavoidable.

In my understanding, the overall influence of the dominant social partners' culture is important but there are also circumstances where they can be put aside, at least for a certain period of time. This happened both in the case of Germany and in the case of Italy before the euro.

As regards Germany, the reunification of the country led to a considerable Keynesian expansion, an increase of national demand of historic proportion and, as an unavoidable consequence, a very significant increase of unit labour costs. Inflation picked up in the country, cost competitiveness deteriorated significantly. As a way of consequence, the trade balance markedly deteriorated and a high current account deficit was posted. The German economy was in an abnormally low competitive position at the start of the euro.

In the second half of the 90's, Italy was in exactly the reverse situation. After having decided that the country should be in the first train of the euro, everything was done in Roma to reach that strategic goal, whatever the difficulties associated with the starting point and the ambition of the Maastricht Treaty criteria as regards inflation and overall fiscal deficit. Contrary to what is often said, the entry point in the euro, namely the cross rate between lira and Deutschemark, was balanced in terms of cost competitiveness, if not to the advantage of the Italian economy. The difficulty came after the start of the euro. Conscious of its loss of competitiveness due to reunification, there was a consensus in Germany to catch up and be back to the pre-unification situation. What I qualify as the dominant culture of German social partners considerably helped in this respect. This was the case before, as well as after the wave of structural reforms launched by Gerhard Schröder in 2003.

As a matter of fact, cost moderation has been constant and persistent in Germany since the start of the euro. A rule of thumb would suggest that the German economy had totally erased its former lack of competitiveness vis-à-vis the average euro area in 2007, before the beginning of the great financial crisis. Italy followed exactly the reverse path. Having followed policies aiming at reinforcing competitiveness before the euro, it considered that, after its introduction, it could rely on the normal spontaneous functioning of its economy. This important change of attitude was generalized in the Euro area. Most of the countries having joined in were relaxing their fiscal policies, encouraged by the position of Germany and France in 2003-2004. Perhaps even more consequentially, they decided, like Italy, to abandon the "competitive disinflation" motto that they had recommended in the run up to the euro.

This explains why the ECB documented a phenomenon which looked dangerous since the inception of the euro: Competitiveness indicators, like the evolution of unit labour costs and external imbalances, were signalling persistent divergences between member countries. Since 1999, Germany has steadily improved its competitive position vis-à-vis the average of the Euro area. Italy and many other countries had deteriorated their relative competitive position year after year from the introduction of the euro and until the 2009-2010 crisis.

This explains why, in my position as president of the ECB, I called upon governments and European institutions, since 2005 and up to the sovereign crisis in 2010, to monitor very closely the national competitiveness indicators, cost indicators as well as external balances and prevent them to be persistently divergent. Unfortunately, no attention was paid to this call until the crisis erupted. In the crisis, the necessity to introduce a new pillar of governance was recognized in autumn 2011 with the setting up of the Macroeconomic Imbalance Procedure (MIP), which entered into force on December 13, 2011. I said often publicly that I considered the MIP as important as the Stability and Growth Pact (SGP) to ensure the long-term cohesion of the Euro area.

Going back to Italy and Germany, and the difference between their social partners cultures, one would expect a relatively frequent issuance of the following MIP recommendations in "normal times".

To Italy: "Beware of your tendency to lose competitiveness, including cost competitiveness, in comparison with the average of the Euro area. Your competitive position has already been eroded. It is important that you embark on a recovery of lost competitiveness. This should be pursued through many actions. Amongst the most important ones are the progress of productivity on the one hand and the moderation of unit labour cost on the other hand, so that their increase would be below the average of the area. By way of consequence your national inflation should be below the average of the Euro area for a certain period of time".

To Germany: "Beware of your tendency to improve permanently your competitive position, including your cost competitiveness, vis-à-vis the average of the Euro area. In the medium and long run, all economies that are members of the Euro area must oscillate around the average cost competitiveness of the single currency area. Good management of the private corporate sector, productivity progress, elimination of non-productive spending justify higher national real growth and higher standards of living. But national unit labour cost increases cannot be systematically below average. Even more when a country is in a highly competitive position inside the Euro area and is posting an important current account surplus. In such an economy, it would be appropriate for the unit labour costs to grow faster than the average of the area. By way of consequence, it would be appropriate for the national inflation rate to be higher than the average of the area".

This last remark is extremely important. A highly competitive national economy must give room for the other members to be able to improve their own relative competitiveness inside the area. In terms of cost competitiveness, these necessary improvements require unit labour cost increases and national rates of inflation in these less competitive economies to be lower than average. And naturally, lower than in the highly competitive economy, whose unit labour cost increase and national rate of inflation signal a *de facto* ceiling for the entire Euro area. This entails considerable consequences for monetary policy. Inflation in the area is the weighted average of all national inflations. This requires half of the weighted average to be higher and the other half to be lower than the stable inflation objective. The central bank cannot fulfil its primary mandate of price stability if at any time the de facto ceiling is at or lower than the objective.

In this book, Germany and Italy are emblematic illustrations of the situations in which all other countries are placed over a medium and long period of time. As an average, half of the time, the national inflation of a particular economy must be over the target and below target the other half of the time. This is true for all economies. This balance should be attained without crisis, domestic or external shocks. The collective success of the single currency depends on its capacity to agree on a governance of the area, which would deliver such individual and collective balances over time.

It is a big challenge for the Euro area economic governance and more particularly for the Macroeconomic Imbalance Procedure. The procedure has to tell Italy that its national inflation should be below 2% half of the time over the long term. It has to tell Germany that its own inflation should be higher than 2% half of the time. In both cases, this runs counter to the present social partners' dominant culture. Not only these recommendations of the Commission and the Council would contribute to the long-term cohesion, prosperity and success of the single currency area in terms of price stability, but they have to be explained thoroughly to public opinion in all countries. We are in a domain where full understanding by social partners and public opinion at large is, in my eyes, absolutely of the essence.

Introduction

Thomas Mayer and Francesco Papadia

When the Bretton Woods system crumbled, and currencies lost their direct link to the dollar and their indirect link to gold, Germany and Italy embarked upon strongly different monetary policies. The divergence was reflected in the evolution of the exchange rates: the German currency rose from 170 lira under Bretton Woods parities to 990 Italian lira per D-Mark at the start of European Monetary Union. A stunning devaluation of the Italian relative to the German currency: about 83 percent! What is behind this development? Does it reflect opposite theoretical concepts and historically constant differences in the institutional setup and the implementation mode of monetary policy? Is there an insurmountable Alpine divide between Italy and Germany that will jeopardize EMU's future?

We have invited 22 experts, mostly from Germany and Italy, to give their views. The essays collected in this book do not pretend to give definitive answers to these questions. However, we can discern from the contributions a few hints. First, there is a difference in the emphasis on rules relative to discretion, which some commentators refer to as a "clash of cultures". It will not come as a surprise to readers that German commentators put more emphasis on rules than Italian ones. Second, and related to the first, there are some differences of view on the relationship between monetary and fiscal policies. While in the Italian approach monetary-fiscal policy cooperation is considered very important, some (but by no means all) German commentators stress the need for monetary dominance. Third, the Italian view is more strongly in favour of putting the central bank in charge of banking supervision. Fourth, there is broad agreement that social and structural economic factors have been important in shaping attitudes towards money and monetary integration in both countries, with German commentators stressing the experience of hyperinflation after WWI and some Italian ones the fascist legacy after WWII. Fifth, some German commentators seem to take a somewhat more skeptical view on the future of EMU than their Italian counterparts. At the same time, however, there is also a considerable overlap of views north and south of the Alps in all contributions. Hence, our key takeaway from the collected essays is that crossing the Alps is not easy, but possible.

In the remainder of this section we give a brief review of the contributions, following their respective narratives rather than their order of appearance in the chapters.

Tobias Piller, Ludger Schuknecht and Otmar Issing discuss the evolution of the Bundesbank as the domestically and internationally highly respected guardian of the D-Mark. During its relatively short history, the D-Mark became the second-most important international reserve currency and the anchor for many European currencies. However, the Bundesbank was feared by some as "the bank that rules Europe", beyond any explicit decision to this effect. Piller identifies the trauma of German Hyperinflation in 1923 as a loadstar for the Bundesbank's post-WWII policy and explains, from this vantage point, the skeptical attitude among many Germans towards the more recent evolution of the policies of the European Central Bank. He also writes of an apparent "obsession" of Germans for price stability and an independent central bank, which gives a sense of the depth of attachment to their currency and central bank, as does the reference by Issing to a "pathological relation" of Germans with their currency.

Ludger Schuknecht shows how the Bundesbank managed to achieve monetary dominance and navigated relatively successfully through the inflationary 1970s. Against this background, it went to great length to enshrine monetary dominance also in the design of the European Economic and Monetary Union. However, both Schuknecht and Piller are skeptical on the preservation of the legacy of the Bundesbank in EMU. "The integration process remains incomplete. This makes it much harder for the ECB to promote monetary dominance than it was for the Deutsche Bundesbank", Schuknecht warns. As it will be seen below, Gunther Schnabl pushes this pessimism one step further, arguing that the gradual transformation of the European Central Bank from a German-type into a French-Italian-type central bank makes it "anything but ready for the next 20 years of monetary union".

Otmar Issing agrees that the successful start of EMU and the credibility which the ECB and the euro enjoyed from the beginning would not have been possible without the widely shared view that the new European central bank was modelled on the German central bank. But he warns that it would be misleading to see the ECB as a clone of the Bundesbank. The European Central Bank has a much broader constituency than the Bundesbank had. Issing, however, rather than reaching the concerned conclusions of Piller and Schuknecht about the quasi-inevitable withering of the Bundesbank values, calls for their preservation through "transparency and wise decisions".

Thomas Mayer points to the post-WWII emergence of a liberal economic order, in the spirit of the "Freiburg Ordo-Liberal School", as a major contributor to Germany's "economic miracle" and the ascendance of the Bundesbank. In line with the ordo-liberal tenets, Ludwig Erhard, the country's first Minister of Economics and later Chancellor, firmly believed that economic policy should provide the institutional framework and sound money for private economic activities, while refraining from meddling in these activities. Mayer fears that these principles have been lost in the course of the Financial and Coronavirus Crises.

Pierluigi Ciocca sets the long process of monetary unification in a broader, long-term picture of the Italian economy. His perspective is definitely an Italian one, but it is not so different from that taken by Hans Helmut Kotz, as will be seen below. In particular he stresses that the desire of Banca d'Italia to achieve monetary stability was often frustrated by incompatible fiscal, wage and structural developments. In terms of intellectual underpinnings, Ciocca stresses the diversity of economic models used by the bank but also the rigour of its methodological approach, combining into what he denotes as "theoretically careful and empirically grounded eclecticism". Ciocca also finds the main limit of the Bundesbank model in its disregard for Keynes' main insight, that, investment oriented, fiscal expansion is, in some circumstances, essential.

Lorenzo Codogno presents "some stylised considerations on how the experience and history of the Banca d'Italia over the decades before monetary union helped it in the design and actual construction of the European Central Bank and in shaping how the monetary union has developed". He stresses that one critical component of the Banca d'Italia experience, since its foundation in 1893, was the need to consider jointly the macroeconomy and the banking sector. It is on the basis of this experience that Tommaso Padoa-Schioppa insisted that financial regulation and supervision should be unified in a monetary union and that supervision should, contrary to the Bundesbank model, be the responsibility of the central bank. It is a pity that he would unexpectedly die before seeing this development come true, with generalized support. Banca d'Italia was also keenly aware of the importance of a sound institutional framework, to which it contributed over the decades. Codogno also stresses, along similar lines as those developed by Ciocca and Kotz, that "monetary policy alone was not enough to stabilise the system" and that the quest of Banca d'Italia for stability was frequently impaired by imprudent fiscal and wage policies as well as external shocks.

Giulio Tremonti takes, consistently with his long government experience, a fully political approach to the issue of EMU architecture. To argue his point, he looks at three periods: The Age of Peace (1943–89), The Age of Globalization (1992–2007) and The Age of Crisis (2008–20). He is particularly critical of the prevailing narrative during the Globalization Age, emphasizing that he, among other Italians, stressed the "dark side" of globalization. Basically, his criticism is that there was too much emphasis on economic, rather than broader societal and political, factors and too little governance of the process. Thus, the Age of Globalization nurtured the Age of Crisis. An episode that Tremonti recalls in vivid terms is the Trichet-Draghi letter of 5 August 2011, addressed to Prime Minister Berlusconi, that he identifies as a soft "coup d'état". Tremonti welcomes the European response to the COVID crisis in the fiscal domain: both the suspension of the budgetary rules and the Recovery and Resilience Fund. But he stresses that this is not enough, and even the euro is not enough. He calls for more: "what is needed in the growing vacuum forming around the euro is politics". And this must include a "common European commitment to, and investment in, defence and security".

Federico Fubini starts his contribution with a bang: "the 'divorce', that freed Banca d'Italia from any obligation to buy newly-issued government bonds in excess of market demand, was a failure". This is a conclusion at variance with a number of other contributions in this volume, such as Codogno and Kotz. The rest of his article is dedicated to supporting this surprising conclusion. The basic arguments that he develops, matching long but illuminating quotations from Mussolini speeches with utterances from representatives of democratic Italy, is that Italy has maintained, albeit under a different and less visible guise, the corporatist culture developed by Fascism. The "divorce" succeeded in the narrow monetary area but failed in a broader context as it did not, indeed could not, really break the corporatist approach prevailing in Italy. This is a critical difference between Italy and Germany: in the latter country the Allies, after the end of the war, dismantled Nazi economic institutions, but they did not do the same in Italy, letting Fascist institutions survive.

Harold James starts by comparing the northern, "Germanic" economic philosophy with the southern, "Latin" philosophy: the northern vision is about rules, the southern one emphasizes discretion. However, he notes that the division between the two views is also visible within countries: the German government eventually abandoned its moral hazard concerns and supported the action of the ECB breaking the spiral of the Euro Crisis; some parts of Italian public opinion supported the strategy of "tying hands", aimed at gaining the credibility that purely discretionary policies could not reach. The Euro Crisis led to a clash of cultures, which manifested itself first in the question of what sort of rules were needed to prevent rescue operations from creating moral hazard and then of who made and enforced the rules. The clash ended in a revulsion of the principle of conditionality, which became clear in the Coronavirus crisis. The question of "how to build consensus and civil community" remains open, says James.

Gertrude Tumpel-Gugerell takes up the issue of "clashes of culture" dealt with by James, making it more operational. Indeed, she identifies four such clashes which economic policy in the euro-area had to confront. All of them have to do with the definition of the responsibility of national with respect to European institutions and, specifically, in three of the four cases, with the responsibility of the central bank. The first clash is whether the central bank should intervene when negative developments in the bond market of one or the other member of the euro area endanger monetary union. The second clash of culture has to do with the division of responsibilities between national and European fiscal policy, in particular in crisis times. The third clash of culture is about the role of the central bank in assuring the stability of the financial sector, as opposed to the responsibilities of private agents and national governments. The fourth clash of culture relates to the responsibility of the central bank in stabilizing aggregate demand. Tumpel-Gugerell does not provide her definitive view on these four clashes of culture, but stresses the need to understand and bridge these cultural differences and offers her article as a contribution in this direction.

Fabio Colasanti dwells on the attitude of public opinion in Italy towards Germany and, in particular, the Bundesbank. He illustrates how legitimate complaints, exaggerations or genuine fake stories came about, stressing the need to understand the first while debunking the second and the third. The economic difficulties of Italy, in the nominal field in the 1970s, 1980s and 1990s and in the real field more recently, "created a strong reaction – a mixture of envy and an inferiority complex – that led a large part of the Italian public to seek out an explanation in events taking place outside of the country and to thereby find foreign scapegoats. Many felt that it could not be that Italy, with its incredible cultural past, was doing so badly economically and socially". One case of gradual development of a fake story reported by Colasanti is about "Italy having paid for German reunification", where the true fact that interest rates in Europe were too high because of the consequences of reunification morphed in the view that Italy had actually financially contributed to the cost of German reunification.

Ivo Maes elaborates on the internal dimension of the differences towards European monetary integration, expanding the point made by James about differences within both Germany and Italy. Foreign policy views and makers were crucial in both countries in charting the EMU project at history making junctures, like the creation of the EMS and the Maastricht treaty. The foreign policy paradigms that informed the views and behaviour of the political authorities, in Germany and Italy, were shaped by widespread pro-European attitudes and a federalist approach, deeply rooted in the history of both countries. The prime ministers of both Germany and Italy followed the foreign policy views at the crucial moments of the construction of monetary union. In contrast, the institutional framework of EMU was strongly shaped by the economic policymakers, in particular the Bundesbank. These policymakers were, especially but not exclusively in Germany, much more skeptical.

Francesco Papadia asks whether the higher monetary stability in Germany than in Italy after the collapse of the Bretton Woods system is a constant feature in the monetary history of the two countries. The answer is a definite no: since their national unification in the second half of the nineteenth century and until nowadays, even disregarding the German hyperinflation of 1923 and the instability during the years preceding the 1948 monetary reform, there has been less monetary stability in Germany than in Italy. The concrete implication Papadia draws from this result is that there is no ineluctable failure in merging into a single currency countries with very different monetary histories. What is critical is that the variables setting monetary policy, and in all likelihood fiscal policy as well, are appropriately chosen. The fact that Italy and Germany have never had as much monetary stability in their national history as they are having with the euro is an encouraging sign in this respect.

André Sapir points out that, although France and Italy had different internal dynamics, they defended the same "monetarist" approach during the Maastricht negotiation, which held that nominal convergence was not an indispensable precondition for monetary union and that the credibility of the new common central bank would achieve the objective of price stability regardless of past economic performance by the members of the monetary union. By contrast the "economist school", sponsored mainly by Germany and the Netherlands, insisted that monetary union could only come as the final 'coronation' after a successful process of economic convergence. The Maastricht agreement was a compromise between the monetarist position, with a strict timetable for the introduction of the single currency, and the economist position, asking for strict convergence criteria before adopting the single currency. Sapir also notes that actual policy performance is more important than formal declarations. So, Denmark, after having obtained an opt-out in the Maastricht Treaty that did not oblige it to adopt the euro, had no problem in maintaining its currency inside the Exchange Rate Mechanism during the 1992 crisis, because of its commitment to prudent policies. Italy, instead, while committed to adopt the euro, entered the crisis in precarious conditions and with a domestically divided attitude towards exchange rate stability, finally succumbing to market pressure.

Daniel Gros stresses the importance that economic models had in determining the budgetary rules in EMU. To be sure, there was a discussion between Germany on the one side, and France and Italy on the other: political leaders in the former country wanted an assurance that fiscal policies would remain prudent, while those in the latter two countries wanted to preserve the freedom to run larger deficits. However, the latter lost out in the debate because the underlying intellectual framework of the time – inspired preeminently by US academics, but also eagerly adopted by central bankers and some economists in Italy – saw little value in discretionary fiscal policy and emphasised the importance of 'rules versus discretion'. This was particularly important in a monetary union encompassing a number of sovereign countries, where external effects of domestic fiscal policies are particularly strong, while one cannot count on financial markets disciplining imprudent fiscal policies.

Hans-Helmut Kotz starts from an illustration of the secular fiscal developments in Italy and Germany, noting that the behaviour of fiscal variables was similar until the late 1960s. Since that time developments were very different, while responding, in both countries, to social pressures: fiscal developments are not exogenous policy variables, but the product of deeper, underlying phenomena. In particular differences in institutions governing or impacting labor markets and the way to solve conflicts about income distribution have consequences for both fiscal and monetary policy. Banca d'Italia had the same desire to achieve price stability as the Bundesbank, but was confronted with different, less favourable trade-offs. According to Kotz, internal structural economic differences between Italy and Germany, and not the Alps, are the dividing line. The difference in monetary developments in Germany and Italy between the demise of the Bretton Woods period and the birth of the euro has ultimately deeper reasons than just fiscal developments.

Lucio Pench carries out a forensic analysis of public finance developments in Italy and Germany since the beginning of the 1960s identifying five periods: the 1960s, the 1970s, 1980-mid 1990, mid 1990-2007 and 2008-2020. While in the 1960s, as also noted by Kotz, the two countries had similar fiscal developments, the 1970s saw the beginning of the differentiation between Italian and German developments. In the 1980-mid 1990 period both countries, albeit with different success, tried to regain monetary stability but "the pursuit of nominal convergence coincided, however, with an explosion of the divergence in the public debt trajectories of the two countries". In the second half of the 1990s and until the beginning of the Great Financial Crisis in 2007, the Great Moderation was visible in both Italy and Germany, and nominal stability was this time accompanied by a convergence, albeit partial, of Italian public debt towards the level prevailing in Germany. In the last period, Italian public debt first grew, then stabilized before jacking up again when the COVID-19 crisis struck. Pench then illustrates how the initial push towards higher debt levels caused by primary deficits between 1960 and 1990 perversely interacted with the "snowballing effect", in later periods, given by a nominal cost of debt higher than income growth, making the Italian attempts at stabilizing the debt-to-income ratio a kind of Sisyphus torture, while Germany's fiscal situation remained overall much more stable.

Klaus Masuch investigates the interaction between monetary and fiscal policy, stressing the need for them to work "hand in hand". Indeed, in his view, policy cooperation has become more important as interest rates have approached the lower boundary (which may be below zero) and monetary policy alone has become less effective as a result. With this approach, Masuch goes beyond the stark alternative between fiscal and monetary dominance, proposing a more articulated policy set-up, in which the two policies exploit, so to say, their comparative advantages. This creates, however, problems in a monetary union, where the central bank has to deal with multiple sovereign fiscal entities. In an environment of very high sovereign debt in a few countries, debt restructuring or a tax on private wealth may have to come on the agenda to pave the way for future economic growth.

How will EMU cope with the numerous challenges already visible today or coming up in the next 20 years? Gunther Schnabl comes to the definitive conclusion that EMU, and specifically the ECB, is not up to the task. The basic reason is that "[…] the common central bank was gradually transformed from a German-type into a French-Italian-type central bank model", less and less trusted. It is remarkable that this conclusion is diametrically opposite to that of Ciocca according to whom "many Italian economists therefore miss the pre-1998 Banca d'Italia, which in many respects they linked to the Fed". In addition, the central bank is now burdened with additional tasks "such as stabilizing the financial system, safeguarding the euro and even protecting the climate". He identifies the euro as a straightjacket in a much less than optimal currency area, which suffers from significant divergence in real economic developments. While a break-up of the euro-area "would help a return to the pre-euro currency competition, which would foster growth and welfare in Europe", it would also lead to strong turbulences in financial markets and growing political uncertainty. As intermediate solution, Schnabl demands more exchange rate flexibility, possibly through the introduction of national parallel currencies alongside the euro.

Pier Carlo Padoan offers a conditional answer to the question whether the ECB is ready for the next 20 years of monetary union, quite in contrast with the much more definitive, negative, view of Schnabl. Padoan looks at developments in the euro-area from an economic policy perspective, consistently with his experience as economic minister, but not forgetting the analytical perspective of the former economics professor. Consistently with the history-oriented conclusions of Ciocca, Codogno and Kotz, Padoan stresses that "monetary policy alone cannot bear the burden of supporting the EZ economy. ECB action must be complemented with fiscal and structural policies". In the fiscal area, in particular, Padoan sees the need for a common fiscal capacity. The Next Generation EU plan is a welcome, significant step in this direction. However, the "ECB will be ready for the next two decades of monetary union also to the extent that the contribution of policies other than monetary policy will take on a larger role than in the past in the support to growth and stability". This will also allow the ECB to gradually unwind its unconventional policies.

Sabine Seeger takes a normative approach to the question of the international role of the euro. She explains how the euro has already established some of the conditions leading to an international role: its stability, the substantial advances on banking union, the large economy that it serves but is at the same time its basis, its second place, after the dollar, as international currency, its use as a linchpin for a number of currencies outside of the euro-area, the changing attitude towards the international role of the euro by euro-area governments as well as the European Central Bank. In prospective terms the Next Generation EU plan can likewise reinforce the international role of the euro. Seeger also notices, however, the remaining limitations hampering a wider international role for the euro, recalling the missing "unions" identified by the five Presidents report of 2015. Seeger does not shy away from noting, as also Tremonti concluded, that a common foreign and security policy is also needed to fully support an international role for the euro. At the end, however, there is a tone of confidence in her article that, although gradually, Europe will be able to establish the basis for a stronger international role of the euro.

Stefano Micossi shares much of the analysis of Seeger, but he adds a critical question: do "we Europeans really want this greater international role for our common currency, given its broader implications for internal macro-economic and regulatory policies"? If the desire was there, the preconditions for this greater role for the euro could be, although in a progressive way and with some difficulties, created. As also noted by Seeger, the euro is clearly the second most important international currency, albeit at quite some distance from the dollar. The euro area economy is large and open, but its capital market has not grown, in size and sophistication, as the Capital Markets Union project promised. An asset with the liquidity and the size of the America treasury paper is still missing and various initiatives to gradually create it have not led to decisive progress as yet. While the outstanding hurdles could be surpassed, with sufficient determination and common engagement, Micossi confesses his inability to answer the question whether Europeans really want their currency to take a larger global role. Hence the remaining question mark to the title of his article.

Chapter I

After Bretton Woods:

German-Italian Monetary Policy Divergence

Pride and Prejudice in Italy

Fabio Colasanti[1]

Italian economic policy changed significantly during the fifty years since the end of the Bretton Woods system (August 1971). As policy moved progressively towards macro-economic stabilisation and towards monetary union in the nineties, the importance of exchange rate stability grew, together with the constraints that it entailed. At the same time, the increase in economic integration within western Europe and the reluctance of the United States to resume the responsibilities it had under the Bretton Woods System, meant more and more exchange rate stability within Europe. This implied the acknowledgment of the growing importance of Germany as an economic partner and that of its currency as the hub of any exchange rate policy.[2] This was the period in which Italians started to perceive the Bundesbank as "the bank that ruled Europe"[3] and Germany's economic policy as the de facto reference for Europe.

---

1   Fabio Colasanti is an economist who spent many years with the European Commission. He headed the department called "Enterprise" from January 2000 to June 2002 and, from July 2002 to March 2010, he was in charge of the department for "Information Society and Media". This second department's task was the development of European regulatory policies for electronic communications and for the audio-visual sector as well as the control of their application in the Member states. The department was also in charge of promoting the take up of Information and Communication Technologies throughout the EU.
Previously, he had spent almost twenty years working on economic and monetary issues during the years of the European Monetary System and the period leading to the creation of the European monetary union. In 1985-87, he was a member of the European Commission's "Spokesman's Group" and, in 1999, he was the deputy head of the office of the President of the European Commission, Romano Prodi.
At the beginning of 2010 he became member of an international group tasked with the elaboration of proposals for the future of ICANN and the definition of its role in managing the internet.
From April 2010 to March 2016, he was the president of the International Institute of Communications (London, UK). From 2014 to 2020 he was a member of the Board of Rai Way (a company listed on the Italian stock exchange). He is also one of the organizers of the Villa Vigoni 'Vigonomics' seminar on the euro.

2   One of the first official and explicit recognitions of this fact can be found in the speech by the Governor of the Banca d'Italia presenting its 1974 Report. "With an overall trade volume not much lower than that of the United States and with the share with the other European partners double than the American one, economic activity in Germany constitutes the most important external factor for the economic trends of the countries of the European economic community. Banca d'Italia, *Considerazioni finali sul 1974*, p. 16.

3   This is a reference to the book by Marsh, David, *The Bundesbank. The bank that rules Europe*, Heinemann, 1992.

This created a situation where Germany and the Bundesbank progressively appeared to large parts of Italian public opinion to be responsible for incorrect or, at the very least, unpopular economic policies. This continues to largely be the case even in the current situation of monetary union where the economic importance of Germany remains significant, but where the Bundesbank has lost much of its reference role of the past. The economic events of this period have been at the origin of differences of opinion, of a few legitimate grievances and of a lot of exaggerations or even outright fake stories that still infest the Italian political debate on monetary union and on the future of the European Union.

There are many reasons why these exaggerations or completely fictional narratives appeared, but the most important ones are emotional. Stabilising the external value of the lira increasingly meant stabilising its exchange rate in relation to the Deutsche Mark. Yet, this endeavour was spectacularly unsuccessful with the Italian lira depreciating by around 82 per cent relative to the DM between the end of the Bretton Woods system and the introduction of the euro. Each phase in this downward spiral was accompanied by strong political tensions.

In addition, from the 1990s Italy entered a period of very slow growth. Between 1991 and 2019, Italy had the lowest rate of economic growth of all European countries: on average just below 0.7 per cent a year. It actually grew less than Greece, notwithstanding the eight years of recession experienced since 2008. During the same period, Italy had a rate of growth lower than that of the group of the other 18 members of today's euro area every year with the sole exception of 1995. On average, over those 28 years, the rate of growth of the rest of today's euro area was higher than that of Italy by about one percentage point a year. In 2019, before the Coronavirus Crisis, Italian GDP per head in real terms was at a level roughly equal to that of 2000.

These very negative trends created a strong reaction – a mixture of envy and an inferiority complex – that led a large part of the Italian public to seek out an explanation in events taking place outside of the country and to thereby find foreign scapegoats. Many felt that it could not be that Italy, with its incredible cultural past, was doing so badly economically and socially. The reasons for the recent dismal results must be found in the rules of the game (the functioning of the economic system), in some external arrangements (globalisation, the euro), in the bias of the referee (the European Union), and in the fouls committed by other players (above all, Germany and France).

The attitude of Italians towards the European Union has been measured by regular Eurobarometer surveys carried out by the European Commission. In 1974, 77 per cent of Italians considered that being part of the Economic Community was positive for the country. This descended to 69 per cent in 1983 and only 51 per cent in 1999. In December 2019, only 38 per cent of Italians "trusted" the European Union while 52 per cent did not.[4]

No comparable surveys on Italians' trust of Germany have been carried out over a sufficiently long period of time, but the fall in trust in the EU certainly follows a pattern similar to that of Germany. A Pew study carried out in 2017 of the G20 countries shows that 79 per cent of French interviewees trust Ms Merkel "to do the right thing in international affairs". The corresponding figure for the UK is 68 per cent, but the figure for Italy is only a meagre 39 per cent.[5] In 2020, a survey (on which more detail will come later) found that a majority of Italians believed that Germany was "strangling" Italy.

The currency crises of the seventies (1972-1978)

A summary of the main events of the last fifty years is necessary to highlight the origin of some of the legitimate grievances and the extent to which some of these are often exaggerated. The summary will also show the origin of some of the fake stories that are still found in the current political discussions in Italy; fake stories that often consist of the identification of a foreign scapegoat.

During the seventies, Italy was experiencing high social turmoil. Its economy had experienced strong growth in the previous two decades, but most of the main features of a modern welfare state were still being introduced. The period of strong growth had led to a strengthening of labour unions and of their activism. Legislation to protect labour unions had been introduced in 1970[6] and the wage indexation system was strengthened in 1975. Under these conditions, the reaction to the two oil shocks triggered a strong attempt to protect incomes through state handouts. The budget deficit in this period was very high[7] while monetary policy was constrained through various instruments including the obligation of the Banca d'Italia to buy the state bonds that had not been bought by the market during the regular auctions. This resulted in a strongly negative average real interest rate on public debt.[8]

---

4   Eurobarometer 1, July 1974 (actually the question at the time was about being "in the Common Market"); Eurobarometer 19, June 1983; Eurobarometer 50, March 1999 and Eurobarometer 92, December 2019.
5   https://www.pewresearch.org/fact-tank/2017/07/05/on-world-affairs-most-g20-countries-more-confident-in-merkel-than-trump/.
6   The so-called *Workers' Statute* (*Statuto dei lavoratori*), law n. 300 of 20 May 1970.
7   The budget deficit increased from 6.6 percent of GDP in 1972 to 8.1 in 1978. The average value for the period was 7.3 per cent of GDP.
8   The negative average real interest rate on the Italian public debt was more than ten per cent for the period with a peak of more than 14 points in 1974 (nominal average public debt rate of interest deflated by the GDP deflator).

The rate of inflation became much higher than in the other European Community member states, with the exception of the United Kingdom.[9] This resulted in a loss of price competitiveness which led to high pressure on the exchange rate. Notwithstanding some modest attempts to stabilise the exchange rates in Western Europe ("the Snake"), between August 1971 and December 1978 the exchange rate of the lira in relation to the DM depreciated by almost 60 per cent.[10] This obviously contributed to a classic inflation-depreciation-inflation spiral.

The reserves of the central bank could not allow unlimited interventions in the currency markets. Both the European Economic Community and the IMF expanded their existing lending facilities and created new ones. Italy received loans from both organisations. These loans were accompanied by economic policy conditions verified through a group called "Group de la Genière" (named after the governor of the French central bank who headed it) which was essentially the "Troika" of those days.

However, given the inadequacy of the size of these facilities,[11] Italy had to arrange additional bilateral loans from individual central banks. Italian public opinion was particularly struck by the loan granted at the end of August 1974 by the Bundesbank for the equivalent of two billion dollars, as this was obtained against the guarantee of 515 tonnes of Italian gold held in Fort Knox. The importance of this loan, however, should not be exaggerated. In its annual report, in May 1975, the Governor of the Banca d'Italia indicated that the official debts of the bank were equal to around 15 billion dollars.[12]

The European Monetary System (1979-1991)

In March 1979, after an unexpected delay due to French dissatisfaction with some arrangements regarding the agricultural sector, Italy entered the European monetary system (EMS). The tensions created by the difficult management of the EMS and its realignments strengthened the resolve of the Italian governments to move to a single currency.

---

9   The Italian inflation rate went over 10 per cent in 1973 and reached a peak of over 21 per cent in 1980. The average increase rate of consumer prices for the 1972-1978 period was above 14 per cent. In Germany, thanks to a more restrictive policy orientation, the corresponding average value was just over five per cent, in France it was 9.9 per cent while in the UK it was 13.8 per cent.

10 In August 1971, 181.2 liras were needed to buy a DM. In December 1978, the figure had risen to 448.1.

11 Italy received around 1.4 billion dollars from the European Community and drew 1.2 billion dollars from its IMF facilities.

12 *Considerazioni finali sul 1974*, 31 May 1975, p. 19.

Economic policy, which had already become moderately restrictive towards the end of the seventies, was more clearly oriented towards reducing inflation and stabilising the exchange rate. At the beginning of 1981 the government granted more independence to the Banca d'Italia by relieving it of the obligation to buy bonds not acquired by the market at the regular auctions. This led to a rise in interest rates[13] and substantially increased the weight of interest payments on public expenditure.[14] Budget deficits became even higher.[15]

During the 1980s, the importance of capital movements as a determinant of the exchange rate grew substantially. The lira was subject to strong pressure on many occasions and its central rate was devalued a number of times in EMS realignments. Foreign exchange interventions took place very often and the EMS credit facilities replaced the IMF and European Community loans of the seventies.

Eleven realignments took place during this period and all took place between September 1979 and January 1987. The Italian authorities tried to compensate only part of the lost price competitiveness through devaluations of the central rate of the lira.[16] They attempted to use the exchange rate as a stabilisation tool.[17] At the same time, this meant keeping track of the monetary decisions of the Bundesbank much more closely than during previous years. The DM was the real pivot of the EMS.[18] "During the period in which Italy was part of the exchange rate mechanism of the EMS, monetary policy had found its main reference in the respect of this constraint".[19]

Realignments became important political events, the occasion of lengthy and complicated discussions, and created substantial tensions between the governments of participating countries. Logically, most realignments involved a revaluation of the DM and

---

13 The average real public debt interest rate (GDP deflator) went from being negative by more than 8 per cent in 1979 to being positive by one per cent in 1991. It further increased to around 5 per cent in 1992 remaining between four and six per cent until the start of monetary union.
14 The percentage of current public expenditure absorbed by interest payments increased from 14 per cent at the beginning of the period (1979) to almost 21 per cent at its end (1991).
15 During the 1979-1991 period the net borrowing requirement oscillated between eight and twelve per cent of GDP (the period average was just above 10 per cent).
16 See, for instance, "The Italian lira: the exchange rate and employment in the ERM", by three Bruegel researchers that shows that the realignments had little effect on the Italian labour market, https://www.bruegel.org/2017/01/the-italian-lira-the-exchange-rate-and-employment-in-the-erm/.
17 See, for instance, Rossi, Salvatore, *La politica economica italiana dal 1968 ad oggi*, Laterza, 2020, p. 68-69.
18 "The Bundesbank turned the original concept [for the EMS] on its head by making the strongest currency the yard stick for the system". Pöhl, Karl-Otto, *Speech at St. Paul's church in Frankfurt*, 27-8-1991 quoted by Marsh, David, *op. cit.*, p. 233.
19 Rossi, Salvaore, *op. cit.*, p. 102.

a devaluation of the Italian lira. The discussions also concerned the position of other countries and issues of image became almost as important as economic considerations. Realignments would be announced on a Friday evening and involved the ministers of Finance meeting in Brussels over the weekend.

One anecdote highlights the political tensions created by these occasions. During the realignment of March 1983, the French finance minister, Jacques Delors, left the meeting on the Sunday morning and made some very harsh remarks about the "arrogance" of some other participants and returned to Paris. The other ministers remained in the Centre Borschette in Brussels, not knowing if or when Mr Delors would return. On Sunday evening it was decided to close the foreign exchange markets on Monday 21st. On Monday morning, Mr Delors returned to Brussels and an agreement was reached.

The sometimes important changes in the market values of the participating currencies were problematic for many sectors. They often led to accusations of competitive devaluations. After the September 1992 realignment there was substantial tension between France and Italy, with the former threatening to take protective measures. The agricultural sector, on the other hand, was partly shielded by the parity changes through the introduction of a complex system of Monetary Compensatory Amounts (MCA).

All EMS central banks were trying to keep their exchange rates as stable as possible. But this meant trying to keep the exchange rate stable in relation to the DM. This led to a situation where the Bundesbank was logically determining its monetary policy on the basis of the needs of the German economy and where the resulting monetary conditions in Germany had to be more or less replicated in all other EMS countries.

This meant that central banks had to adjust their monetary conditions following every change operated by the Bundesbank, and they had to do it rapidly. Fons Verplaetse, governor of the Belgian central bank from 1989 to 1999, stated in an interview that the monetary autonomy of his bank was limited to 15 minutes from the moment they were informed of a change having taken place in Germany! This, he stated, was the time within which the Belgian central bank had to adjust its interest rate policy to avoid serious tensions on foreign exchange markets.

The situation became very delicate in 1990 following German reunification. The need to massively help the former Deutsche Demokratische Republik led to a huge increase in German public expenditure and the Bundesbank was forced to counter this with substantial increases of its interest rates. A better solution would have been a revaluation of the central rate of the DM. This would have deflected part of the increase in internal demand towards higher imports, with positive effects on the rate of growth of the other European countries and would have reduced the need for the Bundesbank to tighten its monetary policy. At the time, various rumours suggested that the German authorities had confidentially explored the possibility of a realignment limited to a revaluation of the DM, but that this had been refused by some other countries, especially France, afraid that such a realignment would still be seen as a devaluation of their own currencies and by the insistence of others to keep the parity with the DM.[20]

The absence of this realignment led to a situation where, for a relatively long period of time, interest rates in many European countries – and not just among the countries officially participating in the EMS – were much higher than the economic situation of the countries would have warranted. Ironically, the final chapter of the report of the Banca d'Italia for the year 1992 (the *Considerazioni finali*, which conveys the political messages of the governor) contains a paragraph where the governor of the Banca d'Italia calls on Germany to put an end to the deterioration of its budgetary balance and stresses the need for its improvement to make room for private investment.[21]

In 1990, in the discussions among economists it was often stated that German reunification had led to an increase of Italian exports towards Germany, but that the benefits of this increase had been offset by higher than necessary interest rates. Often the expression used was that these higher interest rates constituted a price Italy and other countries were "paying" for German reunification. These discussions led to the appearance of the fake story of Italy having actually paid cash for German re-unification. In a less extreme version of this fake story, the investments made in the former DDR by some Italian groups were also billed as "payments towards German re-unification". As a consequence of this rumour, many Italians still believe today that Italy has actually contributed financially to the cost of German reunification. This false story has been peddled by many people including well-known politicians and former ministers.[22]

---

20 The story is indirectly confirmed by Rossi, Salvatore (*op. cit.*, p.113) when he explains the advantages of such a unilateral revaluation and regrets that this had not been allowed to happen by "the ESM constraint, rendered very tough by the French opposition to a devaluation of their currency, unfortunately considered a symbol of grandeur".
21 *Considerazioni finali*, Rapporto sul 1992, 31 May 1993, p. 322.
22 In his book *Bugie e Verità*, Mondadori, 2014, Giulio Tremonti writes that "German unification has been financed by the euro and with the euro" (p. 64). In a footnote he attributes this idea to Tony Judt who, he says, had written in "Postwar" that through the manoeuvre of interest rates Kohl exported the price to pay for the unification of the country, forcing the European partners to bear its weight. In this section of his book Tremonti does not discuss or explain the mechanism through which the cost of unification was

Fabio Colasanti

The crisis of 1992 and, finally, monetary union

The exchange rate stability between 1987 and 1991 in the EMS was certainly due to a growing convergence of the orientation of the economic policies of the participating member states. Italy had embarked on a determined course of stabilisation. France had abandoned the expansionary dreams of the first Mitterrand years and Belgium had been shocked by the devaluation of its currency in 1982. However, the underlying divergences continued and pressure on the existing exchange rate parities was increased by capital movements, which had been liberalised to a very large extent.

September 1992 saw a major crisis in the EMS which led to the British pound, which had entered the EMS in 1990, leaving the system together with the Italian lira.[23] Obviously, such an event had enormous political impact. In 1993, it was even decided to substantially widen the EMS fluctuation bands (to +/- 15 per cent). A new crisis hit the Italian lira in 1995 during a period of general instability created by the Mexican crisis. Between August and December 1992, the lira lost around 15 per cent of its value compared to the DM. During the year 1993 it lost a further 8 per cent and by April 1995 another 15 per cent.

In the world of social media, the crisis of 1992 is usually attributed to George Soros and other "speculators". In reality, it was just a crisis waiting to happen. Italian economic policy had continued to be incompatible with exchange rate stability.[24] The

---

supposed to have been exported. Later on, in the book, in the chapter dedicated to Germany, he simply recalls that "as it has been seen before", German unification was not financed only by Germany, but also by the rest of Europe. In fact, his quotation is not completely correct. Tony Judt did write "In effect, Helmut Kohl exported the cost of his country's unification and Germany's partners were made to share the burden" (*Postwar*, Heinemann, p. 643), but this sentence comes at the end of a paragraph where he correctly explains what happened. More recently, the Corriere della Sera published a special report on German reunification written by Milena Gabanelli and Danilo Taino. https://www.corriere.it/dataroom-milena-gabanelli/germania-est-ovest-caduta-muro-berlino-costo-riunificazione/817c3d32-f8db-11e9-8af8-3023352e2b21-va.shtml. The contents of the article are very imprecise, and the newspaper gave it the title *Germania: quanto è costata alla Germania, all'Europa e all'Italia la caduta del muro* (How much the fall of the Wall has cost Germany, Europe and Italy).

23 The Italian lira formally left only the exchange rate arrangements of the EMS.
24 The Conclusions of the May 1992 Ecofin Council contained a sharply-worded recommendation to Italy to put its public finances in order. "The council conducted a review of the progress made in implementing the Italian programme of Economic Convergence 1992-1994. […] Six months after the presentation of the programme, the evolution of the key variables for nominal convergence is falling short of the stated targets. The budgetary situation and outlook, in particular, give cause for serious concern. The disappointing outcome of the State Sector Borrowing Requirement in 1991 and other developments since the presentation of the programme imply that meeting the deficit target for 1992 now calls for a substantial

uncertainty created by the June 1992 Danish referendum, the difficult Italian domestic political situation (the killing of two anti-mafia magistrates and the beginning of "Mani Pulite") and the weakness of the dollar created a combination that made the crisis impossible to avoid.

It is difficult to deny that monetary union was finally implemented only because it had already been decided with the highest degree of formality (with the signing of a new Treaty). Had the 1992 crisis taken place one year earlier, the outcome of the negotiations may well have been different.

The 1992 crisis constituted a significant blow for reciprocal trust. The Italian side was incensed by the refusal of the Bundesbank, during the last days before the mid-September 1992 crisis, to grant the short-term financing foreseen for the situation where a currency had reached its lowest fluctuation level.[25]

After the nadir of April 1995, the lira started appreciating again, thanks also to the strong measures taken to stabilise the economy. In October 1996, Italy re-joined the EMS narrow fluctuation bands so as to be able to respect the exchange rate stability criterion of the Maastricht Treaty. By this time, the currency had recovered about 15 per cent of its worth in relation to the DM but was still about 24 per cent lower than its value at the beginning of 1992.

---

additional adjustment package. Such a package must amount to well above lira 30 000 billion in the second half of the year. The size of the adjustment required calls for exceptional measures going beyond the normal framework of fiscal policy as conducted so far". In the days after the Council meeting, an amusing story started to circulate among people working in the economic department of the European Commission. The Italian Permanent Representative, Mr Federico Di Roberto, had apparently asked for a meeting with Pascal Lamy, head of cabinet of President Delors. During the meeting he was said to have expressed his surprise about the fact that the European Commission, that usually collaborates strictly in the drafting of the Council conclusions, had allowed a text written in such an undiplomatic language. Mr Lamy had reportedly suggested an improvement in the internal coordination within the Italian government and had informed the ambassador that the text had been drafted personally by the Italian finance minister, Guido Carli, who had asked for the help of his peers to obtain a change of policy in Italy.

25 Rossi, Salvatore, *op. cit.*, p. 43. "Between September 12 and 16, the situation precipitated on the foreign exchange markets, not least because of a lack of cooperation within the EMS", Salvatore Rossi, *op. cit.*, p. 90. The *Considerazioni finali* of the governor of the Banca d'Italia for 1992 (delivered on 31 May 1993) contain a softly worded but clear message. Discussing the needs for the successful functioning of the EMS the governor stated that more than new rules "all the cooperation that the existing rules allow and foresee (was necessary); this cooperation was missing during the last crisis. […] It is necessary to have an element of collective management of the system, in assessing the appropriateness of the exchange rates, in agreeing possible changes and in the defence of the parities considered correct", p. 320.

After some informal contacts, there was a meeting of the Monetary Committee that agreed on a new central parity for the lira corresponding to 990 lira for one DM. This value was 1.2 per cent higher than the average market value for the month before the agreement (September). German and, above all, French industrialists would have preferred a higher parity (around 950 lira for one DM) whereas Italian industry had been dreaming of a new parity well over 1000 lira for one DM. The fact that in the media these parities were expressed in lira per DM demonstrates the pivotal role played by the German currency in the EMS and on foreign exchange markets.

This negotiation, which was certainly of great importance, received wide press coverage. This led to the impression among the less-informed parts of Italian public opinion that the conversion rates with the euro had been the subject of extensive negotiation and that they were not simply the market rates observed on the foreign exchange markets on 31 December 1998 at noon (as had been the de facto agreement in Maastricht six years prior). This led to a widespread fake story that still circulates today about Romano Prodi having negotiated the wrong conversion rate for the Italian lira whereas Germany had negotiated a much better one for itself.[26]

The negotiations of the monetary union had also given Italian public opinion mixed impressions. All along, the Bundesbank had been perceived as being very reluctant. Tommaso Padoa-Schioppa summarized very well the view of the Italian negotiators when he wrote "The Bundesrepublik Deutschland was split between a political level that was working on monetary union half-time, clearly favourable, perhaps even ready to accept it immediately, but not to impose it and a technical level that was working on the subject full-time, but was much more reluctant".[27] The view of most of the Italian press was more negative. Especially during the last phase of the negotiations there was a general belief that the Bundesbank and the German authorities were setting the bar for participation in the first group deliberately high so as to exclude Italy.

The government of Romano Prodi had initially contemplated the idea of joining after the first group, maybe in 2000/2001, together with Spain and Portugal. Mr Prodi was very surprised when, during a meeting in Alicante in September 1996, Mr Aznar expressed his confidence that Spain would be able to satisfy all the convergence

---

26 In fact, Italy entered monetary union in a much better competitive situation than Germany. This was due also to the large depreciations of 1995, only minimally corrected by the October 1996 new central rate. In 1998 and 1999, the Italian current account balance was positive. Germany, on the other hand, was coming from a long series of negative current account balances. The first German current account surplus was recorded in 2002.

27 Padoa-Schioppa, Tommaso, *La lunga via per l'euro*, Il Mulino, 2004, p. 309 (section written with Lorenzo Bini Smaghi and Francesco Papadia).

requirements and that it could join in January 1999 with the first group. He then received the same message from the Portuguese authorities. This led to his decision to embark on a very strict budgetary policy course that, together with the substantial drop in interest rates on Italian government bonds, produced a spectacular turnaround in the Italian borrowing requirement (from 7.2 per cent of GDP in 1995 to 1.8 per cent in 1999). The 1996 budgetary package contained a tax that was dubbed "Tax for Europe" by the press.

In October 1998, the Eurobarometer survey showed that Italians were the European citizens most in favour of the euro by far: 88 per cent felt favourably.[28] In reality, Italians knew very little about the euro. Entering the monetary union had never triggered a significant public debate. They were instead rejoicing at having escaped relegation to the European economic second league. Having managed to snatch the maintenance in the first league from the jaws of the opposition of northern Europeans was seen by many as one of Romano Prodi's main achievements.

Monetary union

The passage to the euro did not put an end to the recriminations and criticism towards Germany and the other northern members of the monetary union voiced by large parts of the Italian public. The main debate concentrated on the effects that a common currency was having on external price competitiveness and on the current account. The most obvious consequence of the decision to enter monetary union was that the external value of the euro would probably have steered a middle course between the trends of the DM and lira, had they continued to exist. Yet this consequence seemed to have dawned on many – including the Italian governments of the first years of the euro – only over time.

Between the beginning of monetary union and the outbreak of the 2008 financial crisis, Italy had lost almost 10 per cent in price competitiveness compared to its main trading partners, taking the consumer price index as a proxy, and almost 25 per cent using unit labour costs.[29] This obviously compounded the difficulties created by the world-wide crisis. Italy was also hit by the 2012/2013 recession originating from the fallout of the Greek sovereign debt crisis. These two recessions led to a correction of the loss in price competitiveness of the first decade of monetary union and Italy's real effective exchange rate in 2019 was almost back at its level of 1998/1999. This happened the "hard way" through unemployment and almost no wage increases. Inflation was reduced almost to zero. Fur-

---

28 Eurobarometer N° 50, p. 63 https://ec.europa.eu/commfrontoffice/publicopinion/archives/eb/eb50/eb50_en.pdf.
29 Bruegel data base https://www.bruegel.org/publications/datasets/real-effective-exchange-rates-for-178-countries-a-new-database/ REER monthly CPI-based: loss of 9 per cent between December 1998 and January 2008. Loss of 24 per cent measured by the ULC (REEL-ULC Quarterly) between 2000-I and 2008-I.

thermore, due also to the weakness of internal demand, Italy has had an external current account surplus since 2013, reaching three per cent of GDP in 2019. However, even before the outbreak of the Coronavirus crisis, Italy had not yet reached its real GDP level of 2007.

The very depressing performance of the Italian economy since the Nineties and especially over the last ten years is at the root of a lot of frustrations which have fuelled new recriminations and accusations. This has, once again, led to the exaggeration of factors that were legitimate concerns, from the existence of a possible deflationary bias in the construction of the monetary union to the persistently high current account surpluses of Germany. In the past decade, Italian public debate concentrated very often on real grievances that might explain five to ten per cent of Italy's problems and largely ignored the other causes.[30] However, the Italian appreciation of the euro, even if much lower than the incredibly high levels of 1998, is still high: 61 per cent of Italians were still in favour of remaining in the monetary union in December 2019.[31] The desire not to be seen as "having been relegated" probably still plays an important role.

Germany was legitimately criticised in 2003 when the European Council decided not to follow the proposal of the European Commission and impose sanctions against Germany and France for breaching the Stability and Growth Pact. However, many forget that this decision – later condemned by the European Court of Justice – had been made possible by the rotating Council presidency that was held by Italy at the time.[32]

When the feared "contagion" from the Greek sovereign debt crisis reached Spain and Italy in 2011, a story made the headlines in Italy: Deutsche Bank had provoked or exacerbated the increase in the spread between Italian and German bonds by dumping billions of Italian bonds on the market. Various Italian politicians denounced the action. A small Italian court in southern Italy, that had already tried to win notoriety by launching an inquiry against the major rating agencies (an inquiry that led to nothing), launched a new inquiry against Deutsche Bank. The Italian market supervision authority, the Consob, asked for explanations as did the Italian ministry for Finance.

---

30 Interesting analysis of Francesco Papadia on Italian economic growth and the euro, Bruegel, 2017 https://www.bruegel.org/2017/07/italian-economic-growth-and-the-euro/.
31 Eurobarometer 92.
32 In his book *Bugie e verità* (Mondadori, 2014), Giulio Tremonti has a chapter on Germany where he criticises many aspects of its economic policies. On page 136, he observes that it was Italy who had avoided European sanctions against Germany in 2003. He obviously refers to his own action as chair of the Council meeting that decided not to take a position on the proposal of the European Commission to sanction France and Germany for their violations of the Stability and Growth Pact.

In December 2017, the Italian director general for public debt, Maria Cannata, had a hearing in the Italian Parliament.[33] Asked again about the sale of bonds by Deutsche Bank in 2011, Ms Cannata explained that Deutsche Bank at the time had just acquired Deutsche Post. This organisation had a large amount of Italian public bonds in its portfolio. As a result, the group now held a much larger amount of Italian bonds than its internal rules recommended. Deutsche Bank had therefore sold 4.9 billion euros of Italian bonds in the first half of 2011, but it had done so attempting to minimise the effects of these sales on the market (an action that clearly also served its own interest). It had sold the bonds on platforms where it was more difficult to identify the seller and it had continued to buy Italian bonds where the transactions were more transparent. During the period of these sales the Italian spread had not changed. The spread started rising in July 2011, well after the sales by Deutsche Bank. In the second half of 2011, only Deutsche Bank had actually increased its holdings of Italian government bonds by 1.1 billion euros. Notwithstanding these facts, the sales by Deutsche Bank still feature prominently in Italian political debates.

Other exaggerations surround the issue of the German current account surplus. This was clearly a problem. It was a symptom of poor coordination of economic policies within the monetary union. The European Commission, the IMF and the OECD have regularly criticised this surplus. Nobody was asking Germany to curb its exports, but everybody was suggesting a stronger expansion of its internal demand that would have led to higher imports.

This legitimate criticism led many to conclude that Germany had no right to criticise Italy for its non-respect of the budgetary rules, given that Germany was not respecting the European rule on the current account surplus. Obviously, these people were missing the point that the budgetary rules of the monetary union were enshrined in the Treaties and had been reinforced by an intergovernmental treaty, the "Fiscal Compact". The excessive macroeconomic imbalances procedure, instead, was introduced through secondary legislation in 2011. It is based on the respect of acceptable ranges for various macro-economic indicators (14 of them) and does not contain the threat of sanctions of the severity foreseen for violations of the budgetary rules. Since the introduction of this procedure, Germany has been regularly found in violation of the current account surplus indicator. But more important is the fact that Italy was also regularly found in violation of various indicators and, in some years, the number of indicators violated by Italy was higher than that of the German breaches.

---

33   Audizione della dottoressa Cannata, 14 Dec. 2017. http://www.parlamento.it/application/xmanager/projects/parlamento/33_-_DEFINITIVO.pdf.

Finally, there is the fact that a large part of Italian public opinion has sided with Greece during its crisis, choosing to see the country as the victim of the rapacity and selfishness of its euro area creditors. One particular fake story that emerged during this crisis is that of European aid having ended up essentially in the pockets of German banks. Euro area banks have indeed received a large amount of money (possibly up to 46 billion euros) through the reimbursement of Greek government bonds they had bought. But this was the direct result of the initial decision to avoid a Greek default. This position had been taken by the ECB and had been supported by France and Italy.

These players were afraid that a Greek default might trigger a major crisis in the European financial system, and that a Greek default might be something akin to the bankruptcy of Lehman Brothers. They were also afraid that the first default of a member of the monetary union might open the door to other defaults and trigger a "contagion", as later events indeed confirmed. On the other hand, the IMF and Germany had been in favour of an immediate restructuring of the Greek public debt.

The initial course of action changed as awareness increased of the seriousness of the Greek public finance and economic situation. During a now famous promenade on the strand of Deauville in October 2010, Chancellor Merkel was able to convince President Sarkozy of the need for restructuring Greek debt, an operation euphemistically labelled "Private Sector Involvement". This set the ball rolling for the recall, in 2012, of the Greek bonds still on the market and the cancellation of bonds for a value of 126.6 billion euros. This decision and its terms and conditions were heavily criticised by many, but if money from the euro area loans reached the banks this was certainly not due to German pressure. In any case, the exposure of French banks towards Greece was higher than that of the German banks.

More important is the fact that the share of aid from the euro area to Greece that was paid to euro area banks is much smaller than often stated. Official statistics do not allow it to be determined which banks received what; they only present figures for the exposure of a national financial system to a country. In February 2016, I published a paper showing that, even under a series of unfavourable assumptions, the share of the aid under the three assistance programmes to Greece that may have reached euro area banks could not be higher than around 17 per cent of the total.[34] Roughly half of the financial help to Greece was used to (partially) repay the public debt or to directly recapitalise the Greek banks. Most of this money went indeed to the Greek banks as they were very large holders of Greek debt and required substantial aid on various occasions, especially after the debt restructuring of 2012. Among the non-Greek banks there was also a large number of American, British and Swiss banks.

---

34 "Financial Assistance to Greece. Three programmes", European Policy Centre, Brussels: 2016, http://www.epc.eu/en/Publications/Financial-assistance-to-Greece~2579c0.

The myth of the aid given to Greece being used almost uniquely to help the bank originates essentially from two papers from ATTAC Austria and Yannis Mouzakis.[35] The calculations by Mouzakis were used also by the Truth Committee of the Greek Parliament,[36] Joseph Stiglitz and many others. In Italy these figures were regularly quoted by the former prime minister Massimo D'Alema, who maintained that "out of the 250 billion euros lent to Greece, 220 went to the banks". "We have not financed Greek pensions; we have financed the German banks".[37]

This story received substantial support from an unexpected source. On 3 May 2016, the Handelsblatt made headlines when it published a two-page summary of a study by professor Jörg Rocholl and one of his assistants, Axel Stahmer, both from the European School of Management and Technology in Berlin. They stated that less than 10 billion euro of the 260 billion lent by the euro area countries had been used to support the Greek economy. The news was widely reported by the German press, by Deutsche Welle, by the Guardian and most of the Italian press. In essence, they were maintaining that, after the end of April 2010, Greece should not have paid any of its public debt, should not have paid any interest on its debt – including to the IMF – and that Greece should not have recapitalised its banks. All this had not helped the Greek economy. In addition, they had made an important methodological error, which had been made also by Mouzakis.[38]

I contacted professor Rocholl and the Handelsblatt. After a second series of observations from my side, the exchange was interrupted with a message stating that "one intention of writing our paper is to invite fellow researchers to comment on our

---

35 https://www.attac.org/en/Stories/greek-bail-out-77-went-financial-sector and https://www.macropolis.gr/?i=portal.en.the-agora.2080.
36 http://www.cadtm.org/Preliminary-Report-of-the-Truth.
37 https://www.youtube.com/watch?v=pWLm895H2Zs.
38 How the money was spent by the Greek government in meaningful categories can be derived only from the documents prepared by the IMF and European Commission: the analysis of the so called "financing needs". These documents provide a breakdown of what the Greek government presumably had to fund. Rocholl and Mouzakis both attempted to calculate the amounts "left" for the Greek economy by subtracting from the total loan disbursements the items of expenditure, identified in the financing needs, that they felt were not in the interest of the Greek people and calculating what was left. However the "financing needs" for the 2010-2015 period were higher than the disbursements by the lenders by slightly more than 50 billion euros as the Greek government was able to find this amount through the raiding of the liquidity of all public bodies, the use of its IMF balances, some commercial credit, SMP and ANFA profits, privatization receipts and an increase in the issue of short-term bills. Any residual calculated in this way is bound to be smaller than the real figure by 50 billion euros. Rocholl and Stahmer, given their extreme assumptions about what was not in the interest of the Greek economy, were even forced to use a lower figure for the cost of debt restructuring in 2012 (29.7 billion euros instead of the full 41.0) to avoid being left with a negative residual!

findings". The Handelsblatt never replied. It is always difficult to kill a good story. For a large part of Italian public opinion this contribution was the final confirmation of their beliefs: the authors of the sixteen-page study were researchers at a German management university and the story had been given prominence by a German economic newspaper. It was the equivalent of a signed confession.

I have mentioned just a few examples of the many accusations against German economic policies that circulate in Italy and originate from the last fifty years of economic history. Some may appear ludicrous and not even worthy of a reply. But the problem is serious. In April 2020, a survey conducted by the company EurometraMR (its best-known representative is Roberto Mannheimer)[39] yielded some very worrying results: 70 per cent of respondents agreed with the statement that "Germany is strangling Italy", with only 16 per cent taking the opposite view. According to the survey, people agreeing with the statement were concentrated in the so-called populist parties (Lega, Fratelli d'Italia and Cinque Stelle), but also a majority of the Forza Italia voters shared this opinion. About 50 per cent of Partito Democratico and Italia Viva voters agreed with the statement.

This is just one survey, perhaps a biased one, and it must have been influenced by some initial blunders by France and Germany in the response to the Coronavirus pandemic. Surely the proposals by France and Germany on how to respond to the Coronavirus crisis and their role in securing the approval of the Next Generation EU package will have changed the situation significantly. But there is still a lot of information work to do. Villa Vigoni could help in this task.

---

39 Eurometra, *L'Europa alla prova del Coronavirus*, 9 Apr. 2020, https://www.eumetramr.com/it/leuropa-alla-prova-del-coronavirus.

The Bundesbank between Bretton Woods and Economic and Monetary Union – a German Perspective[1]

Ludger Schuknecht[2]

1. The challenges and legacies of the Deutsche Bundesbank

The role and performance of the Deutsche Bundesbank between the end of the Bretton Woods era and the beginning of EMU were extremely fortunate but also controversial. Good institutions, a favourable political and societal constellation, a market-oriented pragmatic strategy, and probably also some good luck came together for the Deutsche Bundesbank to master five big challenges:

- First, it helped rebuild the German economy and heal the wounds of Nazi rule.

- Second, it tackled the destabilisation risks in Germany after the end of Bretton Woods with pragmatic monetarism.

- Third, it underpinned the stabilisation of Europe in the 1980s and 1990s by being an anchor of price stability.

- Fourth, it mastered the integration of the Eastern German economy into a re-united Germany.

- Fifth, its federal, institutional setup (giving the German Länder banks equal voting rights) provided the blueprint for European Monetary Union and its success in preserving price stability made sure that EMU got off to a good start.

On this path through almost three decades, however, the Deutsche Bundesbank fought some important "battles" and caused major grievances at home and abroad. In retrospect, their outcome probably determined significantly where we are today. The first major "battle" over stability was in the early 1980s (the earlier post-Bretton

---

1   I am grateful to Otmar Issing and Francesco Papadia for their helpful comments.
2   Ludger Schuknecht was Deputy Secretary-General at the OECD and Chief Economist of the German Federal Ministry of Finance advising on matters of fiscal and economic policy, the international economy and with responsibility for the finance track of the G20 process. He has held posts at the European Central Bank, the World Trade Organization and the International Monetary Fund. His latest book is "Public Spending and the Role of the State" (2020) with Cambridge UP.

Woods stabilisation seems to have been surrounded by much less conflict). Following overly lax policies in the late-seventies economic recovery, the Deutsche Bundesbank tightened monetary reins while the second oil crisis caused a major recession. This did not sit too well with the German government at that time, and it drew quite some criticism from other European countries. But it put Germany and Europe on the stability course of the 1980s.

The second major "battle" arose with German unification, which had given rise to significant inflationary pressures and in some respects irresponsible policies. The Deutsche Bundesbank responded with tighter monetary policy at a time when the business cycle was weak in other countries. This again upset the German government and Germany's European and transatlantic allies and contributed to the EMS crisis in 1992/93. However, the Deutsche Bundesbank prevailed. This, in turn, precipitated the extremely successful stabilisation of the 1990s and a world of firmly entrenched monetary dominance.

Initially, these battles dismayed the proponents of curtailing Deutsche Bundesbank power (first via the EMS and then EMU), notably France and Italy. But they probably increased these countries' political resolve for EMU and reduced the German government's opposition to move forward with monetary union and to 'clip the wings' of 'the Bank that rules Europe'[3] – the political imbalance within Europe had become too great.[4] However, building EMU on the Deutsche Bundesbank model seemed a fair price for a reluctant German population giving up both the Mark and the dominance of "its" Deutsche Bundesbank. All this allowed EMU to get off to a good start.

2. Monetary dominance by evolution rather than by design

The Deutsche Bundesbank was probably lucky three, if not four, times over to allow it such a "run", such a favourable evolution for a quarter of a century. First, it had gained independence against quite some opposition in the 1950s. However, independence was more limited than many people think – no exchange rate policies, no banking supervision – and political factors seem to have had some influence on Deutsche Bundesbank policies just as it should be for an institution accountable to the public and the legislature.[5]

---

3   Marsh, David, *The Bank that Rules Europe*, London: Mandarin, 1992.

4   Issing, Otmar, "Why did the Great Inflation not happen in Germany?", *Federal Reserve Bank of St. Louis Review*, Mar./Apr. 2005.

5   Maier, Philipp and Jakob de Haan, *How Independent is the Bundesbank Really? A Survey*, in de Haan, Jakob (ed.), *The History of the Bundesbank. Lessons for the European Central Bank*, London and New York: Routledge, 2000; Berger, Helge and Friedrich Schneider, *The Bundesbank's Reaction to Policy Con-*

Second, the collective German public and media remained in favour of price stability throughout the post-war period and did not waver even in the recessions of the 1970s and early 1980s. This was not only because of the hyperinflation experience in the early 1920s. Another repressed hyperinflation (though visible in the black market) in the 1940s, a prohibition of indexation, tax reasons, such as the taxation of fictitious (inflation-related) profits, and savings accounts as preferred store of value contributed not only to a psychological but also to an economically motivated aversion to inflation.[6]

Third, the preference for price stability helped Germany build a culture of reasonable fiscal policies and responsible wage setting that facilitated the Deutsche Bundesbank to build its reputation until the end of the Bretton Woods system.

Fourth, the Deutsche Bundesbank needed to assert itself and underpin its credentials for price stability exactly at the moment when everybody wanted more stability in the turbulent early 1970s, with rising inflation and the first oil crisis. So, this first challenge was perhaps easier to master than the following ones, and the Deutsche Bundesbank could "grow on its challenges".

The Deutsche Bundesbank's success in maintaining price stability, the rise of the Deutsche Mark dominance and the move to European Monetary Union over this period were all closely intertwined in a perhaps unique, unrepeatable historical context and dynamics. There was no constructivist master plan but rather an evolution of institutions and policies in a changing national and international environment. All historical accounts point to a step-by-step approach by all actors with partly conflicting short-term interests along an unclear path with frequent surprises. But still there seems to have been a strong compass of "Ordnungspolitik" in the Deutsche Bundesbank that had already marked Ludwig Erhard's post-war market-oriented economic policies.

3. The 1970s and 1980s: trial and error, policy battles and the right compass

In the midst of the post Bretton-Woods turmoil, the Deutsche Bundesbank pioneered pragmatic monetarism as its monetary strategy. However, this did not come about by grand design and neither was it a mere "coincidence".[7] The Deutsche

---

    flict, in de Haan, Jakob (ed.), *op. cit;* Issing, Otmar, *The European Central Bank as a New Institution and the Problem of Accountability,* in de Haan, Jakob (ed.), *op. cit.*

6   Tödter, Karl-Heinz and Gerhard Ziebarth, *From Low Inflation to Price Stability in Germany: Measurement, Costs and Benefits*, in de Haan, Jakob (ed.), *op. cit.*

7   Von Hagen, Jürgen, *Geldpolitik auf neuen Wegen (1971-1978)*, in Deutsche Bundesbank (ed.), *Fünfzig Jahre Deutsche Mark. Notenbank und Währung in Deutschland seit 1948*. Munich: C.H. Beck., 1998.

Ludger Schuknecht

Bundesbank initially even flirted with and introduced monetary and capital controls in 1971-73, but that did not work well. Money growth and inflation had been quite out of control when, in 1973/74, the oil crisis struck and further boosted an already significant rate of inflation (Fig. 1). Moreover, at first, German fiscal and wage policies also moved away from a stability orientation.

		Germany			Germany	USA	France	Italy
	Fiscal balance	Wage growth (annual %)	Money growth target (annual %)	Achieved?		Inflation (annual %)		
1970	0.5	-	-	-	3.5	5.8	5.3	5.0
1971	0.2	12.9	-	-	5.2	4.3	5.4	4.8
1972	-0.4	10.3	-	-	5.5	3.3	6.1	5.7
1973	1.1	13.1	-	-	7.0	6.2	7.4	10.8
1974	-1.7	10.1	-	-	7.0	11.1	13.6	19.2
1975	-5.8	3.7	8	no	5.9	9.1	11.7	17.0
1976	-3.5	7.3	8	no	4.2	5.7	9.6	16.6
1977	-2.6	7.5	8	no	3.7	6.5	9.5	17.1
1978	-2.6	6.5	8	no	2.7	7.6	9.3	12.1
1979	-2.7	8.1	6-9	yes	4.0	11.3	10.6	14.8
1980	-3.0	8.5	5-8	just about	5.4	13.5	13.6	21.1
1981	-4.0	4.9	4-7	just about	6.3	10.3	13.3	18.0
1982	-3.6	2.8	4-7	yes	5.2	6.1	12.0	16.5
1983	-2.9	1.8	4-7	just about	3.3	3.2	9.5	14.6
1984	-2.0	3.5	4-6	yes	2.4	4.3	7.7	10.8
1985	-1.2	4	3-5	yes	2.1	3.5	5.8	9.2
1986	-1.2	5.3	3.5-5.6	no	-0.1	1.9	2.5	5.8
1987	-1.8	4.5	3-6	no	0.2	3.7	3.3	4.7
1988	-2.0	4.3	3-6	just about	1.3	4.1	2.7	5.1
1989	0.1	4.8	ca 5	yes	2.8	4.8	3.5	6.3
1990	-1.9	8.2	4-6	yes	2.7	5.4	3.2	6.5
1991	-2.9	-	3-5	just about	4.0	4.2	3.2	6.2
1992	-2.5	8.5	3.5-5.5	no	5.1	3.0	2.4	5.3
1993	-3.0	2.6	4.5-6.5	just about	4.5	3.0	2.1	4.6
1994	-2.3	1.7	4-6	just about	2.7	2.6	1.7	4.1
1995	-9.5	3.3	4-6	no	1.7	2.8	1.8	5.2
1996	-3.4	1	4-7	no	1.4	2.9	2.0	4.0
1997	-2.8	-0.2	3.5-6.5		1.9	2.3	1.2	2.0
1998	-2.3	2.1	5		0.9	1.6	0.7	2.0
1999	-1.6	3			0.6	2.2	0.5	1.7

Fig. 1: German and international macro data related to Deutsche Bundesbank monetary policy

Source: International Monetary Fund, *International financial statistics. Inflation, consumer prices, annual %*; Destatis, *Bruttolöhne und -gehälter (Inland) pro Beschäftigen*, Baltensperger, 1999.

In this environment, the Deutsche Bundesbank was in a bind. It had got rid of the shackles of Bretton Woods with its intervention requirements and imported inflation – for which it had not been responsible. Now, there was the risk of new shackles from less constrained social partners and politicians that wanted to use the post-Bretton Woods freedom for their (short-term) agenda. And for the instability fallout from that, the Deutsche Bundesbank would be blamed.

Fortunately, the political and popular tide worked in favour of the Deutsche Bundesbank promoting price stability as economic instability and inflation were not popular. However, to prevail, the Deutsche Bundesbank also needed a policy strategy that was communicable and results-oriented, and, thereby, had a good chance of success. After much deliberation, it chose rules-based targeting of central bank money and later, broad money, where some short-term deviation was allowed. Money growth targets emerged from objectives for inflation (in future years), output growth and changes in moey velocity. This was a smart move as it tied the Deutsche Bundesbank to achieving objectives for which the logic seemed quite compelling and which, thereby, were also more time-consistent to anchor expectations. The Deutsche Bundesbank applied market-based measures to control money and liquidity via interest rate policy, reserve requirements and – over time increasingly – open market operations.

The strategy showed good first results in that inflation came down and expectations in the public and political domain became re-anchored in the mid-70s. This was acknowledged abroad and at home, and the government turned to supporting the Bank after the first oil crisis.[8] The GDP deflator as a measure of domestic price pressures declined from 6-8% in the period 1970-74 to around 4% in 1975-78. However, for the first years, the new strategy was implemented with considerable caution in an environment of still expansionary fiscal policies and wage setting, so that monetary targets between 1975 and 1978 were all missed and inflationary pressures resurged before and during the second oil crisis.

Jürgen von Hagen, a respected monetary economist, argued that this track record might have well been the end of money targeting and some Deutsche Bundesbank Council members showed similar scepticism. However, the formation of the European Monetary System (EMS) in 1979 and the second oil crisis with its renewed inflation surge (to 5-6% in 1980-81) changed the game for the Deutsche Bundesbank. The EMS (which was not too burdensome in terms of obligations) created strong incentives for bringing inflation down and anchoring expectations – thereby enhancing

---

8   Deutsche Bundesbank, *Die Deutsche Bundesbank. Aufgabenfelder, Rechtlicher Rahmen, Geschichte,* Frankfurt, 2006.

the Deutsche Bundesbank's reputation and also its leadership role in Europe.[9] The monetarist strategy – refined over time – became the vehicle to do so and, thereby, received a second lease of life.

The Deutsche Bundesbank's policy tightening after the second oil crisis helped achieve its stability objectives, but at the expense of adverse conjunctural effects. This, in turn, raised major opposition from the German government and elsewhere. However, the Deutsche Bundesbank was not alone as the US Federal Reserve led by Paul Volcker also started tightening. Moreover, far worse macroeconomic instability in other countries did not suggest the existence of a readily available alternative and thus helped the Deutsche Bundesbank stay its course.[10]

The experience of the 1980s proved this strategy right. Fiscal and wage policies became more stability oriented, inflation came down and the Deutsche Bundesbank's money targets were met until about 1987. But trouble brewed internationally: the oil price collapse of 1986 and accelerating money growth and inflation thereafter, coupled with financial liberalisation and integration, contributed to pressures for economic overheating. A number of countries experienced boom-bust cycles in asset prices, with recessions and even financial crises around the turn of the decade. The US savings and loan crisis, the Japanese financial crash and crisis, major crises in the Nordic countries and a sharp recession in the UK all happened in the period around and after 1990.

Initially, Germany could partly decouple from these developments. Inflation stayed lower than elsewhere and financial opening did not wreak havoc in housing and financial markets. The Deutsche Bundesbank adjusted its monetary policy instruments with less emphasis on reserve requirements to deal with the greater international banking competition and exercise better monetary control. Still, the new, unstable environment and currency interventions also complicated the control of money supply. Targets were missed in 1986 and 1987, and 1988 was a close call while inflation accelerated.

---

9   Baltensperger, E, "Geldpolitik bei wachsender Integration (1979-1996)", in Deutsche Bundesbank (ed.), *Fünfzig Jahre Deutsche Mark. Notenbank und Währung in Deutschland seit 1948*. Munich, C.H. Beck, 1998.
10   Fig. 1 and Issing, Otmar, *op. cit.*

4. German and European Integration

In this environment, the German unification process started in 1989/1990 and caused more challenges. The first one was operational: East Germany had to be technically integrated into "German Monetary Union". This was a huge task and the Deutsche Bundesbank managed it very well. However, commentators also argued that it was a distraction from the two further, bigger challenges.

Second, this was yet another occasion where policy makers and wage setters tested the resolve of monetary authorities – similar to the early and late 1970s. The German government moved to very expansionary fiscal policies to make unification go "smoothly". Moreover, unions used the opportunity for significant wage increases in East and West.

In order to maintain price stability and anchor expectations beyond the exceptional unification environment, the Deutsche Bundesbank tightened interest rates and liquidity conditions. This upset not only the German government but also Germany's partners and contributed to much turmoil in the EMS. Italy and the UK exited in the autumn of 1992 and instability continued until fluctuation bands were widened significantly in August 1993.

Domestic and international criticism of the Deutsche Bundesbank flew high throughout this period. One can certainly argue that its monetary policies imposed a significant short-term effect on the conjuncture in Germany and within the EMS. At the same time, one should remember that the Deutsche Bundesbank was tasked to follow its mandate, which was primarily for Germany. And it continued to support the EMS parities despite the difficulties that huge interventions caused for monetary management. More importantly and as mentioned, it probably created a very positive long-term effect by re-establishing monetary dominance. Fiscal policy makers and wage setters became more responsible and monetary policies loosened as of late 1992. The Deutsche Bundesbank and the Deutsche Mark were undoubtedly at the peak of their influence – roughly 18% of global foreign reserves were in Deutsche Mark in that period.

The third challenge was the move to European Monetary Union. The writing of EMU had been on the wall of the Deutsche Bundesbank perhaps as early as 1989 with the Delors report and certainly with the Maastricht Treaty of December 1991, when policy makers moved towards EMU also to tackle the political imbalance in the EMS and in European central banking.

Nobody likes to see their own power dismantled. Especially the Landeszentralbanken, which until 1999 sat at the monetary policy table, were sceptical. So, enthusiasm for EMU was naturally limited at the Deutsche Bundesbank, as the historical accounts state. But there was also more anxiety than enthusiasm in Germany as a whole over giving up "part of its birth right as a re-forged nation",[11] and many newspapers and tabloids expressed the public's scepticism quite drastically.

With this in mind, one has to praise the Deutsche Bundesbank for its constructive criticism and fairness in the run up to EMU. It supported the convergence process and even ran ads in favour of EMU, as Deutsche Bundesbank President Schlesinger "looked with hope at European monetary integration". The Deutsche Bundesbank was de facto strongly pro-Europe by relentlessly criticising the lack of political union to accompany monetary union, even if the intention of some was perhaps to fire up the opposition against EMU. The record of price stability, the institutional design and the credible convergence process – instrumentally supported by the Deutsche Bundesbank – got EMU off to a good start.

5. Conclusion

The Deutsche Bundesbank's monetary strategy of pragmatic monetarism served Germany and its partners well in controlling inflation and anchoring expectations. EMU started with the clear expectation of monetary dominance. However, the experience of EMU also shows how difficult it is to "create" a monetary order that will enhance both stability and growth. Just as with the Deutsche Mark, the design of EMU could not anticipate all contingencies and challenges of later years. One challenge has been well known: the lack of political union. The Stability and Growth Pact, the obligation of economic policy coordination and the no-bailout/no monetary financing/ no preferential access clauses (Art. 123-125 of the Treaty) were meant to compensate for that. However, their success is debatable, and the integration process remains incomplete. This makes it much harder for the ECB to promote monetary dominance than it was for the Deutsche Bundesbank.

---

11   Marsh, David, *op. cit.*

The Banca d'Italia-Tesoro Divorce and the Fascist Legacy

Federico Fubini[1]

When the editors called me to ask for a contribution to this important German-Italian project, I immediately felt the need to warn them: I am not an economist, I am just a journalist; I can describe reality as I understand it with my own tools. They immediately reassured me, explaining that diversity of approaches was appreciated. They placed only one condition: I would have to discuss, at least in part of my contribution, the theme of the so-called "divorce" of 1981 between the Treasury and the Banca d'Italia.

I therefore take advantage of my role as a journalist as a convenient excuse to jump immediately to conclusions that I present in a somewhat provocative way: the "divorce", that freed the central bank from any obligation to buy newly-issued government bonds in excess of market demand, was a failure.

It did not fail so much from a theoretical standpoint, as the systematic recourse to debt monetization would certainly have been a mistake. It was not a failure from the point of view of the credibility of the central bank as an inflation-fighter, either: its credentials, if anything, were strengthened by the February 1981 exchange of letters in which then-Treasury Minister, Beniamino Andreatta, and governor of the Banca d'Italia, Carlo Azeglio Ciampi, agreed that the bank did not have to buy all unsold government securities at auctions. In part thanks to the perception that the Banca d'Italia was going to be more independent, inflation decreased rapidly in Italy from about 20% in 1981 to less than 5% in 1986 (it must be said, however, that the first significant drop precedes the "divorce" by at least one year).

So why exactly did the "divorce" prove a failure? Despite the emphasis given at the time, the entire operation turned out to miss its implied fiscal-policy goals. The "divorce" was meant to create funding constraints that would force the government

---

[1] Federico Fubini (Florence, 1966) is an economics and finance writer and deputy editor-in-chief with Italy's "Corriere della Sera". He worked in Brussels as a reporter during the 1990s and early 2000s. In the following years he covered all the largest economic events, from the Great Recession to the Covid Crisis and the related EU response. He is the award-winning author of six books and ten widely downloaded Amazon Audible audio podcasts on the most relevant economic issues of our time.

to pursue greater budgetary discipline. Instead, the opposite happened. The attempt to introduce market-based constraints on the abuse of public spending did not work out as intended. The Italian public deficit rose from about 7% of GDP in 1980 to nearly 11% in 1981, and above 12% in 1985, remaining in double digits until 1993, a year after a violent crisis of the European Monetary System. As for public debt, during the post-war era it has never risen so rapidly as it did in the 1980s (with the unfortunate exception of the pandemic of 2020). Government debt doubled as a share of GDP in the thirteen years following 1981. In part, this was due to a gradual decline in inflation, which during the 1970s and early 1980s had contained public debt growth by acting as a hidden tax on savers.

So, the general failure in bringing about fiscal discipline with the "divorce" warrants some more examination. It is not just that the reform remained informal and incomplete, to the point that it allowed the Banca d'Italia to continue discretional interventions at auctions until 1994 and left the Treasury free to access automatic financing through its own account with the central bank. In fact, the root of the problem goes beyond the institutional set-up: the introduction of some partial market-based constraints on government bonds issuance proved fundamentally insufficient to correct imbalances in the Italian decision-making process.

How was such a failure even possible? The "divorce" probably did not correct the trajectory of public finances because the social, cultural and political forces from which it was supposed to stem were too strong. They were endemic and deep-rooted. As Tommaso Padoa-Schioppa used to say, stability as a choice belongs to society as a whole, not to the central bank or any other institution taken in isolation.

Therefore, we need to understand why Italian society as a whole decided, fundamentally, to keep dumping the cost of its problems on public debt. It's a question that challenges us, as Italians, to this day. Here, too, I draw legitimacy from my professional profile to jump to a provocative conclusion: that episode in 1981 is emblematic of the entire parable of post-war Italy that was – and in part, remains – strongly influenced by the legacy of fascist-era economic institutions. Here we find a decisive difference with Germany, where allied forces dismantled the economic institutions of National Socialism as much as its political ones. In Italy, on the contrary, the very fragility of post-war society in a context of great strength of a Soviet-leaning communist party led the allies to interfere as little as possible with the Italian economy. That became apparent ever since 1944 as American forces entered Rome. Let's not forget that all workforce dismissals were made illegal from August 1945 to two full years later (just as has been the case during the 2020 pandemic).

Corporatism survived in post-war Italy, adapting to the new context. A heavy State presence in the economy remained with the survival of IRI ("Istituto per la Ricostruzione Industriale", Institute for Industrial Reconstruction), while control of the banking sector remained largely in the hands of the government. The extreme centralization of all wage settlements was also a fascist-era feature that survived in post-war Italy, with a semi-public role conferred to trade unions and employers' associations that drew their origins from the 1930s. The public administration, by and large inefficient since unification, was allowed to continue its ways. Professional guilds maintained their control on the provision of services, with their rent-seeking zeal becoming a driving factor behind lengthy judicial processes.

Such features did not hinder economic growth in the 1950s and for most of the 1960s, when the country's productivity was still benefiting from a catch-up effect in technology and competitiveness was ensured by lower labor costs relative to peers. However, as Italy entered a middle-income trap at the end of the 1960s, the political class responded by mostly eschewing necessary reforms and instead loosening the public purse. A dangerous mix of blue-collar protests in 1969, far-left and far-right terrorism, and two successive oil shocks in the course in the 1970s led unstable coalition governments to prioritize consensus-seeking measures over modernization.

The fascist-era economic institutions I mentioned became so inherent to the custom and mentality of the nation, that they are no longer even perceived as a legacy of the Mussolini years. They are perceived by many as the "normal" state of things or the way things should be. But, in order to understand how this came about, let us take a step back by half a century from the moment of the "divorce". Let's go back to the time when it all started.

November 14, 1933 is an important day for the fascist regime. Benito Mussolini is due to speak to the Council of Corporations, the body collecting official representatives of the productive sectors that by then were part and parcel of the State. At this point in time the United States and the whole world were nearing the trough of the Great Depression, before the New Deal made its mark. This particular meeting takes place in the assembly hall of what is now the Ministry of Economic Development, then the Ministry of Corporations. At this moment Mussolini himself holds the interim as Minister of the Corporations.

In front of the Council of Corporations, Mussolini speaks for 70 minutes on the 13 of November 1933, "with a voice that was sometimes hard and sometimes deep in sound just as if came from afar" (Corriere della Sera). What follows are the essential passages of that speech. I left it as it is, without alterations, if not for some minor lexical adaptations to today's language (soon you will understand why):

Federico Fubini

Is this crisis that has been gripping us for four years a crisis 'in' the system or 'of' the system? The crisis has penetrated so deeply into the system that it has become a crisis of the system. Today we can say that the capitalist mode of production is outdated and, with it, the theory of economic liberalism that illustrated it.

Mussolini goes on:

I would distinguish three periods in the history of capitalism: the dynamic period, the static period, and the period of decadence. The dynamic period is the one that goes from 1830 to 1870. It coincides with the introduction of the mechanical chassis and the appearance of the locomotive. The factory is the typical manifestation of industrial capitalism, this is the era of large margins, and therefore the law of free competition and the fight of all against all can play in full. Even this time has its share of the fallen and the dead, but the Red Cross will take care of them. Even in this period there are crises, but they are cyclical ones, neither long nor universal. Capitalism still has such vitality and such strength that it can overcome crises brilliantly. During these forty years the State observes, is absent and the theorists of liberalism say: you, the State, have only one duty, to make sure that your existence is not even felt in the economic sector. The better you govern, the less you deal with economic problems. But after 1870 this period changes. The first symptoms of tiredness in the capitalist world are felt. The era of cartels, trade unions, consortia, and trusts begins.

But what is the consequence? The end of free competition. Having narrower margins, the capitalistic enterprise finds that rather than struggling it is better to strike agreements, to find allies, or merge in order to divide up markets and share the profits. At last this coalition-based capitalist economy turns to the State. What does it ask from it? Customs protection. Liberalism is struck to death.

At this stage, supercapitalism draws its inspiration and justification from the utopia of unlimited consumption. The ideal of supercapitalism would be the standardization of the human being from cradle to grave. Supercapitalism would want all men to be born of the same length, so that standardized cradles could be made; it would want children to desire the same toys, men to go dressed in the same uniform, all to read the same books, all to be of the same taste in movies, all to desire a certain automobile.

This is in the logic of things, because only in this way can supercapitalism make its plans. When does capitalist enterprise stop being an economic fact? When its dimensions lead it to be a social fact. This is the moment when the capitalist enterprise, when it is in difficulty, throws itself into the arms of the State. This is the moment in which the intervention of the State takes shape and becomes increasingly necessary. And those who ignored it are searching for it with a great deal of effort. We are at this point: if in all the nations of Europe the State fell asleep for 24 hours, that parenthesis would be enough to bring about a disaster. By now there is no economic field where the State should not intervene. If we wanted to give in by pure hypothesis to this last-minute capitalism, we would arrive at state capitalism, which is nothing but the reverse of state socialism. This is the crisis of the capitalist system taken in its universal meaning. But for us there is a specific crisis that particularly concerns us as Italians and Europeans. There is a crisis that is typically European. Europe is no longer the continent that directs human civilization. There was a time when Europe dominated the world politically, intellectually, economically. Europe can still attempt to regain the helm of universal civilization if it finds a minimum of political unity.

Let's ask ourselves now: is Italy a capitalist country? Have you ever asked yourself this question? If by capitalism we mean that set of uses, customs, technological progress now common to all countries, we can say that Italy is also capitalist. But if we go deeper into it, Italy is not a capitalist country in the current sense of this word.

Italy in my opinion must remain a country with a mixed economy, with a strong agriculture; a small and medium healthy industry, banks that do not engage in speculation.

In the statement that I presented last night the Corporation was defined as we want to create it. The Corporation is made in view of the development of wealth, political power and welfare of the Italian people. These three elements are linked to each other.

What must distress our spirit is the misery of healthy and valid men who seek work in vain.

I do not dwell on the conciliatory tasks that the Corporation can carry out, and I do not see any inconvenience in the practice of consultative tasks. Already now, every time the Government has to take measures of a certain importance, it calls those concerned. If tomorrow this becomes mandatory for certain issues, I see nothing wrong with it, because everything that brings the citizen closer to the State, everything that brings the citizen inside the cog of the State, is useful for the social and national purposes of Fascism.

When the Great Council (Gran Consiglio del fascismo, the party's ruling body, editor's note) was created on January 13, 1923, political liberalism was buried. Today we bury economic liberalism. The Corporation plays a role on the economic field as the Grand Council and the Militia did on the political field. Corporatism represents a disciplined economy, and therefore also a controlled economy, as one cannot think of a discipline that has no control. Corporatism overcomes socialism and overcomes liberalism as well, by creating a new synthesis.

We have rejected the theory of the economic man, the liberal theory, and we have been inhabiting it every time we have heard that work is a commodity. The economic man does not exist, there is the integral man who is political, economic, religious at a time.

So Mussolini spoke on 13 November 1933.

Now, let's leave aside the rhetorical emphasis. Mussolini resorts here to some tropes that are not very distant from what we hear in today's Italy – not only in Italy, to be honest – among the enemies of globalization and the market. Let's take a few examples. "Capitalism is over, we must look for another model: a different model that is made of feeling part of a community".² And again: "A State that is capable of becoming an entrepreneur is what we need today. Moreover, I do not think that having followed the philosophy of total liberalism, of leaving it to the market without intervening, has produced great results".³ Or else: "Globalization requires us all to be equal, obedient to an imposed model to be predictable and therefore controllable".⁴ Finally: "To protect the welfare of citizens, the State cannot be only a regulator. In exceptional times such as the present one it can also play a role in the economy, in strategic sectors. After all, what Italy does, other countries do as well".⁵

To be sure, those were the intellectual premises from which the founder of Fascism set out to rewrite the laws through which the Italian economy was to function. Part of his views survived him. The key to everything is a deep suspicion towards the market and private initiative, and a strong determination to involve the State and politics into business activity. This is how Mussolini responded to the Great Depression.

Admittedly, the Duce was not a unique and isolated case on the international stage. In the United States, in June of 1933, Roosevelt had launched the National Recovery Authority and inaugurated the New Deal. But there is a particular difference between Roosevelt and Mussolini, among many, that I should stress here: the US president wanted to save the market economy and political liberalism by intervening to create jobs; Mussolini aimed to replace the market economy system with new institutions he created himself.

I am increasingly convinced that many features of Mussolini's design for the economy – not politics – have largely survived in democratic Italy and explain the imbalances that the "divorce" of 1981 failed to overcome.

But let's go back to that moment for now, November 1933. Luigi Einaudi, then senator of liberal, pre-fascist Italy, follows Mussolini's speech from his studio in Dogliani. Or perhaps from the one in Turin, who knows. Einaudi explains how the new National Council of Corporations, the institutional embodiment of Italian corporatism, issues "mandatory and rigidly centralized rules on working conditions and production coordination, to which all companies must adhere. Trade unions and professional bodies become part of the State".

Continues Einaudi: "The interest of the individual citizen in his freedom of thought, meeting, and expression will be subordinated to the economic organization of Italy on the

---

2 Beppe Grillo, YouTube, 15 Feb. 2013.
3 Cgil leader Maurizio Landini, Repubblica.it, 23 Jul. 2020.
4 From an article in the newsletter of rightwing party Fratelli d'Italia "Sovrana bellezza", 4 Feb. 2020.
5 From the speech by Giuseppe Conte at the Ambrosetti Forum, 5 September 2020, Cernobbio (CO), Italy.

one hand and the needs of the Fascist Party on the other. But can a political system based on economic groupings (corporations, editor's note) ensure all the needs of citizens? If the State identifies itself so much in the control of industry and in the maintenance of individual well-being, then it must accept responsibility for the economic situation at all times". This for Einaudi was "the Achilles' heel" of Mussolini's public interventionism.

Now let's take a small step forward. "Corriere della Sera" on May 16, 1937 devotes a front-page story to the "transformation of the IRI into a permanent organ". So the Istituto per la Ricostruzione Industriale, also born in the first months of 1933 with a view to nationalize a large part of industry and banks during the Great Depression, became a permanent feature. At its birth it had absorbed the Liquidations Institute, born in 1926, which was still managing assets that had soured around the end of the First World War. But when Fascism crumbled in defeat, it left in its wake two economic cornerstones: corporatism instead of the market-based relationships between employers and employees, as well as producers and consumers; and direct state ownership of large industrial concerns and the banks.

What became of these two pillars of Fascist Italy?

Let's start with the fate of IRI. Following Liberation in 1944, Rome was under the provisional rule of the Allied Control Commission (ACC, the Allied Control Commission that had the supervision of the entire center-south of the Peninsula). As Pierluigi Ciocca admirably recounts in his "History of IRI",[6] the American commanders entrusted an assessment on the fate of the Institute to a young officer who had already been assistant to the Treasury secretary and would later work at the World Bank in Washington: Andrew Kamarck. Americans knew nothing about IRI. They wondered if they should dissolve it.

Kamarck talked about it at length with Donato Menichella, who had long been general director of the Institute alongside Alberto Beneduce during the 1930s and 1940s, until the Nazi occupation of Rome (and would soon return to his role, before becoming director general and then governor of the Banca d'Italia). In the end Kamarck asked Menichella to draft a memorandum on IRI, in which the Italian economist was to overlook the involvement of the institute in the colonial, autarchic and war events of Fascism. Rather, he focused on the IRI's raison d'être as a substitute – at first temporary, then permanent – for a capitalist system that was in deep crisis. Menichella wrote: "The Italian State found itself as the owner of the shares of the three main banks in the country and of many large industrial shareholdings". It sounded almost as if it had all happened in spite of itself. He hinted that State involvement was due more to chronically incapable entrepreneurs than a real political will of interfering. But Menichella could legitimately boast that public intervention had somehow kept the Italian economy on its feet in the 1930s. American Allied commanders

---

6   Ciocca, Pierluigi, *Storia dell'IRI. L'IRI nell'economia italiana*, vol. 6, Bari: Laterza, 2015.

worried about the social impact of a dismantlement of IRI, in a country that was starving and was marked by the massive presence of a pro-Stalinist communist party. In short, the Finance Sub-Commission of the Allied Command decided to put the fate of the entity to the Italians themselves. Thus, the IRI was saved.

How about corporatism? To understand what happened at that juncture between fascist and democratic Italy, let's read what economist Libero Lenti had to say. Lenti was a rare figure as an academic and scholar untainted by compromise with the regime. In "Corriere" of 16 March 1946 he published a front-page editorial under the title "Trasformismo economico" (referring to Italian parliamentary practice of "trasformarsi", switching sides in order to stay in power as times change). Lenti wrote: "Everyone agrees on the need for a structural reform of the State. But most keep an eye only on the political side of the issue. They neglect to consider the economic side".

Lenti saw things differently, "all the more so at a time when organizations, that are now parasitic for economic life, tend to survive", he wrote. In his 1946 story he referred to "particular groups that press for indefinitely maintaining forms of power conquered at an exceptional time". This problem, he wrote, "is further complicated by the existence of an infinite number of corporative or quasi-corporative bodies which, having become privileged bodies, derive from the State the authority to impose costs and taxes to the detriment of producers and, ultimately, consumers. This is an effective form of collective value-destruction". These bodies, concluded the Corriere's columnist, "in order to survive, are ready for every transformation [...]. This is a continuous transformation from autarchic tasks, to fiscal, commercial, political, statistical, political ones". "Fascism has left us many of these legacies unfortunately".

Lenti grasps an important point. Suffice it to say that to this day, in 2020, the journalists' guild is a quasi-government body with powers to impose compulsory taxation: membership is mandatory (alas) and if one refuses to pay the guilds fee of one hundred euros per year, in theory, one is not allowed to work as a journalist and payments of pension contributions, even when actually made, are also null and void. The same applies, of course, to a large number of still-existing professional guilds. Lenti had understood that corporatism of fascist origin, born in rejection of the market economy, was going to survive in democratic Italy. This was bound to contribute to undermining the country's prosperity once the boom years petered out.

Here lies the background that helps us understand why an inter-institutional arrangement such as the "divorzio" could not possibly change the country's trajectory. Mindsets and economic structures were too deep-rooted. The four decades to follow would challenge, and shake, them both to their core.

Are the Germans Obsessed with Inflation and Central Bank Independence?

Tobias Piller[1]

It seemed like an obsession for Germany's partners during the construction of the monetary union: The principles which Germany wanted to see fully anchored in the Treaty for the monetary union were an uncompromising fight against inflation and, connected to this, the guarantee of full independence for the central bank. Especially in southern Europe, the German requests were received rather as a pain in the neck, based on an historic experience with inflation in the distant past that had led to an obsession with Bundesbank independence.

Germany's self-assuredness about the institutional architecture of its monetary system – combined with some aversion of others towards this attitude – made the way the Germans felt about the D-Mark and the Bundesbank seem like a hardly understandable mixture of national tradition and folklore.

1. Bundesbank fighting for Independence

But, as a deeper look into the historic and structural conditions will show, the folkloristic interpretation of the German attitude is a misperception. Historical developments created a desire for an independent central bank. Later, the independence of the Bundesbank became in some way even legendary. Also this notion did not come from nowhere. What was behind it is revealed by an episode about an open conflict in 1956 between the powerful Chancellor and an unforgiving top management of the Bundesbank.

---

1   Tobias Piller describes since 1992 the Italian economy, companies and finance as a correspondent for the daily newspaper Frankfurter Allgemeine Zeitung. He is particularly interested in the Italian role in the Monetary Union, the export potential of Italian companies and sectoral clusters, and the problems of the Mezzogiorno. Since 2012, he is also reporting on the economy of Greece. Tobias Piller joined Frankfurter Allgemeine Zeitung in 1989, working on the newsdesk, reporting on Eastern Germany after the fall of the Berlin Wall, and on the car industry. Before, he graduated as an economist, after studying at Regensburg University and London School of Economics. During his years in Rome, he committed himself to sustaining the working situation of all foreign correspondents. Between 2007 and 2017, he was elected six times as President of the official Foreign Press Club of Italy, "Associazione della Stampa Estera in Italia".

The protagonist on one side of this episode was Konrad Adenauer, Chancellor of Western Germany since the re-foundation as a democratic state in 1949. In the middle of the 1950s, he was at the apex of his power. Adenauer tried to maximise economic growth in order to leave the misery of wartimes behind and to speed up the recovery of post-war Germany. On this course, he saw the central bank as an obstacle, even though the Bundesbank was not yet officially founded. The function of the central bank was in the hands of the "Bank deutscher Länder" (BdL), the Bank of the Federal States, which was in charge when, in 1948, the new German currency, the "D-Mark", was introduced ahead of the foundation of the Federal Republic of Germany in 1949. In 1956, the representatives of the Federal Government had the legal right to speak at the Governing Council of the BdL and to ask for a postponement of any decision for at least eight days. Adenauer sent his Minister of Finance and the Minister of the Economy to the meeting of the Governing Council to ask the BdL to postpone any decision on higher interest rates and for the permission to park the financial surplus of the Federal Government directly with commercial banks. The Governing Council replied with an outright "no" to the latter request. Moreover, it denied the Government the right to ask for the postponement of the rates decision on the grounds that the Ministers had already asked to postpone the meeting of the Governing Council for several weeks. After the Ministers had left, the Council decided a hefty rise of interest rates by a full percentage point, doing the opposite of what had been desired by Adenauer.[2]

Chancellor Adenauer reacted harshly. When he addressed the Association of German Industry, the "BDI", he fumed that "we have an organ, which is not responsible to anyone, not to parliament and not to government. All the bigger is the responsibility that every member of such an organ has to bear [...] There has been a big blow to the German business cycle, and who will be left behind are the small enterprises [...] The guillotine would hit ordinary people". In Adenauer's opinion, the BdL in Frankfurt did not understand politics. "And when politics is unstable, the economy cannot be stable".[3]

The famous "guillotine-speech" of Adenauer, however, led to some dissenting public voices, which sound familiar today: "As far as the policy of the Central Bank is concerned, the verdict of a lack of political thinking can be easily interpreted as the desire that central bank policy should follow the needs of politicians. And some 'political catastrophes' started with a central bank that was 'thinking politically'", wrote Erich Welter, editor of Frankfurter Allgemeine Zeitung. His conclusion was: "The most important thing is that, at least, the central bank will not let itself get involved in daily tactics and will not change its mind about the task to keep the value of money stable. Because by doing this, it is making its best contribution to an economic strategy".[4]

---

2 Protocol of Bank Deutscher Länder from the meeting on the 7 Mar. 1956, from the Archives of Bundesbank.
3 Text of speech in FAZ, 30 May 1956.
4 Welter, Erich, Editorial in FAZ, 22 Mai 1956.

In the end, even the powerful Chancellor Konrad Adenauer could not do anything but respect central bank independence. This was enshrined in the law for the Bundesbank, the "Bundesbankgesetz", which preceded the change of name of the BdL to "Deutsche Bundesbank" in 1957. Only in theory could Adenauer's Government have acted differently on the grounds that the law regulating the Bundesbank is not part of the Constitution and hence can be changed by simple majority in Parliament. In practice, after the historical experience the Germans had gone through, no politician would have dared to question the independence of the central bank, because he would have faced strong popular resistance.

These events led to Paragraph 12 of the Bundesbank Law on "the relation of the Bank and the Federal Cabinet", which says:

> Without prejudice to the performance of its functions, the Deutsche Bundesbank is required to support the general economic policy of the Federal Cabinet. In exercising the powers conferred on it by this Act, it is independent of instructions from the Federal Government. [5]

Certainly, Adenauer never again sent ministers to a meeting of the Governing Council of the Deutsche Bundesbank. Nevertheless, there have been further conflicts between governing politicians and the Bundesbank, especially when it raised interest rates, as in the late 1950s and 1960s, to counter inflationary pressures during years of vivacious growth. The first President of the Bundesbank, Karl Blessing (1958 to 1969), even dared to write to Chancellor Adenauer prior to the election campaign of 1961 to warn him about the dangers of loose fiscal policies caused by the electoral cycle.[6] Blessing did not refrain from asking for discipline in setting salaries and prices. In his view, rising prices would lead to lower activity in the real economy. In addition, he warned: "Anyone who speculates that we, the central bank, will pull the chestnuts out of the fire by opening the taps of money, is mistaken".[7] Later on, during the elections of 1972, the then Social Democratic Chancellor Helmut Schmidt found a polemic answer to the plights of the policy of the independent Bundesbank: "It seems to me that the German people can stand five per cent inflation more easily than five per cent unemployment".[8]

Further differences arose during the 1990s, when the central bankers judged the fiscal policies of the Federal Government during the post-unification years as too loose. Bundesbank President Karl Otto Pöhl (1980 to 1991) resigned in reaction to the conversion rate of 1:1 between the East German Mark and the D-Mark, which led to big increases in East

---

5   This "Bundesbank Act" has been revised in the meantime, with the insertion of the fact that Bundesbank acts "as part of the European System of Central Banks".
6   Deutsche Bundesbank, *50 Jahre Deutsche Mark*, München: 1998, p. 206.
7   Blessing, Karl. Editorial in FAZ, 2 May 1958, p. 7.
8   FAZ, 9 Aug. 1972, p. 1.

German salaries, taking them far beyond East German levels of productivity. In the view of Pöhl and the Bundesbank this was irresponsible as it would overburden the East German economy and stifle the recovery. Even the appearance of any Bundesbank decision seemed to be important: When in 1999 Finance Minister Oskar Lafontaine, an adherent to the Keynesian school, repeatedly asked publicly for lower interest rates, Bundesbank President Hans Tietmeyer explained during a background meeting in Rome: "Even if there are enough reasons for lowering interest rates, there will not be any decision, as long as a member of Government is expressing the demand for this step in public. Such a move will come only after he has remained quiet for a reasonable time". The Bundesbank simply wanted to avoid at all costs any impression that it might follow suggestions from the Government.

While many European countries suffered from high inflation in the 1970s and 1980s, sometimes in double digits, the Bundesbank had at least some relative success in containing the surge of prices. The trust and goodwill gained by the Bundesbank during the first decades of its existence could also be registered at a few extraordinary occasions: During a large part of 1994, German inflation was pushed up by the effects of unification and Government spending, ending up above the inflation rate in France. Nonetheless, German government bond yields remained at 6.68 per cent, below those of France at 7.52 per cent. This meant that investors kept their faith that the Bundesbank would hold inflation in Germany lower than in France over the long-run, even if this led to higher real interest rates in Germany than in the neighbouring country.

2. The roots of inflation

Maybe there was no other country where the idea of independence for the central bank had such strong support that even a powerful head of government would not dare to touch it. Outside Germany, many believed that this attitude was due to an obsession of Germans caused by the historic experience of hyperinflation, far away in history. But anyone who studies the historic events would have to concede that it was precisely the way the Reichsbank operated which proved to be fatal for the development of inflation. The two devastating waves of the debasement of money – in 1923 by hyperinflation and during WWII by repressed inflation that led to currency reform – were due to the fact that the central bank had been too much under the influence or direct control of Government. In this way, it was natural that a fundamental principle of central banking and of the constitution of money was violated.

What gives value to money – paper notes or virtual numbers in balance sheets – is the principle that the amount of money in circulation should reflect the amount of goods and services produced. This was not the case in the German economy in the times of the First

World War and had fatal consequences. Before 1914 the Reichsmark was tied to gold. So, in theory, the central bank was obliged to exchange any banknote for gold. To give credibility to this link the central bank needed to hold one third of the value of all circulating banknotes in gold. With the start of the First World War, the obligation to exchange paper money into gold was abolished. Initially, the obligation to match one third of the volume of paper money with gold reserves remained in place. But rules and central bankers were still too orientated towards the concept of paper money, to understand that virtual money in bank accounts started to enlarge the mass of money in circulation. For this reason, credit money in bank accounts was not included in the promise of the exchange for gold. Thus, the link between money and gold was broken without it even being noticed.[9]

The gateway for the inflationary developments which were to come was the obligation for the Reichsbank to finance short term gaps in the government budget. The government had the right to issue promissory notes and exchange them for cash at the central bank. These promissory notes did not bear interest and were initially intended as a short-term stop gap for the government. Within few years, however, their role became ever more important. Instead of repaying the promissory notes, the Government simply renewed them. Initially, there was the obstacle that the total amount for the emission of promissory was limited to 475 million Reichsmark, but this limit was soon abolished.

Within a few years, the balance sheet of the central bank lost most of its solidity. Before, the amount of paper money in circulation was guaranteed by one third in gold and the rest by (private) bills of exchange, backed by at least three guarantors. These bills – and their cash equivalent – reflected real activity in the economy. But soon after the start of the First World War, the Reichsbank started to accept promissory notes from the Government in exchange for money without limits. Additionally, parallel money in the form of "Darlehenskassenscheine" (bills of debt) was introduced for settling liabilities to public institutions. The Reichsbank started to accept even those questionable titles for exchange into money.

Government war expenses were increasingly financed by government borrowing from the Reichsbank, which was tantamount to financing the war by printing money. Monetary financing of government expenses continued after the end of the war, when the Government had to pay for invalid soldiers, widows and orphans, and compensation for, e.g., the confiscation of commercial vessels. In addition, fresh money was necessary simply for public investment and other expenditures to create new jobs at a time of high unemployment.[10]

While monetary financing of public spending by the Reichsbank boosted the money supply, the supply of goods dropped dramatically. Moreover, during the war a large part

---

9 Blaich, Fritz, *Der Schwarze Freitag. Inflation und Wirtschaftskrise*, München, 1985, pp. 19-22.
10 Blaich, Fritz, *ibidem,* pp. 33-44.

of national production was deviated to military use. For civil economic activities, including agriculture, productivity and output shrank. The economic historian Fritz Blaich wrote that at the end of the war, the supply of goods for civil use in the German market had shrunk by one third. Thus, a huge monetary overhang had been created. This meant that the reduced supply of goods could not match a hugely increased offer of money.[11]

The overhang became even more dramatic after 1918. While the financing of public deficits by the Reichsbank continued, the supply of goods shrank even more when Germany had to start war reparation payments. The economy received another blow in 1923, when French troops occupied the Ruhr area to enforce reparation payments and cut off the rest of Germany from the most important source of industrial production.

The occupation of the Ruhr area triggered the burst of the monetary overhang. Hyperinflation wiped out all private monetary savings in the course of 1923. Daily life became a challenge during this year. As inflation raced ahead, people had to rush to get part of their salary paid every day and to spend it immediately. Shopkeepers, bakers and butchers found out that Friday's earnings were largely wiped out when the cash was taken to the bank on Monday. A large part of the activities in the economy revolved around printing, counting and distributing ever growing mountains of paper money with rapidly dwindling purchasing power (see table 1).[12]

Date	Price of	
	1 kg of Ryebread	1 kg of Beef
	Marks	Marks
03.01.1923	163	1.800
04.07.1923	1.895	40.000
06.08.1923	8.421	440.000
03.09.1923	273.684	4.000.000
01.10.1923	9.474.000	80.000.000
22.10.1923	1.389.000.000	10.000.000.000
05.11.1923	78.000.000.000	240.000.000.000
19.11.1923	233.000.000.000	4.800.000.000.000

Tab. 1: The Great German Inflation
Source: Blaich, Fritz, *Der Schwarze Freitag*, München, 1985, page 31.

---

11   Blaich, Fritz, *ibidem*, pp. 20-22, 38-39.
12   Blaich, Fritz, *ibidem*, pp. 9-17, 31.

Monetary financing of government spending played a similar role during and after the Second World War, until 1948. But this time the monetary overhang – temporarily kept under control with rationing and food stamps – was eliminated by currency reform before it was allowed to boost prices. This – and the quick return to a market economy – created favourable conditions for an economic recovery that many regarded as a miracle. Part of this miracle was the appearance, one year before the foundation of the Federal Republic of Germany in 1949, of a new currency with a stable purchasing power. The new "Deutsche Mark" soon became a symbol of recovery and a reason of pride for many Germans who had to grapple with the atrocities committed in their name (and often their acquiescence) during the war.

3. The German Understanding of the Role of the Central Bank

To many other nations the German allergy against inflation appeared strange. They had got accustomed to elevated but contained inflation and even saw it as useful for stimulating economic growth and reducing the real value of debt. Hence, the German attitude was seen as oversensitive and almost irrational.

Against this, the experience of the effects on inflation of weaknesses in the institutional architecture of the central bank remained engrained in the collective memory of Germans. Or, putting it the other way round, they became convinced that only a "really" independent central bank could guarantee price stability.

This was the reason why the German negotiators of the Maastricht Treaty sought to transfer the concept of central bank independence towards the European Monetary Union (EMU) – and with it some of the credibility and "goodwill" of the Bundesbank. From an economic point of view, the Germans felt no urgency to establish a monetary union. They did not see any short-term advantages, like perhaps many Italians did. For the latter, EMU was connected with the hope of containing public debt. For instance, after the end of his term as President of the Republic, Carlo Azeglio Ciampi said: "Without the euro, Italy would have ended up like Argentina".[13] In exchange for moving ahead with EMU, Germany was able to set some conditions for the design of the monetary union in the negotiations of the Maastricht Treaty concluded in 1992. The most important conditions were the independence of the future European Central Bank and the ban of outright financing of states by the central bank.

---

13   Ciampi, Carlo Azeglio, Cited in FAZ, 2 Jan. 2007.

Tobias Piller

In the latest European Treaty, from Lisbon in 2007, the formula from Maastricht was still preserved in the first paragraph of Article 123:

> Overdraft facilities or any other type of credit facility with the European Central Bank or with the central banks of the Member States (hereinafter referred to as 'national central banks') in favour of Union institutions, bodies, offices or agencies, central governments, regional, local or other public authorities, other bodies governed by public law, or public undertakings of Member States shall be prohibited, as shall the purchase directly from them by the European Central Bank or national central banks of debt instruments.

In the two decades since the start of European Monetary Union, however, many principles and ways in which the European Central Bank is run have been changed. A prominent change is the way with which the ECB has bought and is still buying government bonds. These bonds are bought in the secondary market, but it is clear to all actors in the financial markets and governments (like the Italian one) that the purpose is to create a backstop for public debt. Governments of heavily indebted countries, such as Italy, want to ensure that there will never again be doubts about their solvency and ability to roll over expiring bonds. Italy was several times at the brink of not being able to refinance its debt (e.g. in 1993 and 2011). Today, the Italian government can fund its activities at highly favourable rates, even though rating agencies deem it at the margin of investment grade, as long as the ECB includes Italian government bonds in its programmes.

Certainly, there have been good reasons for the European Central Bank to embark on extraordinary instruments in extraordinary situations. In 2012, ECB President Mario Draghi feared that doubts about the sustainability of public debt in several southern European countries could tear the monetary union apart, and he made his famous promise to do "whatever it takes" to save the euro. And during the Coronavirus crisis, the ECB, now guided by Christine Lagarde, returned to the recipe of buying massive amounts of public debt.

At the end of 2019, the European System of Central Banks held 23 billion euro of public debt under the label "Government debt", but 2,100 billion euro of government bonds under the label "Securities held for monetary policy purposes" on its balance sheet. Thus, the central bank has bought more than one fifth of the 10,023 billion euro total public debt of the 19 member states of the Monetary Union. The purchase programs for public and private bonds led to an extraordinary increase in the total assets of the European System of Central Banks. At the start of EMU in 1999 with 11 member states, the consolidated balance sheet of the Eurosystem reached 807 billion euro, equivalent to 12.5 percent of the total Gross Domestic Product (GDP) of the member states. At the end of 2019, the balance sheet total was 4,671 billion euro, or 39.2 percent of the GDP of the presently 19 member states.

Against the background of the historical experiences, doubts and worries about the long-term effects of these central bank policies are more widespread in Germany than in other European countries. Unfortunately, these fears have been hijacked by German nationalist parties, which taints the legitimacy of critical questions about the future. Nonetheless, they should be answered. In the short run, there seems to be little danger of inflation because of the huge mass of money created during the last years. At the moment, it would be difficult for anyone to raise prices for goods or services. There is global competition and little scarcity of means of production as well as high price transparency created by the internet. There are no expectations of price increases among consumers which would fuel inflation. However, huge money supply and zero interest rates stimulate asset price increases, and financial market operators rely on the central banks of the world to insure their asset holdings so as to avoid turmoil which could spread to the real economy.

Where will this lead to in the long run? Some decades ago, monetarists would have predicted that a rise in monetary supply would surely trigger inflation. Still today, in Argentina, Turkey or Zimbabwe anyone can see the inflationary effects and the free fall of exchange rates as results of governments taking political control of the central banks. Zimbabwe just recently experienced hyperinflation.[14] But surely, the European Monetary Union is different from Zimbabwe.

In any case, there are warning signs against the ECB going on for too long with purchases of government bonds and the supply of money at zero interest. The problem is that many institutions, politicians, investors, and banks are getting used to these policies so that, from their point of view, they should never end. Could there be an occasion for a change of the present policy in the future? For politicians of an indebted country or managers of investment funds, the moment for change is never right and there will always be a reason to continue as before. Bundesbank President Jens Weidmann warns that in this way the central bank will eventually be captured by institutions which have become addicted to the extraordinary measures of policy easing introduced in recent years:

> In perspective, I see the problem that the rise in public debt makes the risk of fiscal dominance more urgent. There could be growing pressure on Central Banks to leave interest rates low, and thus also the financing costs of States – even if this was not appropriate any more from the point of view of monetary policy. We must be very clear that we will not subordinate monetary policy to the needs of fiscal policy [...] At the moment, we have a constellation, where fiscal policy and monetary policy go into the same direction. But we should not create the impression as if this would always be the case. If in the future there will be conflict, independence and backbone are necessary to pursue the objective of price stability.[15]

---

14 "Zimbabwe's currency: A mouthful of zollars", where zollars refer to "Zimbabwean dollars". *The Economist*, 25 May 2019.
15 Weidmann Jens: Interview to Börsenzeitung, 8 Oct. 2020.

By now, more than two decades after the start of the monetary union and even more years after the negotiations of the Maastricht Treaty, the bargaining power which Germany possessed before the signing of the Treaty and the start of the monetary union, seems all gone. The vote of the President of the Bundesbank counts now as much as those of the Governors of the Central Banks of Malta or Luxemburg, the smallest countries in the euro-area, in the Governing Council of the ECB. Some commentators welcome the thought that the voice of Bundesbank is part of a small minority for some time now in the ECB, often overwhelmed by a majority with different objectives. German unease with the course of the ECB has also led to a series of resignations, including the former ECB Chief Economist Jürgen Stark (2011), the President of Bundesbank Axel Weber (2011), and the German member of the ECB Executive Board, Sabine Lautenschläger (2019).

It did not go down well with other Europeans, when one of the most respected German institutions, the Federal Constitutional Court, dared to look back at the European Treaties from which the Monetary Union and the European Union originated, especially as regards the legal prohibition for the ECB to finance Governments. The German Constitutional Court did not take a fundamentalist view. It just requested that a temporary suspension of Article 123 of the Lisbon Treaty in an emergency should be accompanied by an assessment of proportionality. In other words, there should be a transparent cost-benefit-analysis of all instruments employed to fulfil the ECB's mandate. The reactions were devastating: One line of argument was that a national court would not have the right to control whether the German prerequisites for agreeing to the monetary union – which in Germany were "conditions sine qua non" – would still be met. Others decried an alleged breach of the independence of the central bank, but they obviously meant independence from earlier agreed legal principles, so that the present, more politically motivated majority in the ECB-Council could decide whatever they believed to be useful.

In fact, the majority of the Governing Council of the European Central Bank seems to give a lot of importance to "thinking politically". Is this exactly what the first President of the Bundesbank decried, or are conditions different today? For now, things have gone relatively well for the European Central Bank during turbulent times. However, the test for its independence is yet to come, and there is no guarantee that in the long run inflation will not rise. If there was a persistent rise of inflation, say to 5 percent or more, the institutional set up and the legitimacy of euro and European Central Bank could be put to a very strenuous test by Germany and Germans.

Chapter II

Exploring the Reasons of the Alpine Divide

On the Origins of the German and Italian Policy Paradigms towards European Monetary Integration

Ivo Maes[1]

1. Introduction

Germany and Italy are both founding members of the EU. Both countries enjoyed relatively stable and supportive attitudes towards European integration among the elite and also more widely in public opinion. Germany has, of course, been a more powerful actor in the European Union system than Italy. In the literature on European monetary integration, Germany and Italy are mostly strongly contrasted. This article argues that there were important similarities in the policy paradigms towards Economic and Monetary Union (EMU) between these two countries. The paper distinguishes between the policy paradigms of foreign policy-makers and economic policy-makers and traces the origins of these paradigms in the national institutional settings. Indeed, the state structures in both countries are characterised by a division of power amongst institutional policy-makers.[2] Both countries are relatively young nation states, a contrast, for instance, with a country like France.[3]

In both Germany and Italy, there were disagreements between economic and foreign policy-makers on issues of European monetary integration. At crucial moments, like the creation of the European Monetary System or the Maastricht Treaty, foreign policy-makers played a crucial role in the advancement of the EMU project. Naturally, it is not always easy to delineate exactly foreign and economic policy-makers. In both countries the nucleus of the foreign policy-makers was the Foreign ministry, while the central bank was at the core of the economic policy-makers. Foreign policy-makers, under the influence of a European federalist vision, were strongly in favour of European monetary integration. These foreign policy beliefs were crucial in charting

---

1 Ivo Maes is Senior Advisor at the Economics and Research Department of the National Bank of Belgium and a Professor, Robert Triffin Chair, at the Université catholique de Louvain, as well as at ICHEC Brussels Management School.
2 Maes, Ivo and Lucia Quaglia, "Germany and Italy: Conflicting Policy Paradigms Towards European Monetary Integration?", *Constitutional Political Economy*, Vol. 17, No. 3, Sep. 2006, pp. 189-205.
3 For a comparison of France and Germany on EMU, cf. Maes, Ivo "On the Origins of the Franco-German EMU Controversies", *European Journal of Law and Economics*, Vol. 17, No 1, Jan. 2004, pp. 21-39. For a comparison of France and Italy on EMU, cf. Quaglia, Lucia and Ivo Maes, "France and Italy's Policies on European Monetary Integration: a Comparison of 'Strong' and 'Weak' States", *Comparative European Politics*, Vol. 2, No. 1, Apr. 2004, pp. 51-72.

EMU policy at decisive moments and they were rooted in the historical legacy of both countries. Germany and Italy were both created in the second half of the nineteenth century and marked by fascist regimes in the twentieth century. After the Second World War, the mainstream political leaders in both countries supported the process of European integration as a way to rehabilitate their countries in the international community. Moreover, since both Germany and Italy were "frontier" States in the Cold War, European integration was also a way to anchor democracy. The vast majority of political elites in both countries shared a federalist approach to Europe, in contrast with France. The pro EMU policy paradigms of foreign policy-makers in Germany and Italy contrasted, during most of the post-war period, with the more sceptical beliefs of economic policymakers. In both countries, economic policy-makers, at different moments, had doubts whether enough "convergence" had been reached to make a more stable exchange rate system sustainable. In the 21st century, with a disappointing economic performance and the rise of the migration issue, populism gained influence and euro-sceptic positions have become more popular, especially in Italy.

2. State structures in Germany and Italy

Germany is characterised by power-sharing institutions within a federalist state structure with checks and balances. Unlike many other European states, such as France, the nation state had much less deep roots in Germany (or Italy). Moreover, the experience of national socialism marked a fundamental break with the past in Germany. As national socialism had shown the dangers of a centralisation of power, a crucial element of the new economic and political system in post-war Germany was "decentralisation". This was a reaction against the centralisation of Hitler, but it was also the result of American influences in the reconstruction of West Germany, which resulted in a federal State, federal central banking system, anti-cartel policy, etc. Decentralisation not only applied to the political organisation of the country, such as the federal structure of the state, it was also a basic principle of the organisation of economic policy. So, the central bank was responsible for monetary policy, but not for banking supervision.

The German state structure is a clear example of institutional pluralism.[4] The prime minister, the Chancellor, controls several resources and holds sway over the policies and the direction of the government, though they are also highly constrained by the constitution, the statute law, co-governing forces and veto players.[5] Potential veto players are

---

4   Strum, Roland, "Policymakers in a new political landscape", in Padgett, Stephen, William E. Paterson, and Gordon Smith, *Development in German politics 3*, Basingstoke: Palgrave, 2003, p. 102.
5   Schmidt, Manfred, *Political institutions in the Federal Republic of Germany*, Oxford: OUP, 2003, p. 26.

empowered by German federalism and the predominance of political parties. Individual ministers initiate policies themselves, however, in case of conflict with the Chancellor or within the cabinet, the Chancellor has generally the last word.

Germany's economic system in the post-war period can be characterised as a "social market economy", combining the principle of freedom in the market with that of social balance. In contrast to "laissez-faire" capitalism, the concept of the social market economy requires above all a clear legal and political regulatory framework, or "Ordnungsrahmen".[6] Ordo-liberal economists emphasise the interdependence between the economic order and all other forms of order (i.e. legal, social and political).

A constitutive element of the social market economy is monetary stability.[7] Monetary stability is important for economic reasons, as inflation damages the steering function of the price mechanism and creates uncertainty, which hurts investment. It is also important for social reasons, as inflation causes a redistribution of income, to the disadvantage of the weaker groups who cannot protect themselves. Memories of this were still vivid in Germany, with the hyperinflation of the 1920s. The task of ensuring monetary stability became the responsibility of the independent Bundesbank. There is also an affinity with the German "federalist" approach of preferring decentralised and compartmentalised structures.[8]

The Bundesbank is widely regarded as one of the most independent central banks in the world. The relationship with the political authorities, first and foremost the government, is complex. The Bank enjoys a high degree of independence from the government, and before EMU had exclusive responsibility for monetary policy, as well as a strong say in exchange rate policy and international monetary agreements. The Bank exerted its influence also beyond monetary policy in a strict sense, as it was vigilant about the effects of budgetary and income policies on price stability.

Before EMU, the federal government had the prime responsibility for external monetary relations. The choice of the exchange rate regime and the decisions on parity realignments were made by the Federal government. However, since exchange rate policy has a direct effect on monetary policy and price stability, the central bank exerted a strong influence also on these decisions. The central bank was furthermore responsible for the day to day management and currency interventions.

---

6   Tietmeyer, Hans., *The Social Market Economy and Monetary Stability*, London: Economica, 1999, p. 6.
7   *ibidem*, p. 138.
8   *ibidem*, p. 165.

The federalist German philosophy went along with a positive view towards European integration, supporting the transfer of sovereignty to supranational European institutions. Moreover, the belief that European security and Franco German reconciliation were the most vital of all interests for Germany was widespread.[9] This was at the core of the foreign policy paradigm in Germany.

Former German Chancellor Helmut Schmidt, in an article in *Die Zeit* of 29 September 1995, also underlined the motive of safeguarding peace: "The progress made in European integration [...] corresponds to Germany's vital, long-term strategic interest in ensuring peace if our country wishes to avoid a third anti-German coalition. All Chancellors from Adenauer to Kohl have been guided by this insight [...] Compared with this essential goal, all the nit-picking about the technical details of monetary union [...] is of secondary importance".[10]

The period 1989-1990 was characterised by dramatic political changes in Europe. With the fall of the Berlin Wall in November 1989, the issue of German unification came suddenly to the forefront. The German government's policy line could almost be summarised in Thomas Mann's dictum: "Wir wollen ein europäisches Deutschland und kein deutsches Europa". German unification and European Monetary Union would become intertwined.

It can be interesting to contrast Germany with France, one of the oldest nation states in Europe, with a long tradition as a strong, centralised state. As remarked by Rosanvallon,[11] the 'State' preceded the nation in France and gave France a coherence and an identity. The Revolution of 1789 abolished the monarchy and reduced the role of religion, placing 'Reason' at the centre of French society. This further reinforced the role of the state in French society. It gave birth to "la tradition républicaine", focused on the 'one and indivisible' republic, with the primacy attached to the sovereign nation as the source of legitimacy. With the Fifth Republic, France became a presidential republic in which the president is elected directly by its citizens. The head of state enjoys a strong leadership role in line with the Napoleonic and centralist traditions. French policy-makers have generally been more reluctant to transfer sovereignty to the European level – they favoured an intergovernmental Europe. For French policy-makers, European monetary integration was also a way to obtain a more symmetrical international monetary system. De Gaulle had always been critical of the central position of the American dollar

---

9   Küsters, Hanns Jürgen, "Walter Hallstein and the Negotiations on the Treaties of Rome 1955-57", in Loth, Wielfried, William Wallace and Wolfgang Wessels (eds.), *Walter Hallstein. The Forgotten European?*, London: Macmillan, 1998, p. 62.

10 Bernholz, Peter, "The Bundesbank and the Process of European Monetary Integration", in Deutsche Bundesbank, *Fifty Years of the Deutsche Mark*, Oxford: OUP, p. 734.

11 Rosanvallon, Pierre, "L'Etat au Tournant", in Lenoir, René and Jacques Lesourne (eds.), *Où va l'Etat?*, Paris: Le Monde Editions, 1992, p. 64.

in the Bretton Woods system.[12] EMU could then weaken the supremacy of the US dollar in the international monetary system and reorientate the G5/G7 meetings from an American-German discussion to a "transatlantic" dialogue.

Italy, like Germany, dates its existence only back to the second half of the 19th century and national identity is still not considered as fully consolidated. The state is perceived as having limited legitimation, and the low trust in national institutions was traditionally matched by widespread pro-European attitudes. De iure, the sphere and scope of state action in Italy are broad, however they are undermined by the systemic neutralisation of power between different centres competing for influence. For these reasons, Italy has traditionally been portrayed as a 'weak' state[13] with a porous structure and a dispersed and poorly coordinated set of institutions punctuated by personalism and fragmentation, and a Byzantine bureaucracy. The executive had limited powers vis-à-vis the legislative and the Prime Minister's position within the executive was also relatively weak. Thus, the formal and substantial powers of the Prime Minister and the executive in macroeconomic policymaking, as well as in other policy areas, such as the EMU policy, were quite limited and mainly rested on the Prime Minister's function as arbiter between domestic forces.[14] The archipelago institutional structure also meant that a multitude of economic ministries were involved in macroeconomic policy-making in various ways.

In the post-war period, the Italian central bank had a special position in Italy and was highly respected domestically and internationally.[15] Firstly, the Banca d'Italia secured stability and continuity in the volatile Italian environment with a high turnover of governments, even if substantial changes in the composition of the government majority and political personnel were more limited. Secondly, the Bank is a monolithic institution within which the governor has a very powerful position representing the Bank de jure and de facto and being personally responsible for central bank policy.[16] This contrasted neatly with the weakness of the executive and its strong subordination to the legislature, at least for most of the period considered here. It should be noted that, precisely because the central bank was a robust institution, whereas the remaining parts of the Italian state apparatus were weak, it was able to have a major input in Italy's macroeconomic policy strategy and EMU policy, as also in Germany (where political structures were stronger).

---

12 Maes, Ivo, *Robert Triffin. A Life*, in cooperation with Ilaria Pasotti, Oxford: OUP, 2021 (forthcoming).
13 Ranci, Pippo, "Italy: the Weak state" in Duchêne, François and William G. Shepherd, *Managing industrial change in Western Europe*, London; New York: Pinter, 1987.
14 Dyson, Kenneth and Kevin Featherstone, *The Road to Maastricht*, Oxford, Oxford University Press, 1999.
15 Quaglia, Lucia., "Civil Servants, Economic Policies and Economic Ideas: Lessons from Italy", *Governance*, 18, 4, 2005, pp. 545-566.
16 Eizenga, Wietze, "The Banca d'Italia and Monetary Policy", *Suerf papers on monetary policy and financial systems*, n. 15, p. 13.

A crucial problem for Italian policy-makers, that mainly resulted from the fragmented national institutional framework, were the frequent divergences and inconsistencies between the various macroeconomic policies: fiscal policy, monetary and exchange rate policy and incomes policy.[17] So, inflation and budget deficits were much higher in Italy than in Germany and the Italian lira lost ground against the Deutsche Mark. However, economic policy also evolved over time, becoming more stability oriented in the 1980s and 1990s.

The role of the exchange rate as an instrument of economic policy has been a topic of intense discussions among economic policy-makers in Italy.[18] The Banca d'Italia, in its Annual Report published in May 1969, at a time when Italy's external position was strong, was one of the first official actors to raise the issue of the inflation divergencies in the Bretton Woods system and to discuss potential alternatives like a crawling peg. So, at the Banca d'Italia there was a strong tendency to favour exchange rate flexibility. One of the reasons is probably a strong Anglo-Saxon orientation at the Banca d'Italia (in the Anglo-Saxon academic world the exchange rate is generally regarded as an instrument of economic adjustment). Moreover, especially from the 1970s onwards, Italy's economic performance, especially its high inflation, often made adjustments of the lira parity unavoidable.[19] So, whereas some economic policy-makers in Italy, especially in the 1980s, maintained that the exchange rate could be a tool to impose macroeconomic discipline, others regarded it as a valuable instrument of economic adjustment, which Italy was not ready to give up, and that could be forsaken only after significant convergence had been achieved across European economies. So, economic policy-makers both in Germany and Italy, were taking more "economist" positions than foreign policy-makers.

Italian attitudes towards European (monetary) integration were, in general, more complex than the German stance: there was less consensus and positions shifted over time. However, for most of the period covered by this paper, Italian political, economic and cultural elites, as well as public opinion, supported the process of European integration. Italian governments have traditionally been among the most pro-European and most in favour of transferring sovereignty to the European level.

---

17   Rossi, Salvatore, *La Politica Economica Italiana 1968-98*, Roma: Laterza, 1998.
18   Maes Ivo, "Il pensiero economico italiano e l'integrazione europea (1945-1999)", in Lilia Costabile et al. (eds.), *Gli economisti italiani. Protagonisti, paradigmi, politiche*, Roma: Bardi Edizone, Atti dei Convegni Lincei, 2015, pp. 309-332.
19   The social changes in Italy with the "hot autumn of 1969" were not only more extensive and pervasive than in other countries (e.g. terrorism with the Red Brigades), but also lasted much longer. See Allum, Percy, "Italian Society Transformed", in McCarthy, Patrick (ed.), *Italy Since 1945*, Oxford: OUP, 2020, pp. 10-41.

An important role was played by the Christian Democrats, who dominated the political scene until the 1992 general elections and who were very pro-European. The European "vocation" was also the prevailing ethos of Italian diplomacy, which emphasised that Italy had to remain at the core of the process of European integration. Membership of the European Communities was seen as a way to rehabilitate Italy in the international community after 1945 and as a way to anchor democracy and freedom in a wider European framework.

The similarity of the German and Italian views came clearly to the foreground with the publication of a joint memorandum in 1981 by the German foreign minister, Hans-Dietrich Genscher, and the Italian foreign minister, Emilio Colombo. The document called for stronger cooperation in foreign policy, extending it to security and defence matters, and it also proposed treaty reforms that included more majority voting.

3. Conclusion

To understand German and Italian approaches towards European monetary integration it is important to focus on the policy paradigms of different categories of state policy-makers. State structures in both countries, power sharing in Germany and power fragmentation in Italy, meant that many different institutional actors were involved in policy making on European monetary integration and that there was no clear or monolithic view, in contrast with France. In both countries there were important and systematic differences of opinion between economic and foreign policy-makers. Foreign policy views and foreign policymakers were crucial in charting the EMU policy of both countries at history making junctures, like the creation of the EMS and the Maastricht treaty, with the prime ministers taking their view at crucial moments. In contrast, the institutional framework of EMU was strongly shaped by the economic policy-makers, especially the Bundesbank. The foreign policy paradigms that informed the views and behaviour of the political authorities in Germany and Italy were shaped by widespread pro-European attitudes and a federalist approach, deeply rooted in the history of both countries.

Exploring the Reasons of the Alpine Divide: Italian and German Monetary Histories since Unification

Francesco Papadia[1]

In 1973 I started working at the International Cooperation Department of Banca d'Italia, to be later merged with the Research Department, after my postgraduate studies at ISTAO, in Ancona, and at the London Business School. I ended my work at Banca d'Italia in 1998, when I moved to Frankfurt, called by Sirkka Hämäläinen to take care of Market Operations of the European Central Bank, a task that I kept until 2012.

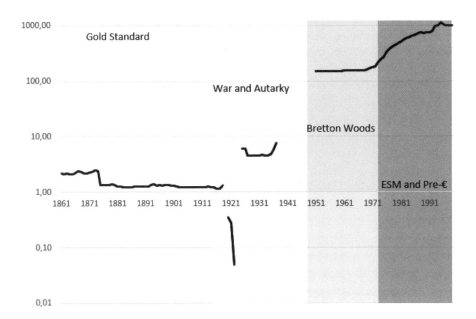

Fig. 1: Bilateral lira/German currency exchange rate. Log scale. Liras for unit of German currency. 1861-1998.
Source: Ciocca, Pierluigi and Adalberto Ulizzi. OECD, *Exchange rates (indicator)*, 2020.

---

1 Francesco Papadia, Senior Fellow at Bruegel. Chair of the Selection Panel of the Hellenic Financial Stability Fund and of Prime Collateralised Securities. Former Director General for Market Operations at the European Central Bank.

Francesco Papadia

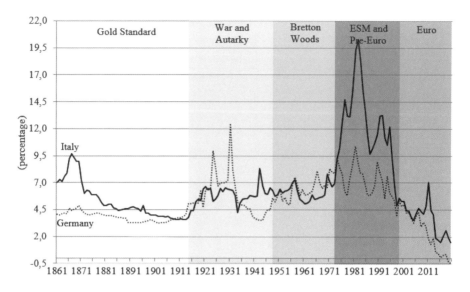

Fig. 2. Interest rates in Italy and Germany. 1861-2020.
Source: Homer, Sidney and Richard E. Sylla, F. Spinelli and Michele Fratianni. International Monetary Fund, International Financial Statistics. OECD Main Economic Indicators – Complete database.

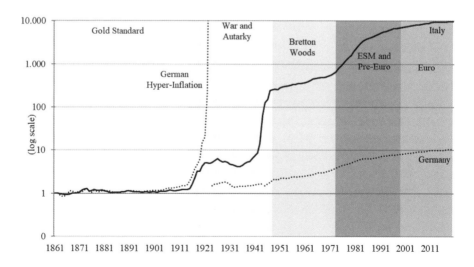

Fig 3. Consumer Price Index in Germany and Italy. 1861=100. Log scale. 1861-2020.
Source: Mitchell, Bill, Jim O'Donoghue, L. Goulding and Grahame Allen. Italian National Institute of Statistics. OECD Main Economic indicators, complete database.

The period with the darker shading in figures 1 to 3 corresponds to my work experience at Banca d'Italia and, much more importantly, to the period in which Italian monetary policy was basically left to the discretion of Italian authorities. Of course, even during this period different incarnations of the European Monetary System somewhat limited this discretion, but not to the degree prevailing in the Bretton Woods fixed parity system.

If one would only look at the darkly shaded 1973-1998 period, they would be impressed, as I was during my career at Banca d'Italia, by the relentless depreciation of the lira against the Deutsche Mark, even if at lower speed over time. The same strong impression would derive from looking at the dark area in figures 2 and 3, with the consistently higher interest and inflation rate, as read from the higher steepness of the curve of the price index, in Italy than in Germany.

Overall, German monetary conditions were much more stable than those of Italy in the years between 1973 and 1988. This is true even if we measure monetary stability not by the level of interest and inflation rates but by some measure of variability, like the variance: in the 1973-1998 period the variance of inflation was 29.69 in Italy and only 3.98 in Germany, the variance of the interest rate was 12.82 in Italy and 2.14 in Germany.

While the time series in Fig. 1 obviously ends in 1998, when both the lira and the Deutsche Mark were substituted by the euro, figures 2 and 3 also report the data for the two following decades. One can, looking at them, still find some trace of a more stable situation in Germany than in Italy, notwithstanding the common currency, in particular regarding the behaviour of the interest rate, because of the large and variable spread between the German and the Italian interest rate.

Impressed by the persistent pattern of less stability in Italy than in Germany, one would be justified in looking for an explanation in constant different features between the two countries: do we have to search for some deep Teutonic or Italian characteristic to explain the diametrically different monetary histories of Germany and Italy? This line of research would seem to be, albeit indirectly and partially, confirmed by the observation[2] that Italy had, in the 1861-1979 period, a rate of inflation nearly 5 percentage points higher than that of France, the United Kingdom and the United States, considered sequentially as the relevant comparator. Consistently the lira had an average annual depreciation in the same period of about 4 percent, while higher nominal interest rates prevailed in Italy.

A look at the period before 1973, indeed one starting around the national unity of the two countries, shows that this line of research is not justified: the continuous devaluation of the lira, the persistently higher rate of inflation and interest in

---

[2] Franco Spinelli and Michele Fratianni, *Storia Monetaria d'Italia,* Etas Libri, 2001.

Italy compared to Germany are artefacts from making the observation period start in 1973. Indeed, even a cursory look at the period before 1973 in figures 1, 2 and 3 destroys the impression of constancy in the different monetary development between the two countries.

Of course, the first, paroxysmic difference is the German hyperinflation of the 1920s: inflation recorded quite an increase in Italy in the aftermath of World War I, but nothing comparable with the German hyperinflation, the virtual annihilation of the exchange rate of the German currency as well as higher German interest rates. Only the currency reform of 1923 tamed these extreme developments. Also, after World War II Italian inflation recorded an increase, but not to the point of requiring a monetary reform, with the introduction of a new currency, like in Germany in June 1948, even if the price control imposed by the Nazis make the reading of inflation in that country very uncertain.

These were extreme developments, connected to historical political events, but they are not the only times in which monetary stability was lower in Germany than in Italy. Indeed, an overall look at the entire period reported in figures 1 to 3 shows that the persistent depreciation of the Italian currency with respect to the German one as well as the higher inflation and interest rates in Italy with respect to Germany are really only a characteristic of the 1973-1998 period.

A closer look at the figures shows that interest rates were higher and more volatile in Italy than in Germany during the "Gold Standard" period, but a look at the German series in that period sheds some doubts about the representativity of the reported interest rate, which remained quasi constant for decades around 4 per cent, while inflation ranged between + 19 and − 10 per cent, which would have resulted in wild swings in the real rate of interest. During the "War and Autarky" period interest rates were more stable in Italy than in Germany, while no significant difference appears during the Bretton Woods years.

Furthermore, the German currency sharply devalued against the lira not only at the occasion of the hyperinflation but also around the middle of the 1870s, while the exchange rate between the two currencies was stable in the remaining part of the gold standard period and during the Bretton Woods years.

Exchange rate developments can be further illustrated looking (Fig. 4) at the effective exchange rates of the Italian and the German currencies, which take into account the behaviour of the exchange rate toward a portfolio of currencies and not just one, as in the bilateral exchange rate.

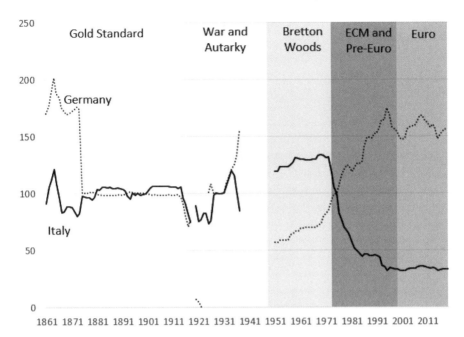

Fig. 4 Effective exchange rate of the lira and the German currency. 1861-2020. 1871=100.

Source: Ciocca, Pierluigi and Adalberto Ulizzi, Exchange rates (indicator), OECD (2020). doi: 10.1787/037ed317-en (Accessed on 27 August 2020).

In the gold standard period, the effective exchange rate of the Italian lira was definitely more stable than that of the German currency, essentially because of the break created by the foundation of the German Reich in 1871. Additionally, in the "War and Autarky" period the German currency was less stable than the Italian one. In the Bretton Woods period, the lira effective exchange rate was more stable, because the Deutsche Mark was already on an upward trend. During the most recent "euro" period, the Italian effective exchange rate was more stable than the German one.

The most trustworthy gauge of monetary stability is the rate of inflation, not only for its meaning but also because it is the variable that can be more precisely measured. There are numerous years in the 1860s and 1870s in which Italian inflation was 3 percentage points, or more, lower than in Germany, the same happened in a number of years of the first three decades of the twentieth century, i.e. not only on the occasion of the hyperinflation. But there are also many years in the pre-1973 period in which Italian inflation was higher than the German one. Furthermore, the fairly frequent years of negative inflation in either country does not allow us to draw inferences about monetary stability just by comparing the respective levels of inflation. A more telling statistic is the variance of inflation, as reported in Tab. 1 for different periods. To avoid the statistic to be basically determined by the two extreme episodes of the hyperinflation of the 1920s and the aftermath of the Second World War, leading to German Monetary Reform, the observations for 1922-1924 and 1944-1948 are excluded.

Period	Gold Standard (1861-1914)	War and Autarky* (1915-1943)	Bretton Woods (1949-1972)	ESM and Pre-euro (1973-1998)	Euro (1999-2020)	1861-1972*	1861-2020*
Italy	13.64	212.00	5.31	29.69	1.15	76.76	63.83
Germany	26.11	397.82	11.03	3.98	0.56	134.78	93.35
Italy/Germany	0.52	0.53	0.48	7.45	2.06	0.57	0.68

Tab. 1. Variance of inflation in selected periods in Germany and Italy.
*Excluding 1922-1924 and 1944-1948.

A few interesting results emerge from or are confirmed by this table:

- The euro period is by far the most stable one, from a monetary perspective, in the more than secular history of the two countries;

- Even eliminating the paroxysmal periods of the hyperinflation and the German monetary reform, the "war and autarky" period was, for both countries, by an order of magnitude more unstable than any other period;

- The "gold standard" period was not, for both countries, that paragon of monetary stability that one may think, confirming that gold anchoring avoided persistent inflation, but not inflation variability;

- The higher monetary instability in Italy than in Germany is not a constant feature in the monetary history of the two countries, indeed it is a characteristic mostly of the EMS and Pre-euro period, even if inflation was less stable in Italy than in Germany also during the euro period, notwithstanding its low level;

- Over the long period of 1861-1972, even excluding hyperinflation and the years before German monetary reform, there was more monetary stability in Italy than in Germany;

- This also applies extending the sample to the full 1861-2020 period;

- Overall monetary stability appears intrinsically intertwined with broader historical developments.

In conclusion, Italian monetary conditions were much less stable than German ones in the 1973-1998 period, in which monetary policy had much weaker constraints than in the preceding Bretton Woods period and before the euro was introduced. However, this was by no means a constant feature in the monetary history of the two countries. Indeed, over a century and a half in which the two countries had a national currency, there was more monetary instability in Germany than in Italy, even omitting the hyperinflation and the 1948 German monetary reform. We therefore should not look for some immutable, metaphysical characteristic of the two countries but rather search for different conditions that explain over time the different performance of the two economies. This is the task for the other chapters in this section. Can one find the reason in different schools of economic thoughts? In fiscal developments? In the institutional monetary setup? In different policies by the respective central banks? In different wage negotiation frameworks and ultimately in income distribution issues?

The concrete implication deriving from our result is that merging in a single currency countries with very different monetary histories is not a recipe for failure and monetary instability if the variables setting monetary policy, and in all likelihood fiscal policy as well, are appropriately chosen. The fact that Italy and Germany have never had as much monetary stability in their national history as they are having with the euro is an encouraging sign, but of course not a proof, that the variables setting monetary policy in the euro area are adequate, even if not optimal. However, this chapter does not permanently settle the question of what the right variables are, it just shows that the search for the reasons of a different monetary performance is legitimate, since there is no destiny condemning Italy to less monetary stability than Germany.[3]

---

3   Further works cited: Beyer, Andreas, Vitor Gaspar, Christina Gerberding and Omar Issing; *Opting out of the great inflation: German Monetary Policy after the break down of Bretton Woods*; National Bureau of Economic Research, Working Paper 14596, 2008; Ciocca, Pierluigi e Adalberto Ulizzi, *I tassi di cambio nominali e "reali" dell'Italia dall'unità nazionale al sistema monetario Europeo (1861-1879)* in Ricerche per la storia della Banca d'Italia, Vol. I, Laterza, 1990; Henry Oliver, *War and Inflation since 1790 in England, France, Germany, and the United States*. The American Economic Review, February 1941, Vol. 30, No. 5; Hetzel, Robert L., *German Monetary History in the First Half of the Twentieth Century*, Federal Reserve Bank of Richmond Economic Quarterly Vol. 88/1 Winter 2002; *id.*, *German Monetary History in the Second Half of the Twentieth Century;. From the Deutsche Mark to the euro*, Federal Reserve Bank of Richmond Economic Quarterly Volume 88/2 Spring 2002; Kole, Linda S., and Ellen E. Meade; *German Monetary Targeting: A Retrospective View*. Federal Reserve Bulletin, vol. 81, no. 10, October 1995, p. 917-931. HeinOnline; Laidler, David E., and George W. Stadler; *Monetary Explanations*

of the Weimar Republic's Hyperinflation: Some Neglected Contributions in Contemporary German Literature; Journal of Money, Credit and Banking, 816-831 30 (4), 1998; Mitchell, Brian *International Historical Statistics*, 1750-1988, New York, Palgrave Macmillan, 1992; O'Donoghue, Jim, Louise Goulding and Grahame Allen, *Consumer Price Inflation since 1750,* London Office for National Statistics, 2004; Sidney, Homer and Richard Sylla, *A History of Interest Rates*, New Brunswick, N.J. Rutgers University Press, 1991; Spinelli, Franco and Michele Fratianni, *Storia Monetaria d'Italia*. Etas Libri 2001.

The Influence of Economic Schools. The Case of Italy

Pierluigi Ciocca[1]

After the post-war inflation and depreciation had been halted in 1947 by the Banca d'Italia led by Luigi Einaudi, the lira remained strong until 1969-73. This was thanks to the progression in firms' productivity and the prudence of Einaudi's immediate successors at the head of the central bank, Donato Menichella and Guido Carli. The effective nominal exchange rate rose by nearly one third. Wholesale prices increased by not more than 1% per year, so that the "real" exchange rate — price competitiveness — remained unchanged.[2]

For the subsequent nearly thirty years the lira then weakened, primarily as a result of non-monetary factors. From the so-called "hot autumn" of 1969, by way of social tensions that extended to armed terrorism, wages exploded with annual rises of more than 20% in 1974, 1977 and 1981. They were not kept within the rise in productivity of firms but driven by the trade unions or incomes policy. In 1973-74 and in 1978-79 the increases in energy prices devastated the Italian economy, which depended more than others on imported oil, owing in part to the population's aversion to nuclear power. For years general government net borrowing exceeded 10% of GDP. The public debt rose to 90% of GDP in 1988 and touched 125% in 1994. Although the economy, despite slowing, kept growing (by 3.8% per year in the 1970s and by 2.4% in the 1980s) the political and institutional spheres did not provide for a return to equilibrium.

Between 1970 and 1984 consumer prices rose by 15% a year. The Banca d'Italia — with severe monetary and credit restrictions which gave rise to unemployment — only succeeded in temporarily reducing inflation: from 26% to 11% during the course of 1975 and then from 23% to 13% during the course of 1977. By gradually raising real interest rates and underpinning the exchange rate, inflation was brought down from 21% in 1980 to 4.6% in 1987 in the wake of the oil counter-shock of the previous year.

---

[1] Pierluigi Ciocca was Head of Market Operations and Economic Research at Banca d'Italia and Deputy Director General of the Bank from 1995 to 2006. He is Member of the Accademia dei Lincei.

[2] Ciocca, Pierluigi and Adalberto Ulizzi "I tassi di cambio nominali e 'reali' dell'Italia dall'Unità nazionale al Sistema Monetario Europeo (1861-1979)", *Ricerche per la storia della Banca d'Italia*, Vol. 1,, Rome-Bari: Laterza, 1990.

Competitiveness was maintained at the cost of a depreciation of the effective exchange rate by 50% from 1970 up to Italy's joining the EMS,[3] and by a further 30% from 1979 to 1990. During those twenty years the lira/deutschemark ratio went from 170 to 732 lire per DM. The limited propensity and the inability of governments to curb the deficit and the debt led in the summer of 1992 to the definitive currency crisis and the dramatic exit from the EMS in September of that horrible year.[4] The lira fell to 1,250 against the mark in 1995 and then recovered to 990 in November 1996, when renewed membership in the EMS was possible with a view to participation in the euro, which was approved in 1998.

The shortcomings of the economic and political-institutional context – less stability oriented than Germany's – were systematically denounced by the Governors of the Banca d'Italia.

Paolo Baffi, 1979:

The crisis has revealed how inflexible and precarious was the edifice that had been constructed, how uncertain the distinction made between market factors and administrative factors, between social requirements and industrial requirements, between the management of public property and the exercise of supervision, between the taking of risks and the desire for guarantees, between the public sector and the private sector and among political control, economic control, administrative control and judicial control.

Carlo Ciampi, 1992:

Too often in the past, the reform of major items of public expenditure and of the procedures for preparing and implementing the budget has failed to materialize; it can be postponed no longer. The fight against tax evasion must be made truly effective[…].

Antonio Fazio, 2005:

Italy's endowment of public capital remains small. In many economically advanced regions, the basic transport infrastructure is inadequate; in the South the supply of electricity and the distribution of water are also insufficient […]. Sufficient and modern infrastructure is indispensable for the growth of tourism […]. In the South the tourist industry is well below its potential.

---

3   The decision to join the EMS divided Italian economists – including Beniamino Andreatta and Luigi Spaventa in Parliament – but many of them agreed with the wider exchange rate band that the Governor of the Banca d'Italia, Paolo Baffi, had recommended and ultimately obtained.

4   One of the leading economists who advised the Government ex post saw the collapse of the lira "a blessing in disguise", "un'astuzia della storia" (Spaventa, Luigi "Quegli straordinari anni Novanta", in Carrubba, Salvatore et al., *Il cammino della lira da Bretton Woods all'Euro*, Milan: Atic Forex, 2007, pp. 83 and 98). But it was then that Italy lost its currency. According to the Banca d'Italia, a controlled and smaller depreciation of the lira would have been possible later, after the necessary budgetary measures had been taken and before, not after, the exchange rate had given way.

The list of citations could be continued with the repeated interventions of Mario Draghi and Ignazio Visco, but for the most part warnings and proposals went unheeded.[5]

Given the structural weaknesses, the inadequate economic policies adopted and the high level of unemployment, monetary policy could only limit inflation and the depreciation of the currency. A specific problem for monetary policy in Italy has always been the search for the "right" interest rate in view of the particularly pronounced variation in productivity across firms and across regions. Even now 95% of businesses (4.2 million out of a total of 4.4 million) still have fewer than 9 workers. The average number for all businesses is very small: 3.8. Among manufacturing firms, the gross value added per worker varied in 2017 from €27,000 for the smallest with less than 9 workers to €69,000 for the medium sized (with from 50 to 249 workers) and to €80,000 for the largest. Medium-sized Italian manufacturing firms are more efficient than their French, English and German counterparts. By contrast, the productivity of the smallest and the largest Italian firms is comparatively much lower. The per capita income gap between the Mezzogiorno and the rest of the country remains wide, exceeding 40%, against a background of twenty years of a basically stagnant Italian economy as a whole.

In addition to protecting, with a varying degree of success, the internal and external value of the currency, from the end of the Second World War the Banca d'Italia, as part of its prudential supervision duties, has pursued the sound and prudent management – stability combined with efficiency – of the banking and financial system.[6] The public resources employed in protecting depositors from the bank failures that occurred between 1950 and 2000, expressed at 1998 prices, did not exceed 2% of that year's GDP. This cost is one of the lowest incurred by the advanced countries in that half century. In the post-Lehman crisis, the impact on the public debt of the support provided to banks amounted, at the end of 2011, to 11% of GDP in Germany and to only 0.2% in Italy. Analogously, even in the new and deep recession of the Italian economy, the public money made available to the banks that ran aground in 2012-13 amounted to 0.8% of GDP, compared with 4.5% for the euro area as a whole.

Setting aside Nobel prizes not granted (de Finetti, Sylos Labini, Pasinetti and Sraffa, who was nonetheless awarded in 1961, after Keynes and before the extension of the Nobel to economics in 1969, the prestigious Swedish *Söderström Gold Medal*), Italian economic culture is of a very high order. Above all it is rich in its multiplicity of approaches, never flattened on methodological individualism, mainstream orthodoxy, marketism, monetarism or Capital Asset Pricing Model (CAPM). The range of paradigms that the

---

5   Carli, Federico and Pierluigi Ciocca (eds.), *La Banca d'Italia e l'economia. L'analisi dei Governatori*, 5 Vols., Turin: Aragno, 2019.

6   Ciocca, Pierluigi, *The Italian Financial System Remodelled*, London: Palgrave Macmillan, 2005.

leading Italian economists have cultivated since the end of the Second World War goes from the classical and Marxist positions to Walras-Pareto, from the various interpretations of Keynes (philologically pure, neoclassical synthesis and "bastard" Keynesianism) to Sraffa, the adversary of the marginalist tradition, to statistical-econometric, historical-economical and institutional analysis, to which the Banca d'Italia has also made significant contributions. In monetary analysis there have been only limited adhesions to the quantity theory of money either in the versions à la Irving Fisher or in the formulations that followed Milton Friedman's restatement.[7]

This culture always attached relevance to the action of the central bank, also in the light of the inaction which frequently characterised governments' economic policies. At the same time this culture did not spare the Banca d'Italia from criticism when it was considered to be overly restrictive (Carli in 1962-63 and in 1975; Baffi in 1977; Ciampi in 1980-86; and Fazio in 1994-97). On the other hand, there was also criticism, and rightly so, of governments' inaction and inadequacy – notably of the Berlusconi/Tremonti governments – and of the more recent positions of the neo-fascist Right, nationalist, anti-EU and anti-euro political groupings. In particular, only rarely were economists' proposals concerning the public finances accepted and implemented. Some economists went so far as to consider the effects of budgetary corrections to be expansionary. The majority deemed them necessary, though not always as rigorous as those proposed by the Banca d'Italia.[8]

The same culture has been largely in agreement with the philosophy of the Banca d'Italia, supporting its role and features: independence; accountability; rigorous economic analysis; dual mandate; complementarity of supervision, monetary policy and lending of last resort; and the discretionary right to purchase government securities both on the secondary market and even at issue, in particular circumstances.

A central bank worthy of that name must not embrace any one specific economic theory. It cannot believe, as the neoclassical school currently prevalent outside Italy imagines, that markets are self-regulating, that the economy is intrinsically stable and that only intervention by the State can destabilise it; that inflation is a monetary phenomenon and not also due to costs, inefficiency of allocative mechanisms and asymmetry in the movement of relative prices; that banks are to be treated in the same way

---

[7] Nardozzi, Giangiacomo, "Moneta e credito: vent'anni di dibattito in Italia", in *Moneta e Credito*, 1993, pp. 379-420; Garofalo, Giuseppe and Augusto Graziani (eds.), *La formazione degli economisti in Italia (1950-1975)*, Bologna: il Mulino, 2004; Roncaglia, Alessandro *L'età della disgregazione. Storia del pensiero economico contemporaneo*, Rome-Bari: Laterza, 2019.

[8] Morcaldo, Giancarlo, *La finanza pubblica in Italia (1960-1992)*, Bologna: il Mulino, 1993 and *Una politica economica per la crescita*, Milan: Angeli, 2005 (especially Chapter 4 and the Appendix).

as other enterprises; that the long-term interest rate depends on saving/investment and not on conventions, liquidity, expectations and the credibility of monetary policy.[9] The central bank cannot think that the flexibility of prices, wages, interest and exchange rates can ensure full employment.

Faced with the reality of the day, often forced to act under time and other constraints, the Banca d'Italia has always felt the need for a theoretically careful and empirically grounded eclecticism. This multifaceted approach has been matched by the autonomy the central bank enjoys in its action. Over and above its de iure independence, the Banca d'Italia has been de facto autonomous from both the political world and the business community. Relations with both have been dialectical and, not infrequently, conflictual.

During the last twenty years the shortcomings of the European System of Central Banks (ESCB) and particularly of its centre of decision, the ECB, modelled on the Bundesbank, have become increasingly clear: the lack of a dual mandate beyond price stability, the lack of competences in banking supervision (until 2014) and in lending as a last resort to intermediaries at risk of insolvency and of infecting the entire system, and the inability to purchase government securities at issue, when really needed.[10] Poorly equipped, the ECB was unable to mitigate the recession of 2008-09, bank failures, and the debt crises of some euro area countries. It was unable to raise yearly inflation rates towards the mythical 2 per cent level. It was unable, even with quantitative easing pushed to the limit of the statute, if not beyond, to support sluggish domestic demand.

The limits to the effectiveness of monetary policy in stimulating investment and consumption in the absence of an expansionary fiscal policy have been known to economic theory since the *General Theory* and have also emerged from central banks experience. The data of the last twenty years for Europe, the United States, Japan and the United Kingdom confirm this. In all these cases the expansion of the monetary base via the balance sheet of the central bank has been accompanied — in addition to the speculative fever of stock exchanges completely detached from the "real" economy — by a slower growth of money supply, even slower nominal GDP growth, and a minimal increase in consumer prices. The gap between the growth rates of the four variables is also evident in the euro area. The growth in the liabilities of the ESCB (9.5% per year) was limited by the contraction of about one third in its

---

9   The reference is to the *safeness* of the long term rate of return on capital, as dependent upon a monetary policy which "appeals to public opinion as being reasonable and practicable and in the public interest, rooted in strong conviction, and promoted by an authority unlikely to be superseded" (Keynes, John Maynard, *The General Theory of Employment Interest and Money*, London: Macmillan, 1936, p. 203).

10 Ciocca, Pierluigi, *Stabilising Capitalism. A Greater Role for Central Banks*, London: Palgrave Macmillan, 2016.

balance sheet between the summers of 2012 and 2014, exactly when expectations of deflation were becoming more intense. In the other counties referred to, the four variables followed a very similar path.

Above all, the ECB should have convinced the governments of the leading European countries to adopt expansionary fiscal policies with an eye – as suggested by Keynes – not on deficits, but on public investment. It would have been enough for monetary measures to support such policies. This did not happen. The ECB ended up acting on its own, with the declared aim of "saving the euro": a political problem indeed that, if it existed, should have been solved at the institutional level, tackled by governments, and not by a technical body such as the ECB. In itself the euro was sound and there was demand for it both within the euro area and internationally. The main macroeconomic effect of quantitative easing was to contribute to the depreciation of the currency (from 1.5 dollars per euro in 2008 to 1.1 in early 2020). Abroad, the devaluation appeared to have been deliberately competitive. Accordingly, Europe came to be subjected to threats of protectionist reaction by the United States, which itself needed to devalue in order to correct the terrifying deficits in its balance of payments and external position (its net foreign debt having reached 50% of GDP).

Many Italian economists therefore missed the pre-1998 Banca d'Italia, which in many respects they likened to the Fed. Moreover, perhaps because neither ordo-liberalism nor the social market economy have a place in Schumpeter's *History of Economic Analysis* or in the subsequent high theory, Italian economic culture did not deem them worthy of consideration. This may partly explain why it continues to wonder on what basis of economic analysis and/or for what political ends Germany, between 1999 and 2019, cut public investment, impoverished its infrastructure without even replacing depreciations, accepted GDP growth that was limited, on the domestic demand side, to little more than 1 per cent per year. The lack of demand in Germany is reflected in a rise in national saving from 22% to 28% of GDP, while investment remained at 19%. This deep void of "absorption" gave rise to abnormal surpluses in the balance of payments and huge exports of capital, at the cost of not using it domestically, even dissipating precious national resources and creating serious problems throughout the euro area.[11]

In line with their rejection of every suggestion of abandoning the EU and the euro, the best Italian economists have appreciated the recent shift imposed by Germany, France, Spain and Italy on a Europe faced with the recession caused by the pandemic, trusting that the propensity to keep domestic demand in line with aggregate supply will be confirmed when the recession has been overcome.

---

11 Bolaffi, Angelo and Pierluigi Ciocca, *Germania/Europa. Due punti di vista sulle opportunità e i rischi dell'egemonia tedesca*, Rome: Donzelli, 2017.

Meanwhile, from the early 2000s,[12] Italy's economic problem was increasingly one of growth. It is not the first time this has happened since the unification of Italy.[13] Since 1861 per capita income has increased 14 times, so much so that Italians have joined the richest 10% of the world's citizens. This progress was mostly concentrated in two historical periods: 1900-13 and 1948-73. The breaks in growth and the contractions recorded at the end of the 19th century, in the 1930s and during the Second World War were followed by formidable recoveries in terms of material wellbeing.

As in the past, the problem of growth with which Italy has again been confronted has its roots deep in the country's economy and society: weak control of public finances; disappointing total factor productivity; lack of infrastructures; uneven distribution of income and human capital; small size of the firms and low degree of competition among them; inadequate legal framework for the economy; North-South economic divide.

With the euro, the EU offered Italy price stability, low interest rates, and close integration of the movements of goods, labour and capital. But these structural opportunities were not taken, owing to the limits in the governance of the economy, to firms' response and to the cultural, institutional and political features of present-day Italy.[14]

Return to growth is therefore a question entirely within Italian society. Apart from the present adverse cycle, it calls on the country's leadership to take long-term action on several fronts. On the essential aspects of this action economists have insisted for years: a rebalancing of the budget and a halt to the increase in public debt, starting from the cut of inefficient current expenditure and success in curbing fiscal evasion; valid investment in material and immaterial infrastructure; a more modern legal framework for the economy; not subsidies but competitive pressure on firms; greater equality in the distribution of income; a new policy for the Mezzogiorno.[15]

If these guidelines are followed, if firms contribute with capital and innovation, if there is encouragement from a Europe and a Germany less insensitive to the common need for expansion, Italian society will be able — as it has shown in the past — to find the road to growth again.

---

12 Ciocca, Pierluigi, *L'economia italiana: un problema di crescita*, Banca d'Italia, 25 October 2003.
13 Ciocca, Pierluigi, *Ricchi per sempre? Una storia economica d'Italia* (1796-2020), Turin: Bollati Boringhieri, 2020.
14 *Ibid.*, especially Ch. 15.
15 Ciocca, Pierluigi, *Tornare alla crescita. Perché l'economia italiana è in crisi e cosa fare per rifondarla*, Rome: Donzelli, 2018.

The Influence of Economic Schools. The Case of Germany

Thomas Mayer[1]

The ordo-liberal economic school rose to considerable influence in post-war Germany. After a temporary attack by Keynesianism during the late 1960s and 1970s, it rebounded in the 1980s and dominated the public economic policy discourse well into the 2000s. But its influence weakened in the wake of the Great Financial Crisis and the Euro Crisis and it seems to have come to an end during the Coronavirus Crisis. In the eyes of this liberal author the demise of the German ordo-liberal school and its influence on economic policy is likely to leave Germany and the European Union adrift.

1. Primacy of politics versus primacy of rules

Nazi Germany was an early adopter of Keynesianism, even before it was officially invented. Immediately after having been appointed Chancellor, Adolf Hitler in March 1933 made Hjalmar Schacht the President of the German Reichsbank. Schacht had been instrumental in introducing the "Rentenmark" in November 1923, which ended hyperinflation, and he had held the position as Reichsbank President already from 1924 to 1930. During his new term in office he revealed similarly creative skills. The economy was in depression and money was scarce. Schacht used an idle private company by the name of "Metallforschungsgesellschaft" (Metal Research Company or MEFO) to issue state-guaranteed bills of exchange, dubbed MEFO-Wechsel, as a means for the government to pay for the purchase of goods.[2]

---

[1] Thomas Mayer is Founding Director of the Flossbach von Storch Research Institute and former Deutsche Bank chief economist. He received a doctorate in economics from Kiel University, is a CFA Charterholder and Professor at University Witten/Herdecke.

[2] The bills carried interest of 4%, had a 3-month maturity and could be renewed 19 times for a 5-year period. See Bossone, Biagio and Stefano Labini, *Macroeconomics in Germany: The forgotten lesson of Hjalmar Schacht*, Voxeu.org, 01 Jul. 2016 https://voxeu.org/article/macroeconomics-germany-forgotten-lesson-hjalmar-schacht.

Suppliers to the government could exchange the MEFO-Wechsel they received as payments from the government against cash at the Reichsbank. The scheme was an early version of today's "Quantitative Easing Programs", although with the difference that government debt accumulation was outsourced to MEFO (so that official debt figures were not affected), and that the issuance of bills was strictly tied to government purchases of newly produced goods. With this Schacht wanted to prevent the emergence of money creation in excess of goods production, which had led to hyperinflation in 1923. The economy recovered and in 1938 Schacht urged the end of the MEFO programme. Hitler disagreed. In 1939, he removed him from the Reichsbank. After the war Schacht was accused of "crimes against peace" at the Nuremberg Trial, but was acquitted.

Despite Schacht's exoneration, the appetite for policies once embraced by the Nazis was weak in post-war Germany. Against this background, Ludwig Erhard, who had run an economic research institute during the war years, rose to the head of economic administration of the American-British occupation zones. Erhard had a predilection for the "Ordo Liberalism" of the Freiburg School of Economics. In that school, a distinction is made between the shaping of an economic order on the one hand and the direct steering of economic processes on the other. The state is tasked with establishing the economic order, notably ensuring the functioning of economic competition, but it should stay out of managing the economic process itself. Its key protagonist, Walter Eucken, summed up the guiding principle of Ordo Liberalism: "State planning of forms – yes; state planning and control of the economic process – no".[3] While in Schacht's world clever management of economic processes had been desirable, clever design of rules allowing competition to operate was essential in the world of Ludwig Erhard. Thus, the guiding principle of economic policy moved from the primacy of politics before the war to the primacy of rules thereafter.

2. *The Keynesian escapade*

In 1947, the German economic administration, headed by Ludwig Erhard, came to the view that a currency reform was needed to neutralise the monetary overhang created during the war. This was not an entirely new idea. Erhard had already worked on a plan towards the end of the war and a group of US economists had done the same. Hence, the allied military commanders quickly agreed. The plan prepared 1946 by US economists – named Colm-Dodge-Goldsmith-Plan after its authors – provided the blueprint. Half of the Reichsmark (RM) money stock in private hands was converted at 10 RM: 1 DM into

---

3   Gerken, Lüder (ed.), *Walter Eucken und sein Werk*, Mohr Siebeck, 1991. For an exposition and critique of ordo liberalism, see also Bofinger, Peter, *German macroeconomics: The long shadow of Walter Eucken*, Voxeu, 7 Jun. 2016, https://voxeu.org/article/german-macroeconomics-long-shadow-walter-eucken.

the new German mark (DM), the other half at 15.38 RM : 1 DM (meaning that 100 RM bought just 6.50 DM). By eliminating the monetary overhang, the new German mark had theoretically much more purchasing power than the old Reichsmark. But would this also prove to be true in practice?

Ludwig Erhard thought so and took the risk of being wrong. He abolished most price controls and allowed vendors to set their prices freely. The result was a surprise for many: Vendors were willing to exchange goods they had held on inventory against the new German mark, supply and confidence increased. Most economic historians agree that currency reform coupled with the abolition of price controls laid the foundation for what was to become Germany's "economic miracle". In the following years the German economy grew at a rapid pace and German economists and policy makers embraced the ordo-liberal theory practiced by Erhard. Eventually, unemployment decreased to an extent that labour became scarce. However, instead of allowing wages to increase to rebalance the labour market, the government, pressed by industry, embarked upon a hiring program of workers, first from neighbouring countries in the European Economic Community and later in addition from more distant countries, such as Turkey, Tunisia, Morocco, and South Korea.

Despite the increase of labour supply, inflation accelerated in the first half of the 1960s and induced the Bundesbank to tighten credit conditions. In 1966-67 the economy fell into a mild recession. The government of Chancellor Kurt Georg Kiesinger, consisting of a "Grand Coalition" between the conservative CDU/CSU and the social-democratic SPD, reacted with a fiscal stimulus programme. The policy was inspired by Karl Schiller, the Minister of Economics from the SPD and a former economics professor. It was executed jointly by him and Franz-Josef Strauss, the Minister of Finance and head of the CSU. Schiller was a convinced Keynesian and strong advocate of counter-cyclical economic policies. His policy convictions were in stark contrast to those of Ludwig Erhard who had loathed demand management by the government. But the stimulus programme helped to get the economy quickly back on track. Keynesianism seemed to have arrived in Germany. Schiller even managed to enshrine Keynesian demand management in a law, dubbed "Stabilitäts- und Wachstumsgesetz" (Stability and Growth Law), which has been in force since 1967.

When Willy Brandt formed the first SPD-led government in 1969, Schiller retained his position as Minister of Economics and in 1971 assumed the position of Minister of Finance on top. For Schiller, anti-cyclical policy meant that the government would adopt a restrictive fiscal stance when the economy was at risk of over-heating. But Brandt wanted to implement his costly policy programmes and resisted Schiller's push for more fiscal restraint as the economy grew strongly. Being a man of convictions, Schiller resigned from his government positions in 1972 and even ended his SPD party membership.

Schiller's resignation was the first blow to the German flirt with Keynesianism. It seemed to suggest that demand management would work in economic theory but not in political practice. Politicians were keen to run government budget deficits during the economic downswing but would resist the consolidation of government finances during the upswing. The result would be ever larger government debt. The fate of Schiller and Schacht seemed to prove the point.

The second blow came as a result of "Stagflation" during the 1970s. In 1972, Helmut Schmidt – who would succeed Willy Brandt as Chancellor in 1974 – alluded to the Phillips-Curve saying that the German people would "tolerate 5% inflation better than 5% unemployment". When both inflation and unemployment reached this mark during his tenure in 1974-82, his credibility as an "economic manager" was dented and Keynesianism discredited. Disenchantment with Keynesianism eventually contributed to the break-up of his social-liberal coalition government in 1982. The liberal Economics Minister Otto Graf Lambsdorff published a letter to Schmidt, in which he demanded a change of course in economic and fiscal policy from Keynesian demand management towards market-liberal supply-side policies. As Schmidt resisted, all liberal ministers left the government, paving the way for a new CDU-led government under Chancellor Helmut Kohl.

3. The battle of Maastricht

As early as 1949, the French politician and economist Jacques Rueff thought that a common currency would pave the way for European integration: "Europe is created through money, or it is not created at all". In 1970, a commission chaired by the Prime Minister of Luxembourg, Pierre Werner, presented a plan to create a monetary union by 1980. A fierce controversy arose between those who believed that once the currency was introduced, the economic conditions for its success would emerge of their own accord and those who disputed this. Members of the first group were called "monetarists". Opposite them, in the second group, were the "economists", who advocated the "coronation theory". Only after the necessary economic conditions had been created was a common currency to come. Werner wanted to proceed with introducing the common currency and creating the conditions for its success at the same time. His ambitious idea was not put to a test. The Werner Plan failed because of the collapse of the Bretton Woods Exchange Rate System in the early 1970s, in which the common European currency was to be embedded. The discussion between the "monetarists" and the "economists" fell asleep, unresolved. Instead of a monetary union a fixed, but adjustable, exchange rate system emerged – first in the form of the so-called "snake" and then of the "European Monetary System" – in which the German mark assumed the role of the anchor currency (and the German Central Bank was seen by some "to rule Europe").[4]

---

4   Marsh, David, *The Bundesbank: The Bank That Rules Europe*, London: Reed Consumer Books, 1993.

The collapse of the "German Democratic Republic" in the late 1980s and the reunification of Germany in 1990 led to the resumption of the project of a common currency. Especially from the French point of view, a strengthened Germany was to be firmly integrated into the European Union. The replacement of the German mark, which many considered to be overpowering, by a European currency was intended to curtail German monetary and economic sovereignty. Chancellor Kohl was prepared to pay this price for the assent of France and other EU countries to German unification.[5] However, on the technical level, the Ministry of Finance and the Bundesbank fought hard to embed German "ordo-liberal" principles into the treaty for a European Monetary Union (which became known as the "Maastricht Treaty"). In particular, the European Central Bank was to pursue price stability as its primary goal, be protected against any political interference in monetary policy and be banned from monetary financing of government debt. Governments were to take sole responsibility for their finances and the stability of their financial industry. Mutualisation of debt was forbidden. In an additional treaty, dubbed the "Stability and Growth Pact", governments had to commit themselves to sound fiscal policies so as to prevent any need for the ECB to act as a lender of last resort to them.

4. The last stand against New-Keynesianism

Contrary to the hopes of some and fears of others, the monetary union had a smooth start and the euro seemed to be well established at its tenth birthday at the beginning of 2009. But this turned out to be an illusion. EMU had benefitted from the expansion of the global credit cycle, allowing private households, companies and states to paper over economic inefficiencies with cheap borrowing. When the credit cycle contracted in the Great Financial Crisis of 2007-08, several euro area states came to the verge of bankruptcy, either because they had overborrowed or had to bail out collapsing banks. Earlier promises and contractual agreements were thrown out the window. To the horror of the German establishment in politics and academics, euro states were bailed-out by newly created euro area institutions and the ECB gradually assumed the role of lender of last resort to states. Christine Lagarde, French Minister of Finance at this time, candidly admitted: "We violated all the rules because we wanted to close ranks and really rescue the euro zone".[6] For the ordo-liberal old guard in Germany, this was difficult to accept.

---

5   *ibidem*; Mayer, Thomas, *Europe's unfinished currency*, London: Anthem Press, 2012.
6   Reuters, *France's Lagarde: EU rescues "violated" rules*, 18 Dec. 2010, https://www.reuters.com/article/us-france-lagarde/frances-lagarde-eu-rescues-violated-rules-report-idUSTRE6BH0V020101218

For some time, the governments led by Chancellor Angela Merkel made some efforts to keep the legal framework of EMU established in the Maastricht Treaty alive. The German Chancellor pushed for a debt restructuring in Greece, insisted on strict conditionality for financial assistance from euro area crisis funds, and rejected the mutualisation of debt through Eurobonds. But these efforts in fact masked a retreat from Germany's earlier ordo-liberal position. Following financial market turbulence after the Greek debt restructuring, Chancellor Merkel agreed that this measure was "exceptional and unique". And she did not oppose ECB President Draghi's positioning of the ECB as a de-facto lender of last resort to euro area states through his promise to do "whatever it takes" to save the euro, which he made in July 2012, against the backdrop of an emerging Italian solvency crisis. Moreover, the German government took the side of the ECB in a trial at the German Constitutional Court, where the plaintiffs argued that the programme to back Draghi's promise (dubbed "Outright Monetary Transactions") represented a transgression of the ECB's statutes. Ironically, the German Central Bank testified for the plaintiffs.

5. Merkelianism

Angela Merkel is likely to have a tenure as German Chancellor that will only slightly fall short of that of Helmut Kohl, Germany's longest serving Chancellor. Kohl had a profound impact on the country through his dash for German unification and his willingness to replace the German mark with the euro. Against this, it seems that Merkel has acted only as an amplifier of existing trends. In the 2005 election she campaigned with an economic programme embracing almost radical free market ideas. Her designated Minister of Finance promised to introduce a flat tax, and she was dubbed the "Maggie Thatcher of Germany". After she had almost lost the election to Gerhard Schröder, the incumbent Chancellor, she ditched her election programme, entered a "Grand Coalition" with the Social Democrats, and moved to the political center. And when environmental issues gained importance in society, she embraced "green policies".

Kay and King[7] distinguish between competent politicians, who base their decisions on thoroughly discussed and developed narratives, and incompetent politicians, who base their decisions on narrow theories and hate dissent. Angela Merkel seems to belong to a third category. She identifies narratives which gain popularity in the electorate and adjusts her policy accordingly. Free from strongly held convictions and too risk averse to develop narratives of her own to shape policies, she goes with the flow of public opinion. Famous examples of this technique include her abrupt change in atomic energy policy

---

7   Kay, John and Mervyn King, *Radical Uncertainty*, London: The Bridge Street Press, 2020.

after the Fukushima nuclear accident in 2011 and her open-arms refugee policy in 2015. She stuck with the former as public opinion remained set against atomic energy and corrected the latter as public opinion turned against an uncontrolled inflow of migrants.

The Coronavirus Crisis set the stage for a change of her European policy. In the wake of the Euro Crisis she had insisted on parsimonious policies in the crisis countries, in line with German public opinion. But during the Coronavirus Crisis German public opinion changed in favour of lavish government support for all those affected by the lockdowns. With the ice of ordo-liberal orthodoxy broken at home, Chancellor Merkel joined forces with French President Macron in pushing for very generous crisis support and reconstruction programmes at the European level.

Public opinion would probably not have turned away from ordo-liberal principles as much as it has, had there not been a change of view among the opinion leaders. In universities and think tanks, ageing economists of the ordo liberal school have gradually been replaced by young economists educated in the New-Keynesian paradigm. Even the Bundesbank has been mellowed by the generational change. The modern New-Keynesians are relaxed about rising government debt and see no fault in the monetary financing of the debt as they regard the risk of a return of inflation as very low. Thus, the expert opinion meshes well with a public opinion, which has learned to appreciate a "free lunch" from the government. And if there are free lunches for the Germans, why should there not be free lunches for all Europeans?

6. *The insecure hegemon*

Some of Germany's European partner countries saw the European Economic and Monetary Union as a device to embed Germany in a union of equals. When it entered EMU in 1999 Germany was even dubbed the "sick man of Europe". In fact, however, EMU has helped to strengthen Germany's economic, financial and political power. Owing to lower inflation and an (from the German perspective) undervalued euro, German industry has gained market shares in the euro area and global economy. Large current account surpluses have made Germany a big creditor (in the euro area notably through the German Central Bank's claims in the interbank payment system Target2 of the Eurosystem, which in November 2020 exceeded one trillion euro). Economic strength and financial power have increased Germany's political sway in the EU.[8] Since Germany

---

8   This does not imply that the Germans are therefore better off. The introduction of the euro has lowered Germany's terms-of-trade below what they would have been in the hard currency regime of the German mark. Thus, German incomes are lower as a result of lower export and higher import prices. Current ac-

has suffered less from the Coronavirus pandemic and is somewhat better placed to cope with the structural changes induced by it, its stature is increasing further. The proverbial "man from Mars" probably would identify Germany as the EU's hegemon.

According to Antonio Gramsci, the hegemon is capable to define his own interests as those of all others. Hence, for Germany to act as hegemon it would need to be capable to define its interests in Europe. The ordo-liberals attempted to do this and thought that the pursuit of their policies would also be in the interest of all other EU countries. However, public opinion is fickle and Angela Merkel's approach to shape policy according to the dominating public narrative of the day makes Germany a very insecure hegemon. France under President Macron tries to fill the void, but it lacks the economic and financial power to assume the role. Thus, the lack of leadership in Europe is likely to fray the EU in a similar way as the lack of leadership in the entirety of the West is presently fraying the Western world. In the eyes of this liberal author the demise of the German ordo-liberals is an important reason for this development.

---

count surpluses are badly invested so that factor income from abroad does not compensate for the domestic income loss. See Hünnekes, Franziska, Moritz Schularick and Christoph Trebesch; "Exportweltmeister: The low returns on Germany's capital exports", *Kiel Working Paper*, no. 2133, Jul. 2019.

Alpine Divide – Is it Mostly Fiscal?

Hans-Helmut Kotz[1]

> Public finances are one of the best angles to understand the social fabric, in particular, though not exclusively, the political mechanisms.
> Schumpeter 1918, *Krise des Steuerstaats*[2]

I. Where should we begin?

Most visibly, at least from a financial market perspective, the Alpine divide – Italy vs. Germany – shows in "lo spread": the difference in yields on sovereign debt (Fig. 1). The premium the Italian sovereign has to pay, compared to German federal government obligations (*Bunds*), reflects almost exclusively[3] relative credit risk, as perceived by market participants. Markets, of course, can err. They put changing judgments on fundamentals, the capacity and willingness of the respective debtor country to pay. More concretely, in the case of Europe's monetary union, this translated into overestimating the preparedness of EMU-partner countries' fiscal authorities or the ECB to help a troubled debtor. Both actions were, of course, prohibited in principle. But here, compliance was not completely credible. For a reason: Bailing-out obviously can be beneficial for creditors, in particular for financial institutions and their stakeholders in creditor countries; it is not completely unselfish. Moreover, financial stability concerns, if they are deemed to be systemic, typically lead monetary authorities to apply unconventional policy tools – playing lender and market maker of both last resort and first resort as well, according to the needs. Indeed, from a historical perspective, such policies have been much less unconventional than often portrayed.

---

1   Center for European Studies, Harvard University, Cambridge, MA and Leibniz Institute for Financial Research SAFE, Frankfurt, Germany.
2   Schumpeter, Joseph, *Die Krise des Steuerstaates*, 1918, republished in Goldscheid, Rudolf and Joseph Schumpeter, *Die Finanzkrise des Steuerstaats*, Hickel, Rudolf (ed.), Frankfurt: Edition Suhrkamp, 1976, pp. 329-379.
3   In risk-adjusted terms, rates for Italian BTPs and German Bunds should be identical. Given that there is no monetary union break-up risk, the only risk investors can claim to be compensated for is default risk, country risk pure, the country premium. The probability of this risk can be backed out of the premium.

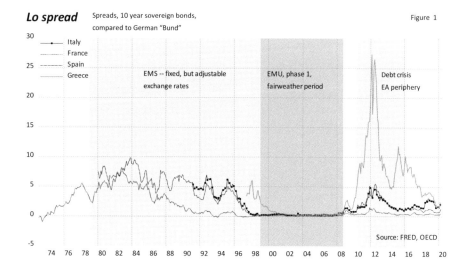

Fig. 1: Spread between respective sovereign and German Bund for selected European countries between the end of the Bretton-Woods-System, the European Monetary System (with exchange rate risk), the first ("quiet") and the second ("troubled") phase of European Monetary Union (with default and redenomination risk).

Under such circumstances, markets' credit assessment could be blunted, 'lo spread' might be compressed. Without the expectation of a backing option, spreads might not only be wider, rising at times precipitously, but capital inflows could also stop abruptly. This roll-over risk is lurking behind the corner for provinces or states in any monetary union *when* its no-bailout proposition is credible. Thus, having relinquished their monetary policy tools, it also concerns euro area member states. In monetary affairs, they have become sub-sovereigns.[4] There is no "national" monetary policy to support the market. When a supra-national backstop is in doubt, this implies a premium over safer debtors, in times of crises a very significant one.[5] In 2012, this phenomenon was dubbed re-denomination risk. For investors, this amounted to an ever more likely threat: a debtor country breaking away from the euro area, subsequently paying its debt in a devalued, new currency. In some cases, the premium for this risk turned out to be higher than the exchange-rate risk premium, prevailing under the fixed, but adjustable peg of the European Monetary System (see again Fig. 1).

---

4   Before monetary union was launched, it was difficult to find satisfying all-else-equal comparators. Spreads on Canadian provinces or U.S. states (after 1837) came to mind. In the first decade of the Euro, spreads where however substantially below those counterfactuals.

5   See De Grauwe, Paul and Yumei Li, "Self-fulfilling crises in the Eurozone: An empirical test", *Journal of International Money and Finance*, 34/2013, pp. 15-36.

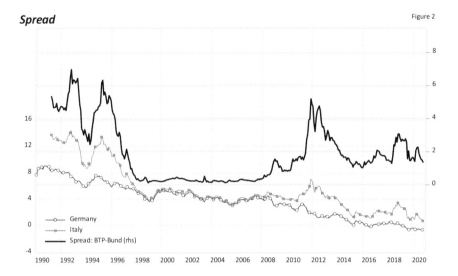

Fig. 2: Yields on Italian and German government bonds (lhs) and their difference, "lo spread" (rhs). Until 1999, this wedge captured largely the depreciation risk of the Italian Lira. In 2010, credit risk re-emerged and at times even a break-up (redenomination) premium was priced in.

In the spring of 2012, spreads between Italian and German government bonds rose to some 550 basis points (see Fig. 2). While Italy managed to stabilize its high debt to GDP ratio (of some 130%) by generating a sufficient surplus in its non-interest accounts, achieving such a debt-stabilizing primary surplus appeared to become ever more challenging with the spread-widening in 2012. This entailed a substantial risk of the crisis becoming self-fulfilling. Given Italy's size, this most probably would have meant "redenomination" or in more graphical terms: break-up.

Be that as it may, "lo spread" has apparently become a metric for everything that has gone wrong with Italy.[6] Alas, the Alpine divide is not only fiscal or budgetary, but also real. Comparatively, Italy has been underperforming most of its European peers, for almost a generation now.[7] Quite interestingly, however, for a substantial period

---

6   See Rubinelli, Lucia, "What an Italian Donkey's Fate Tells Us About the Future of Europe. A fable about Italy, bond yields and politics in the European Union", *New York Times*, 24 Nov. 2018.

7   See Pellegrino, Bruno and Luigi Zingales, "Diagnosing the Italian Disease", *NBER Working Papers*, n. 23964, UCLA and Chicago Booth, 2019; also Gros, Daniel, *What is holding Italy back?*, 2011 https://voxeu.org/article/what-holding-italy-back. Incidentally, during the 40 years before that, Italy's growth in per capita GDP was only surpassed by South Korea, reaching at the beginning of the 1990s the same level as France or Germany; see de Cecco, Marcello, "Italy's dysfunctional political economy", *West*

(from the mid-1990s until the mid-2000s), Germany shared this fate. Indeed, it was barely seen in a more benign light. In too many domains, Germany held the "red lantern", allegedly almost beyond hope.[8] Germany was generally seen as the "sick man of Europe".

This perception has changed since the mid-2000s. Has Germany been performing better because of its comparatively better fiscal policy: Is 'it', the Alpine divide, all fiscal? Is the more robust budgetary position the upshot of better institutions? Has Italy veered off track since it adhered even less to the rules of the Stability and Growth Pact (SGP) than its comparator, whose breaching of the rules in 2003 led to a first reform of the SGP? What are the ultimate drivers of these divergences – the various Alpine divides?

Obviously, I will treat these issues in just very broad strokes. My main point will be that EMU has raised the stakes for economies like Italy, for whom the "vincolo esterno" has been substituted by a rule, the SGP, also external, but much less unforgiving. This answers the question of this section title: We should begin our analysis before EMU was launched.

II. Deficits and debt in Italy and Germany

But when? Looking at deficits and debt (relative to GDP) between Italy and Germany, both follow rather similar trajectories since the end of WWII until the late 1960s, i.e. before the first oil price shock.[9] Admittedly, there's a difference in levels, but this reflects the effects of the London Debt Agreement, which halved German public sector debt in 1953. Just to recall, Germany defaulted twice in the 20th century, Italy did not. In Italy, debt (as a percent of GDP) only started to rise comparatively faster in the late 1960s. Deficits and debt, of course, also rose in Germany, as in other advanced economies. But only after the first oil price shock, hence with a few years' delay, and, most importantly, with much slower pace.

European Politics, Vol. 30, No. 4, 2007, pp. 763 – 783. For Michael Porter (*The Competitive Advantage of Nations*, London: MacMillan, 1990, pp. 421-455), Italy's Northern regions belonged to the dynamic vanguard of advanced economies.

8   See Sinn, Hans-Werner: *Ist Deutschland noch zu retten?*, Berlin: Econ, 7th ed., 2004.
9   This is remarkable, since the differential response to the doubling of oil prices across OECD countries launched these economies on divergent deficit and debt paths, at least for a while.

Alpine Divide – Is it Mostly Fiscal?

In a seminal paper, Alberto Alesina and Roberto Perotti[10] suggested six angles to assess differences in the political economics of public sector deficit and debt trajectories: (1) tax smoothing, to avoid the distortionary effects of tax increases (or procyclical expenditure cuts), (2) intergenerational conflicts about burden sharing (e.g. disputes about pension reforms in pay-as-you-go systems), (3) strategic role of public debt (possibility to reduce the leeway of successor governments), (4) debt bias of coalition governments (heightened temptation to delay), (5) effects of budgetary rules and procedures and (6) political mechanics of fiscal decentralization.

Following Buiatti et al.,[11] who build on very diligent data compiled by Francese and Pace, the tax smoothing argument – or 'how to pay for extraordinary events' – largely seems to hold for a long period of time: debt rose during three distinct phases, after WWI,

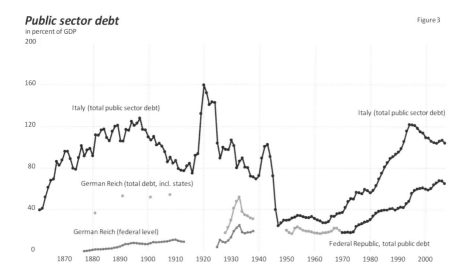

Fig. 3: Evolution of public sector debt (in percent of GDP) in Italy and Germany between 1860 and 2007; with Germany defaulting twice (breaks in series) and set on a different trajectory with the London Debt Agreement of 1953. Since late 1960s, Italy seems to have taken a diverging path; data provided by Maura Francese and Angelo Pace from their paper of (2008), ibid. (FN 10), gratefully acknowledged.

---

10 See Alesina, Alberto and Roberto Perotti, "The political economy of budget deficits", *NBER Working Papers*, n. 4637, 1994.

11 See Buiatti, Cesare, Carmeci, Gaetano and Luciano Mauro, "The origins of the public debt of Italy: Geographically dispersed interests?", *Journal of Policy Modeling*, vol. 36, 2014, pp. 43-62 and Francese, Maura and Angelo Pace, "Il debito pubblico italiano dall'Unità a oggi. Una ricostruzione della serie storica", *Questioni di Economia e Finanza* 31, Banca d'Italia, 2008. Fig. 3 uses their so carefully constructed data. Their support is much appreciated.

after the Great Depression, and after WWII. The 'optimal fiscal policy' or intertemporal burden sharing assessment also carries over to the period up until the end of the 1960s. Afterwards, however, policies to contain unemployment and reduce the output gap by allowing deficits to rise seem to dominate. That's also when the divergence compared to Germany and some other (future) euro area member states started growing. But Italy's participation in the various exchange rate mechanisms (Bretton-Woods, EMS and its different phases) also seems to have played a role, as did divided governments[12].

For Germany, from 30,000 feet high, one might tell a rather similar story. Ever since the London Debt Agreement and until 1972, overall public debt hovered around 20 percent of GDP. Subsequently, as a result of fighting a recession in 1974/75 (demand management), attempts to solidify its welfare state and, perhaps, some push at the end of the 1970s to take a locomotive role, the debt ratio went up to 40 percent. After a few years of stabilization, it shot up again in the immediate wake of debt-financed German unification, now towards 60 percent. However, funding the fundamental adjustment pro-

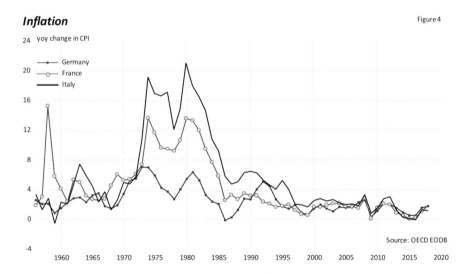

Fig. 4: Between Italy, France and Germany, wage bargaining institutions and monetary authorities responded differently to the two oil price shocks (1973 and 1979): To absorb the (demand and supply) shock, on both occasions the "competing claims" of labor and capital were met in Italy and France with more accommodative monetary policies than in Germany. This, rather mechanically, led to a depreciation of the lira (and the French franc). In the 1990s, France then opted for the politique "du franc fort" or an approach of "dévaluation competitive".

---

12   Galli, Emma and Fabio Padovano, "A Comparative Test of Alternative Theories of the Determinants of Italian Public Deficits (1950-1998)", *Public Choice*, v. 113/n. 1-2, 2002, pp. 37-58.

cess in East Germany through debt would fall under the 'how to pay for extraordinary challenges' category. Also, a substantial part of the financing of the Eastern German current account deficit – the difference between local consumption and local production, in size and duration historically possibly unprecedented – was financed through the social security system, hence not showing up in government debt levels.

While trajectories clearly diverged between Italy and Germany since the late 1960s, one could argue that there was no Alpine divide in principle: budgetary policies were responding to social pressures, which differed.

III. Mediating competing claims, differently

And that's where the divide really comes in. On both sides of the Alps, those pressures were operating on different scales. In this regard, a particularly pertinent indicator is the evolution of inflation.[13] Inflation rates between the two economies started to diverge in the early 1970s (see Fig. 4).

This mirrored substantially different intensities in the conflict between labor and capital about how to divvy up economic value added. Inflation can thus be understood as a mechanism to bring competing claims on GDP in line.[14] Hence, differences in systems of wage negotiations play a decisive role. However, industrial relations in Italy were much less cooperative than in Germany, for example, at the latest since the "autunno caldo" of 1969.

Of course, I do not pass a negative judgment on the reform of labor laws and pensions, which resulted from those conflicts. The point I want to make is that differences in institutions governing or impacting on labor markets come with consequences for both, fiscal and monetary policy in case they aspire to influence macroeconomic outcomes. Most importantly, both fiscal and monetary policy work through a "common funnel" (James Tobin). They are inexorably intertwined.

---

13 Persistent differences in inflation rates across countries, expressing the respective vector of interests within national contexts, have been for some time the focus of research of political scientist. This was the case in particular during the high-inflation 1970s, when analysts often stressed contradicting expectations of stakeholders. Charles Maier, distinguishing between an economic and a sociological explanation, has written a magisterial overview in 1978 (The political economy of inflation, in: Maier, Charles, *In Search of Stability: Explorations In Historical Political Economy*. Cambridge: CUP, pp. 187-224. When the article was republished almost a decade later, he added 2 ½ pages of commented literature.

14 Carlin, Wendy and David Soskice, *Macroeconomics and the Wage Bargain. A Modern Approach to Employment, Inflation and the Exchange Rate*, Oxford: OUP, 1990.

Banca d'Italia, for instance, at least from a short- to medium run perspective, was faced with a trade-off: either risking a deep slump or accommodating the societal stress. And, "cum grano salis", that's what it did. In fact, until 1981 – when the famous "divorzio" between the Treasury and the Bank of Italy occurred – that's what it was basically obliged to do, by way of buyer of last resort at the Treasury's bond auctions.

Only when Italy "tied its hands"[15] by entering the European Monetary System, thus committing to defend its pegged exchange rate, Banca d'Italia gained some autonomy from fiscal policy. At the same time, given that the EMS was asymmetric in practice, for Banca d'Italia membership meant that it was obliged to follow Bundesbank's monetary policy guidance.

However, in this case, there was probably no Alpine divide involved. Banca d'Italia pursued a largely similar objective: the desideratum of price stability, though, again, against different societal background conditions. In any case, during most of the EMS period, Banca d'Italia was able to use Bundesbank's policy guidance as a protective shield within the Italian political economic environment.[16]

However, Bundesbank's policy was self-evidently targeted at its home domain, to which it adapted tools as well as the operationalization (including the quantitative definition) of the primary objective ("Preisnorm, unvermeidliche Preissteigerungsrate"), which was not a quasi-physical constant (the famous 2 percent). The qualifier 'unavoidable' betrays that the Bundesbank accounted for difficulties in pursuing its ultimate objective. Bundesbank's 'monetarism', to which it converted in the mid-1970s, also in response to highly contentious wage conflicts, especially in the public sector, was always "pragmatic" (Helmut Schlesinger). So pragmatic, in fact, that Alan Blinder had difficulties in seeing the difference with a discretionary policy approach.[17] Interestingly, Bundesbank reaction functions (somehow Taylor rules before Taylor), as run inter alia by the important monetary theorist Manfred Neumann, uncovered that the Bundesbank always took note of more than the growth rate of the various monetary aggregates it supposedly pursued as its intermediate objective. From these targets it, of course, deviated half of the time; it did that deliberately, typically referring to "Sonderfaktoren".

---

15 See Giavazzi, Francesco and Marco Pagano, "The advantage of tying one's hands: EMS discipline and Central Bank credibility", *European Economic Review*, v. 32, pp. 1055-75, 1985.

16 Some take a more critical view of Banca d'Italia's approach during that period, see for a very instructive analysis Giannini, Curzio, *L'età delle banche centrali*, Milano: Il Mulino, 2004, pp. 277-307.

17 See Blinder, Alan, "The Rules-versus-Discretion Debate in the Light of Recent Experience", *Weltwirtschaftliches Archiv*, v. CXXIII, 1987, pp. 399-414.

Given differences in economic perspectives and background conditions across the Alps, this monetary policy stance of the Bundesbank implied inconsistencies and, at times, the need in Italy to untie, that is, to devaluate.

The bias for devaluation was regularly the upshot of wages running ahead of productivity, constantly pushing Italy's inflation rates above those of its partners in the EMS. This implied (rather mechanically) a real effective appreciation of the lira. An arithmetical corollary was the loss in price competitiveness, requiring ever so often corrective devaluations, the security valve to make the arrangement palatable.[18]

During German unification, the very large differences in background conditions, calling for opposing policy responses, then led to the EMS crisis of 1992-1993 – and the exit of the UK as well as of Italy from the system.

Germany, on the other hand, was characterized through most of the period since the first oil price shock by some sort of "konzertierte Aktion" or "Bündnisse für Arbeit" etc., at least implicitly. Germany's concentrated and coordinated labor unions understood that they were working in a small, very open economy, the success of which was dependent, at firm level, on its competitiveness. Concurrently, firm owners and managers were fully aware of the fact that productivity and performance on export markets (as well as obviously at home) were dependent on highly qualified and commensurately paid labor.[19]

In any case, wage moderation was an effective functional substitute to budgetary stabilization. At the same time, there was less of a need for inflation as a 'social mollifier' (Martin Bronfenbrenner). This institutional set-up also continued to prevail when Germany entered EMU, probably at an overvalued exchange rate. Within EMU, given its by definition one-size-fits-all monetary policy, this puts pressure on Germany's partners to adjust, in particular in industrial relations. That is, unless a fiscal policy could compensate.

---

18 In the first couple of editions of his excellent *The Economics of European Integration* (Oxford: OUP, e.g. 1994, pp. 13-17), Paul de Grauwe illustrated different preferences between members of a monetary union with the help of a two-panel graph: an equilibrium condition for the exchange rate of the lira and the D-Mark (relative purchasing power parity) as well as *two* Phillips curves, an Italian and a German one. Differences were captured in different profit-share preserving price-level increases. These differences in inflation preferences were, of course, discussed for a long time. De Grauwe refers to work of Herbert Giersch (1973) and Max Corden (1972). One should probably add Richard Cooper (1968) etc. See again, footnote 10.

19 Hall, Peter and David Soskice, "Introduction to Varieties of capitalism", *Varieties of capitalism: The institutional foundations of comparative advantage*, Hall/Soskice (eds.), Oxford: OUP, 2001, pp. 1-68.

IV. Differences in ideas, policy institutions or economic background conditions and perspectives?

The evolution of fiscal balances over time could be reflecting several underlying forces. It could be ideas, leading to different policy approaches. In that case, reference to the respective (national) policy debates is pertinent.[20] On the other hand, it might also be interests, e.g. conflicts about the appropriate role of the public sector in cushioning shocks (stabilization and redistribution) or supporting structural adjustment (reallocation). These contentious issues concern the volume – size of the state – as well as the funding of the provision of public goods. Such policy debates and political economic conflicts largely take place within the perimeter of national politics.

It would be tempting to search for differences in economic philosophies across the Alps. Perhaps, over the last few decades, the public discourse in Italy has been more pragmatic, more Americanized than the Ordo-oriented policy debates North of the Alps. But there is so much overlap and it would be easy to find counterexamples. For instance, while Alberto Alesina was never referring to Ordo positions, his arguments about how to manage public sector debt sound almost stereotypically 'German'. For him, one of the potential reasons for a debt bias resided in soft budget constraints for subnational public sector agents. Obviously, this is as close as one can get to Ordo's 'liability' principle, requesting the same radius for (a) decision making and (b) liability, i.e. owning up to the consequences of one's decisions.

Policy institutions also differ across the Alps. While this amounts to stating the obvious, an interesting question to pursue would be: Why was leaving the euro never debated as a serious policy proposal North of the Alps? To be sure, this option was heavily discounted by, inter alia, Carlo Cottarelli as well as probably all of the contributors to this volume (beginning with Francesco Papadia).[21] Luigi Zingales (2014), however, was reluctant to take such a view. Instead, he argued that the existing set-up of EMU "was unsustainable and damaging for Europe's South, which includes Italy [...] The project can only be saved on condition of radical reforms in the short term".[22] This is, incidentally, a position shared by many French economists (e.g., most recently, Robert Boyer).[23]

---

20 Hall, Peter, *The Political Power of Economic Ideas. Keynesianism across Nations*, Princeton: PUP, 1989 (with chapters by Marcello de Cecco and Harold James on the (rather reluctant) absorption of Keynesian ideas in Italy and Germany, respectively).

21 Cottarelli, Carlo, *What We Owe. Truths, Myths, and Lies about Public Debt*, Washington, DC: Brookings, 2017.

22 Zingales, Luigi, *Europa o no. Sogno da realizzare o incubo da cui uscire*, Rizzoli, 2014 (Kindle edition, pos. 52, my translation). Obviously, no radical reforms were made, still talk of breaking up has faded again into oblivion, spreads testifying to this.

23 Boyer, Robert, *Les capitalismes à l'épreuve de la pandémie*, Paris: La Découverte, 2020.

However, some of the suggestions of Zingales to attenuate tensions within EMU most probably would not garner the agreement of the German Council of Economic Experts, probably reflecting the median view amongst German economists, and possibly even less so the one of the German median voter. In that regard, the "Italian" response to proposals made by a group of French and German economists – themselves a compromise between "French" and "German" approaches – has also been interesting.[24] There appear to be 'national' clusters in economic arguments.[25]

Finally, what concerns variety in policy approaches, differences in economic background conditions evidently should be accounted for. And in this regard, ever since the 2000s, Germany and Italy evolved along different trajectories. The puzzle of Italy seemingly unlearning, at least at the aggregate level, has been diagnosed with an eye on what to do, amongst others, by Ignazio Visco.[26] He emphasizes more specifically the need for investing in knowledge (basic research, education and skills) to counteract the falling total factor productivity. He also highlights the importance of a sound financial system, serving its purpose of allocating societal capital at lowest costs possible.[27] I completely agree with Ignazio Visco's arguments. What I would add, is the need for a sustained, strong public sector effort in research.[28] This is not about competitiveness, but about pushing out the production possibility frontier – respecting environmental constraints.

V. Where does this end?

Finally, this is my answer to the question addressed to me by the editors: No, the Alpine divide is not mostly fiscal. While the state of public finances provides, to make use of Schumpeter's argument in the epigraph, an important analytical angle, one has to acknowledge the interaction between fiscal policy and various societal subsystems. One also has to drill deeper, what Schumpeter obviously did.

---

24   Bénassy-Quéré, Agnès et al.: *How to reconcile risk sharing and market discipline in the euro area*, https://voxeu.org/article/how-reconcile-risk-sharing-and-market-discipline-euro-area, 17 Jan. 2018 and Lorenzo Bini Smaghi, *A stronger euro area through stronger institutions*, https://voxeu.org/article/stronger-euro-area-through-stronger-institutions, 9 Apr. 2018.
25   In this case, I find myself (as so often) in agreement with Lorenzo Bini Smaghi as well as Stefano Micossi, i.e. that inter alia the French-German debt restructuring proposal would be prone to pushing banks and financial markets into bad equilibria when in crises.
26   See Visco, Ignazio, *Investire in conoscenza. Per la crescita economica*, Milano: Il Mulino, 2009 and Visco, Ignazio, *Perché i tempi stanno cambiando*, Milano: Il Mulino, 2015.
27   See also Friedman, Ben, "Is our financial system serving us well?", Daedalus, Fall 2010, pp. 9-21.
28   See Gruber, Johnathan and Simon Johnson, *Jump-Starting America: How Breakthrough Science Can Revive Economic Growth and the American Dream*, Cambridge, MA: MIT UP, 2019.

The common currency, that is the de-nationalization of monetary policy has, unmistakably, changed political-economic landscapes at national levels. In the run-up to monetary union, some in Italy argued that EMU would imply "germanificazione" (and in France, an economist spoke of "la teutomanie") What was not correct about this diagnosis was the understanding that EMU's features would mimic the German institutional set-up. They did not. The implicitly coordinated interaction between fiscal, monetary and incomes policy in Germany was not replicable at the euro area level. Instead, rules were established.

What was, however, correct about the concerns expressed about "germanificazione" was that, to cite Wendy Carlin and David Soskice, "living in the Eurozone with Germany [could] remain a source of tension [for] member states that do not have the wage-setting institutions that make the real exchange rate an effective stabilization mechanism".[29] The plural – institutions – is used on purpose. There are different ways to influence the real exchange rate: the Belgian model differs from the Dutch Polder approach which differs from the German way.[30] In other words: EMU plays out against other varieties of capitalisms.

A convincing approach to solidify EMU's institutional structure has yet to be found. And it seems almost impossible to find common ground about what establishes the minimum conditions for a functioning monetary union.[31] What gives rise to a more optimistic perspective is that preferences seem to vary more within nations than between them.[32] Luigi Zingales' view that "Europe, as it currently exists, is not only not sustainable, but it damages the South of the continent, to which Italy belongs" is shared by many. Not each economic problem is only structural, as "the" Germans (though, not all of them) seem to hold. Neither is each problem a lack-of-aggregate-demand issue. The Next Generation EU plan, launched to address the Covid-19 crisis, which came with asymmetric consequences across Europe, testifies to both points. Germany put up, with no delay whatsoever, a literally unprecedented fiscal stabilization program, and continues doing so. In other places, including Italy, less room of maneuver was available.[33] Nonetheless, Italian efforts also try to address supply-side challenges as they arise from sectors (hospitality, tourism etc.) that will most probably have to downsize substantially.

---

29   Carlin, Wendy and David Soskice, *Macroeconomics. Institutions, Instability, and the Financial System*, Oxford: OUP, 2015, p. 450.
30   See on this, documenting the pertinence of the institutional context for EMU, various boxes in World Bank, "Including Institutions. Boosting Resilience in Europe", *EU Regular Economic Report* 5, Washington DC, 2019.
31   See Hall, Peter A., "Varieties of capitalism in light of the euro crisis", *Journal of European Public Policy*, v. 25, n. 1, 2018, pp. 7-30.
32   See Alesina, Alberto et al. "Is Europe an Optimal Political Area", *Brookings Papers on Economic Activity*, Spring 2017, pp. 169-213.
33   See Julia Anderson et al., *The fiscal response to the economic fallout from the coronavirus*, Bruegel Dataset, 2020 and IMF, *Fiscal Monitor*, Washington, DC: IMF.ch. 1, 2020.

There are, indeed, structural economic differences, and they do show at the level of national budgets. However, here the dividing line is not the Alps. To a substantial degree these divergences are internal. Here it must suffice to just allude to Eastern Germany and the "mezzogiorno". A substantial part of national fiscal issues in Italy seem to be the upshot of regional imbalances.[34] For Germany, this was also the case in the wake of its unification, though it was the federal level which carried the burden – on purpose, not unintendedly. For Italy, Buitta et al. thus call for a hard budget constraint, as do many others. Most importantly, this would imply "that lower-level policy makers should not have access to unlimited credit and central government should not bail them out in every case of fiscal distress".

This is basically reiterating the no-bailout principle. In Europe, as in many other jurisdictions, it was, of course, honored in the breach. However, applying the rule regardless of circumstances would have meant a very substantial hit to creditor institutions, in particular North of the Alps. In other words, the principle comes with escape clauses – "not bail them out in every case" – in the case of systemic crises, when institutions involved are too big and too systemic to fail.

An open issue, raised before European nation states embarked on EMU, was about its consequences in terms of regional disparities. These issues remain open and they foster frustration in many who feel left by the wayside. This is where the discussion about effective regional or place-based policies has to start. Another topic for an Italian-German debate, preferably at Villa Vigoni.

---

34   See Buiatti et al., *loc. cit.*

Differences between Italian and German Public Finances: a Long-Term Economic Perspective[1]

Lucio Pench[2]

1. Introduction

In the current policy debate, Italy and Germany are often considered as representing opposite perspectives on the evolution of Economic and Monetary union (EMU). Fiscal policy in particular is seen as the key area in which the two countries' perspectives most clearly diverge.[3] It is easy to see the divergence between the Italian and the German perspectives on the role of fiscal policy in EMU as mirroring that of their respective fiscal positions, specifically, in terms of public debts: the public debt ratios of Italy and Germany stand at the opposite ends of the spectrum among large EMU economies. At the same time, it may be useful to frame the divergence between the two countries in a long-term economic perspective, possibly with the aim of detecting ways forward. This is indeed the aim of the present piece.

2. A stylised history of public debt in Italy and Germany (1960-2020)

The long-term evolution of public debt in Italy and Germany, namely over the sixty years from the start of the 1960s to the end of the 2010s, shows a common upward trend, in line with the experience of advanced economies. At the same time important differences between the two countries and over time are evident, which make them relative outliers with respect to other advanced economies.

---

1 I thank my colleague Alessandra Cepparulo for excellent research support and useful comments.
2 Lucio Pench has been with the European Commission since 1989. He is Director for Fiscal Policy and the Policy Mix in DG ECFIN. His experience includes being the Commission chief negotiator on the reform of the Stability and Growth Pact, heading the fiscal policy and surveillance unit as well as a stint as adviser in the Group of Policy Advisers reporting to the Commission President. His interests and publications focus on macro-fiscal issues, including in particular the relationship between policies and the EU institutional frameworks. A graduate of Sant'Anna School of Advanced Studies, Pisa, Lucio Pench holds also masters' degree in international relations (economics focus) from the Fletcher School of Law and Diplomacy.
3 Gros, Daniel, "COVID-19 and Europe's New Battle of Ideas", *Project Syndicate*, 23 Apr., 2020.

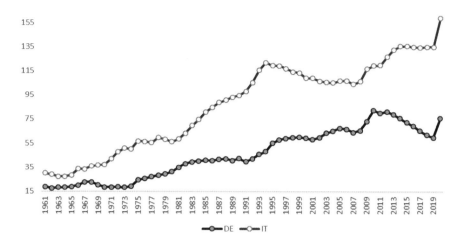

Fig. 1: Gross public debt in Italy and Germany (% GDP)
Source: Mauro, Paolo et al.,[4] European Commission Spring forecast 2020.

A visual inspection of the public debt series for the two countries (Fig. 1) coupled with some elements of historical background[4] allows distinguishing four periods:

- *The 1960s: the low-debt years.* Both Italy and Germany[6] started the 1960s in a very favourable economic and budgetary position, in particular , with low levels of public debt. This reflected two factors:

  1 *The liquidation of public debt that occurred in both countries in the aftermath of World War II.* In Italy, this took place through very high inflation during the war and in the immediate aftermath. In Germany, by way of outright debt cancellation in connection with the currency reform of 1948 (effectively resulting into the conversion of domestic public debt into the newly created Deutsche Mark at a 10:1 ratio);

---

4   Ministero del Tesoro, *Il Debito Pubblico in Italia: 1861-1987*, Roma: Istituto Poligrafico e Zecca dello Stato, 1988; Burret, Heiko T., Lars P. Feld and Ekkehard A. Köhler, "Sustainability of German fiscal policy and public debt: Historical and time series evidence for the period 1850-2010", *CESifo Working Paper*, No. 4135, Center for Economic Studies and ifo Institute (CESifo), Munich, 2013.

5   Mauro, Paolo, Romeu Rafael, Binder Ariel and Asad Zaman, "A Modern History of Fiscal Prudence and Profligacy". *IMF Working Paper* No. 13/5, International Monetary Fund, Washington, DC, 2013.

6   At that time their reintegration in the post-war economic and political order, reflected by the Bretton Woods system of fixed exchange rates against the dollar, was complete and the process of European integration was under way, with the creation of the European Economic community (1957).

2   *Unprecedented growth in the economy* (especially since the mid-1950s), leading external and domestic observers to speak of 'economic miracles', *coupled with prudent public finance policies aiming at favouring investment and competitiveness*. The debt-to-GDP ratio remained at historically low levels in both countries throughout the decade, supported by high economic growth and relatively stable inflation, although Italy recorded an increasing debt ratio from the mid-1960s, reflecting the accommodation of cost pressures from the private sector and expanding demands on the public budget.

- *The 1970s: the 'Great Inflation' years.* The post-World-War II economic regime and pattern of growth suffered a major shock with the end of the Bretton Woods system (1971) and the first oil shock (1973-74), which coincided with a slowdown in growth and an increase in economic instability amplified by divergent macroeconomic responses across industrial countries. As Italy and Germany found themselves at the opposite spectrum of policy responses, in particular, in terms of tolerance of high inflation, currency depreciation and budget deficits, the decoupling between the public debt trajectories of Italy and Germany began to become evident. In this period, the Italian debt-to-GDP ratio accentuated its increase relative to that of German debt as a share of GDP: the difference between the two ratios, which was about fifteen points at the end of the 1960s, reached about thirty percentage points at the end of the 1970s, when the Italian debt ratio approached 60% of GDP.

- *The 1980s and until the mid-1990s: the nominal convergence years.* The 1980s and the 1990s saw a renewed search for macroeconomic stability, following the combination of persistently high inflation and unemployment of the 1970s. In Europe, the search for macroeconomic stability expressed itself in the (re-)creation of a system of pegged, but adjustable exchange rates, the European Monetary System (ESM) and its accompanying Exchange Rate Mechanism (ERM), effectively revolving around the Deutsche Mark (1979). This eventually led to the launch of Economic and Monetary Union (in 1999) among eleven Member States of the European Union, which put a single independent monetary authority (the European Central Bank) in charge of a common currency (the euro), according to the plan set out in the Delors Report (1989) and the legal framework established by the Maastricht Treaty (1992). This period saw a process of 'nominal' convergence (i.e., in terms of nominal variables such as inflation, nominal interest rates, government deficits) with Germany playing the leader and Italy a challenged follower. A reflection of this process is the record of devaluations, both in number and amount, of the Italian lira against the Deutsche Mark during the first period of the ESM (1979-87), and the lira's eventual ejection from the ERM in the 1992 crisis. Periodic devaluations did not fully compensate for higher inflation in Italy relative to its commercial partners: the period of the 1980s and early

1990s sees the reversal of the long-standing historical pattern of real undervaluation of the Italian lira relative to international statistical norm.[7] The pursuit of nominal convergence coincided however with a widening of the divergence in the public debt trajectories of the two countries. At the start of the run-up to EMU in the mid-1990s, the Italian debt ratio stood around a post-World-War-II high of around 120% of GDP, more than sixty points above the corresponding value for Germany (in spite of the debt shock following German reunification in 1990.

- *The second half of the 1990s until 2007: the 'Great Moderation' years.* The period from the run-up to EMU to 2007 was characterised by pronounced macroeconomic stability, in terms of stable growth, low and stable inflation, and convergence of long-term interest rates. The performance of the euro area in this period can be seen as a particularly strong version of the world-wide decline in macroeconomic volatility observed since the mid-1980s and known as the 'Great Moderation'.[8] The achievement of nominal convergence during this period was consistent with a reduction in the differences in the level of public debt between in Italy and Germany, with the Italian debt ratio declining (to close to 100% of GDP in 2007) against a moderate rise in the German debt ratio. The decline in the debt ratio of Italy however slowed down towards the end of the period; the rise in Germany essentially reflected the absorption of the reunification shock and its aftermath.

- *The period from 2008 to current (2020): the crisis years.* The Great Financial Crisis (2007-08) put an end to the Great Moderation. The dramatic rise in risk premia in the economy, as private assets previously deemed 'safe' suddenly ceased to have a market, was compounded in the euro area by a reassessment of the risks of national public debts in the face of the crisis. The difficulties of the banking sector combined with the underlying losses in competitiveness and the absence of any 'monetary backstop' for the government[9] resulted in the euro area crisis (2011-12). This opened a new period of divergence in the public debt trajectories of Italy, at the epicentre of the euro area crisis, and Germany, benefiting from a 'safe haven' effect. The debt ratio, which had risen more markedly in Germany in immediate response to the Great Financial Crisis, climbed in Italy to new peacetime records in connection with the euro crisis. In subsequent years, Italy broadly stabilised its debt ratio, in a context of ultra-loose monetary

---

7   Di Nino, Virginia, Barry Eichengreen, and Massimo Sbracia, "Real Exchange Rates, Trade, and Growth: Italy 1861-2011", *Quaderni di storia economica (Economic History Working Papers)*, no. 10, Rome: Banca d'Italia, 2011.

8   Benati, Luca and Charles Goodhart, "Chapter 21 – Monetary Policy Regimes and Economic Performance: The Historical Record, 1979–2008", *Handbook of Monetary Economics*, 3, 2010, pp. 1159-1236.

9   De Grauwe, Paul, "The Governance of a Fragile Eurozone". *CEPS Working paper*, n. 346, Brussels: Center for European Policy Studies, 2011.

policy by the ECB, while Germany managed a steady reduction toward 'Great Moderation' levels, in contrast with the rest of the euro area. The large ongoing increase in debt ratios due to the Pandemic Crisis appears to have exacerbated the divergence, with Italy's debt ratio nearing its all-time (post–World-War I) high.

3. The drivers of the dynamics of government debt: structural differences between Italy and Germany

To appreciate the economic forces driving the dynamics of government debt ratios, it is useful to look at the components of the debt change and their sub-components.

The debt change is defined as follows:

$$\Delta b_t = p_t + b_{t-1} \cdot \frac{(1+I_t)}{(1+y_t)} + \varepsilon_t \qquad (1)$$

where b_t, p_t are public debt and the primary balance, as ratio of GDP, respectively (with ε_t being a residual reflecting 'below the line' operations affecting the debt but not the recorded balance); I and y are the nominal effective interest rate (average cost of debt) and the growth rate of nominal GDP. The product $b_{t-1} \cdot \frac{(1+I_t)}{(1+y_t)}$ is the so called 'snowball effect' as, assuming a positive interest-interest growth rates differential, it causes debt to grow faster with time (the opposite occurs for a negative-interest growth rates differential).

In turn, the primary balance is the difference between government revenues (t_t) and non-interest expenditure (g_t):

$$p_t = t_t + g_t \qquad (2)$$

And the nominal rates of interest and growth can be decomposed in the real and inflation components:

$(1+i_t)=(1+r_t)(1+\pi_t) \cong 1+r_t+\pi_t$ (neglecting $r_t\pi_t$)

$(1+y_t)=(1+g_t)(1+\pi_t) \cong 1+g_t+\pi_t$ (neglecting $g_t\pi_t$)

where r_t, g_t, and π_t are the real interest, economic growth and inflation rates, respectively.

We review the evolution of the debt drivers in turn for the two countries (neglecting the residual r_t and g_t, and π_t and for simplicity).

Lucio Pench

Primary balance

While the primary balance is the variable that can be more readily traced back to government policies,[10] the description of its evolution does not match that of the evolution of public debt.

The primary balance does not show marked trends in Germany (Fig. 2). Abstracting from cyclical fluctuations, particularly evident at the time of the first oil shock and the Great Financial Crisis (and the preceding expansion) as well as the exogenous shocks of the reunification and the Pandemic Crisis, the primary balance tends to show a small surplus over the longer term. The main exception to this pattern are the 1970s, which were a period of relatively small but sustained deficits. This appears broadly in line with a tax-smoothing behaviour once adjusted for the asymmetric nature of debt shocks. Instead of simply letting bygones be bygones, as pure tax-smoothing would prescribe, the government runs primary surpluses to bring debt down in normal times, to prevent it from creeping up over time as shocks are prevailingly debt-increasing[11] The relative stability of the primary balance in Germany is underpinned by relatively stable expenditure and revenue ratios (Fig. 3).

In Italy, by contrast, the primary balance moves into deficit from the mid-1960s and does not record a surplus until the beginning of the 1990s. In turn, one can distinguish two distinct sub-periods in this long sequence of primary deficits: in the 'Great Inflation' period of the 1970s, the primary balance moves deeper into deficits with large between-year variations. In the subsequent period, characterised by the pursuit of nominal convergence, the primary balance moves steadily in the opposite direction. In the run-up to EMU, as Italy was required to clear the hurdle of the 3% deficit threshold stipulated by the Maastricht Treaty as part of the EMU 'convergence criteria', the primary surplus reaches record highs in the order of 5% of GDP. As the 'Great Moderation' enters its most successful and terminal phase before the Great Financial Crisis, the primary balance declines rapidly. The euro area crisis forces a strong adjustment, following which the primary balance oscillates around a sizeable, but not historically high surplus of 1.5 – 2% of GDP, before plunging to an unprecedented peacetime low with the Pandemic Crisis.

---

10 The primary balance is the driver of the debt evolution that is more directly under the control of the government, since, at least in the medium to long run, it reflects its spending and tax programmes.
11 Escolano, Julio and Victor Gaspar, "Optimal Debt Policy Under Asymmetric Risk", *IMF Working Paper*, no. 16/178, Washington, DC: International Monetary Fund, 2016

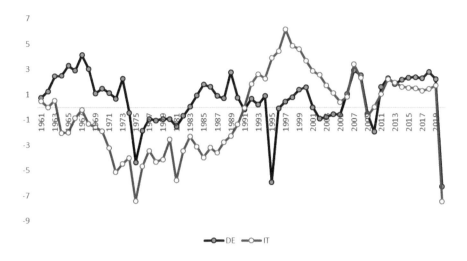

Fig. 2; Primary balance in Italy and Germany (% GDP)
Source: Mauro, Paolo et al.,[12] European Commission Spring forecast 2020.

Primary balance composition

The decomposition of the primary balance bears attention. In Germany, the relative stability of the primary balance is underpinned by relatively stable expenditure and revenue ratios. By contrast, in Italy, persistent significant primary deficits from the start of the 1970s to the end of the 1990s are the results of an equally persistent 'revenue shortfall', where revenues struggle to catch up with expenditure. The eventual closure of the gap comes entirely from the revenue side. Following a short period of containment in the run-up to EMU, the expenditure ratio increases further and exceeds that of Germany. Reversing the initial positions, at the end of the period the Italian economy has a higher burden of taxation than the German economy.

Snow-ball effect and its components

The other main driver of the change in debt, namely, the 'snow-ball' effect, needs to be considered in conjunction with the primary balance (Figures 4 and 5).

---

12 Mauro, Paolo, Romeu Rafael, Binder Ariel and Asad Zaman, *op. cit.*

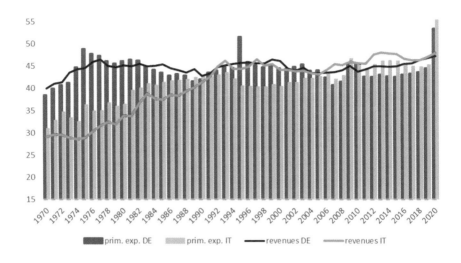

Fig. 3: Primary budget balance decomposition (% GDP): Italy and Germany
Source: Mauro, Paolo et al.,[13] European Commission Spring forecast 2020.

Abstracting from normal cyclical developments (in a recession both the primary balance and the 'snowball effect' will typically contribute to increasing debt, because the negative change in growth increases the interest-growth rates differential), the decomposition of the change in public debt over time highlights the key role of the 'snowball effect' in Italy relative to Germany. In particular, a large negative snowball effect is essential for containing the rise in debt in Italy during the 1970s in spite of record negative primary balances. The same effect works in the opposite direction in the run-up to EMU, making it more difficult to stabilise debt in spite of the achievement of primary surpluses. Periods in which the snowball effect is very small tend to coincide with periods in which the debt is relatively stable. This is more or less the pattern prevailing in Germany.

In turn, the interest-growth rates differential drives the sign of the snowball effect as well as the change in the size of its contribution. The comparison between the two countries (Fig. 6) highlights that, in the passage from the 'Great Inflation' period to that of nominal convergence, the interest rate growth rate differential in Italy swings from largely negative to positive. The change in Germany is much less pronounced.

---

13 Mauro, Paolo, Romeu Rafael, Binder Ariel and Asad Zaman, *op. cit.*

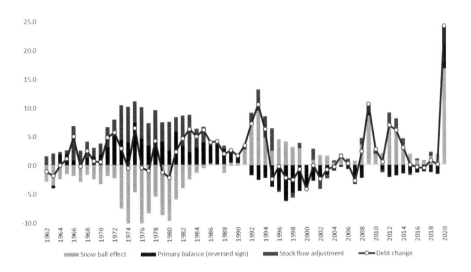

Fig. 4: Decomposition of change in public debt: Italy (% of GDP).
Source: Author's elaboration on Mauro, Paolo et al.,[14] European Commission Spring forecast 2020.

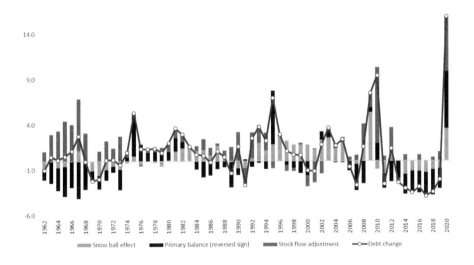

Fig. 5: Decomposition of change in public debt: Germany (% of GDP).
Source: Author's elaboration on Mauro, Paolo et al.,[15] European Commission Spring forecast 2020.l

---

14   Mauro, Paolo, Romeu Rafael, Binder Ariel and Asad Zaman, *op. cit.*
15   *ibidem.*

Fig. 6 Interest rate (average cost of debt) growth rate (nominal GDP growth) differential: Italy and Germany

Source: Author's elaboration on Mauro, Paolo et al.,[16] European Commission Spring forecast 2020.

Conversely, in the aftermath of the Great Recession, the differential settles on negative values in Germany, reflecting both the global decline in interest rates and safe haven effects, contributing to the decline in the debt ratio. The opposite remains the case in Italy, even after the absorption of the spike in connection with the euro area crisis.

The main reason for the large negative differential in Italy in the 1970s is inflation, both expected and unexpected, coupled with financial repression, namely restrictions channelling capital to the governments' funds that, in a deregulated market environment, would go elsewhere, chiefly among them capital controls. In fact, Italy introduced increasingly stringent controls on the outflows of capital in the 1970s, which were only gradually eased in the course of the 1980s and were finally abolished at the beginning of the 1990s, under the concurrent pressure of the run-up to EMU and transformations in the global and domestic business and financial environment. Germany, by contrast, after an experience with capital controls in the opposite direction, namely, to restrict capital inflows, during the late 1960s and the 1970s, eliminated all controls by the early 1980s (Goodman and Pauli 1993). A typical indicator of financial repression is the persistence of negative real yield on long-term debt (Fig. 7).

Fig. 7: Real market long-term interest rate: Italy and Germany
Source: European Commission Spring forecast 2020.

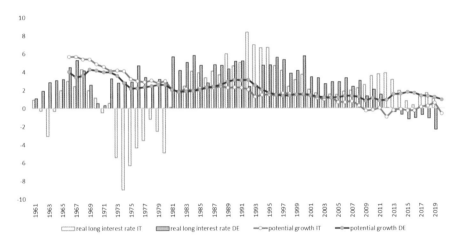

Fig. 8: Real market long-term interest rate and potential growth: Italy and Germany
Source: European Commission Spring forecast 2020.

In the aftermath of the Great Financial Crisis, the other element of the interest-growth rates differential, namely the rate of growth of the economy, can be seen clearly at work to the disadvantage of Italy relative to Germany (Fig. 8). The potential rate of growth of the Italian economy, which exceeded that of Germany in the 1970s and broadly matched it in the 1980s and the 1990s, has been falling behind since the early 2000s and has effectively been close to zero since the Great Financial Crisis.

4. Conclusion

A long-term perspective on public finances in Italy and Germany highlights the similarity of the starting positions of the two countries as they successfully emerged from the post-World-War-II reconstruction. Policy divergence manifested itself since the late 1960s and more clearly during the 'Great Inflation' period of the 1970s. In terms of public finance outcomes, specifically debt dynamics, the divergence between the two countries grows with Italy's pursuit of nominal convergence (inflation and nominal interest) in the 1980s and the 1990s, consistent with the return to a system of pegged exchange rates (ESM/ERM) and ultimately the creation of EMU. The relaxation of the fiscal adjustment effort in the aftermath of EMU-entry and the deteriorating productivity performance have made Italy especially vulnerable to the shocks of the Great Financial Crisis, the euro area crisis and, lastly, the Pandemic Crisis. Without the traditional escape routes of exchange rate depreciation to restore competitiveness and financial repression to stabilise or even liquidate public debt, 'orthodox' fiscal adjustment remains the only way out of fiscal unsustainability. Although, in the aftermath of the Great Financial Crisis, conditions may exist for some return to financial repression across advanced economies,[16] the constraints inherent to monetary union make a recourse to it, as well as to unexpected inflation, to the degree needed for significant debt reduction of the stock of outstanding debt in Italy impossible. Political economy constraints on the size of the adjustment and its composition, together with resistances to structural reforms, may result in fiscal sustainability to be undermined not so much by sudden crisis episodes, as by the underlying decline in growth, of which the high level of public debt is both a cause and a consequence.[17] The situation of Germany, especially after the Great Recession, appears as the 'virtuous' mirror image of that of Italy. However, the common membership in the single currency creates systemic externalities from national sovereign debt risks that cannot be removed through apparently linear solutions such as debt restructuring mechanisms or other strong reinstatements of the 'no-bail-out' principle.[18] At the same time, the large and increasing difference in public debt levels exemplified by the polar cases of Italy and Germany, and more generally between Germany and the other major economies in the euro area, objectively represents a fundamental

---

16   Reinahrt, Carmen and M. Belen Sbrancia, "The Liquidation of Government Debt", *IMF Working Paper*, n. 15/7, Washington, DC: International Monetary Fund, 2015.

17   Balassone, Fabrizio., Maura Francese, and Angelo Pace, "Public Debt and Economic Growth in Italy". *Quaderni di storia economica* (Economic History Working Papers), no. 11, Rome: Banca d'Italia, 2011; Bastasin, Carno, Manuela Mischitelli and Gianni Toniolo, "Living with high public debt, Italy 1861-2018", *Luiss Guido Carli Working paper*, n. 11, Libera Università di Studi Sociali Guido Carli, Rome, 2019.

18   Tabellini, Guido, "Reforming the Eurozone: Structuring versus restructuring sovereign debts", *Voxeu.org*, 23 Nov. 2017; *Id.*, "Risk sharing and market discipline: finding the right mix", *Voxeu.org*, 16 Jul. 2018.

objective obstacle to any plan for a common 'safe asset', without having recourse to guarantees by national budgets or financial engineering solutions.[19] The policy response of the EU to the Great Pandemic, with the creation of an unprecedented debt-based transfer instrument conditional on structural reform (Recovery and Resilience Facility), together with a reinstatement of common fiscal rules focused on reducing excessive debt accumulation, offers hope that the unsustainable divergence between Italy and Germany may be halted and reversed.

---

19   Leandro, Álvaro and Jeromin Zettelmeyer, "The Search for a Euro Area Safe Asset", *PIIE Working Paper*, n. 18/3, Washington, DC: Peterson Institute for International Economics, 2018.

Chapter III

Approaches to Economic and Monetary Union

The Legacy of the Bundesbank

Otmar Issing[1]

1. Introduction

Hardly any central bank in the world has a higher reputation within its country – and beyond – than the Deutsche Bundesbank. In a mixture of irony and admiration, Jacques Delors once said: "Not all Germans believe in God, but all believe in the Bundesbank", and one could add to that its currency, the D-Mark. So, it is not surprising that many Germans felt it was a great sacrifice to give up the beloved D-Mark in exchange for the euro. While in autumn 1995 in Italy, for instance, 68% of the population were for the euro and only 10% against, the figures for Germany were 34% in favour and 45% against.[2] Against the background of dominant euro scepticism, Chancellor Helmut Kohl had taken a very unpopular decision by signing the Maastricht Treaty. Although the history of events tells a different story,[3] there is still a widespread view that giving up the D-Mark was the price to pay for the agreement of European partners to German reunification.

In this context two questions arise:

– How has the Bundesbank gained such a reputation?

– What was the role of the Bundesbank in the process which led to EMU?

---

[1] Prof. Dr. Dr. mult. h.c. Otmar Issing born in 1936 held chairs of economics at the University Erlangen-Nuremberg and Wuerzburg. He was a member of the Council of Economic Experts (1988-1990). From 1990-1998 he was a member of the Board of the Deutsche Bundesbank with a seat at the Central Bank Council. From 1998-2006 he was a founding member of the Executive Board of the European Central Bank, responsible for the Directorates General Economics and Research. He has Honorary Doctorates from the Universities Bayreuth, Frankfurt and Konstanz and received many awards. He was Head of the Advisory Group on the New Financial Order appointed by Chancellor Merkel (2008-2010) and member of the High Level Group of the European Commission chaired by J.De Larosiere (2008-2009). In 2017 he was appointed member of the G20 Eminent Persons Group on Global Financial Governance.

[2] Issing, Otmar, *The birth of the Euro*, Cambridge 2008, p. 21.

[3] *ibid.*

2. The Bundesbank – a unique success story

To understand the psychological attachment of the German people to their currency one has to go back to 1945 and the experience with two currency reforms. Twice in one generation the Germans had suffered from the total destruction of their currency – in 1923 due to hyperinflation and in 1948 in the course of the so-called "stopped inflation", when tight controls prevented prices from rising and the Reichsmark had basically lost its function of medium of exchange. After these experiences, a deep desire for a stable currency had developed. The D-Mark, which arose from the currency reform of 1948, fulfilled this wish and ultimately became the most stable currency in the world, alongside the Swiss Franc. Trust in the currency was a kind of beacon in the darkness left behind by the horrors of the Nazi regime and the lost war – nothing left to be proud of. Much later, as a member of the Board of the Bundesbank, when I spoke of Germans having an almost "pathological relation" with their currency, I pointed to its origin in this episode.

The currency reform had been enacted by the Allies. The Bank deutscher Länder, the predecessor of the Bundesbank, was established in March 1948. Safeguarding the currency was its mandate. And the Americans had insisted on endowing the new central bank with the status of independence. When the former Chancellor Konrad Adenauer attacked the central bank in 1956 because of an increase in its discount rate, he clearly lost the "opinion battle", giving a clear signal of the high esteem the central bank and its currency had already achieved.[4] This position in the minds of the public was so strong that in the law by which the Deutsche Bundesbank was established, the status of independence withstood the resistance of the chancellor.

The Bundesbank law of 1957 is based on two pillars: the goal of safeguarding the currency, which in the course of time was understood as price stability, and the status of independence. What was widely seen as a kind of constitutional act was, in fact, a simple law that could have been changed at any time by a one-vote majority in the federal parliament. However, throughout the existence of the Bundesbank as the guardian of the D-Mark, the potential fragility of this legal basis was never tested. Certainly not all politicians were in favour of an independent Bundesbank – several times it was criticised as being too powerful and undemocratic – but none of them saw any chance to gain popularity by questioning the status of the Bundesbank. A little anecdote might illustrate its unique standing. When Helmut Kohl visited the Bundesbank in 1996, at the occasion of the 65th birthday of its president Hans Tietmeyer, he remarked: "As a politician and chancellor I was not in line with all decisions of the Bundesbank. But as a German citizen I am glad that we have an independent central bank". This position stands in stark contrast to the situation in other countries.[5]

---

4 Issing, Otmar, "Central Bank independence and monetary stability", *Occasional Paper 89*, London: Institute of Economic Affairs, 1993.
5 *ibidem*.

The experience of German reunification in 1990 confirmed that the D-Mark was also highly regarded by the citizens of the GDR, who for decades had to live not only under a communist regime, but also with a weak and unconvertible currency. Demonstrators in the streets in 1989 held placards saying: "If the DM does not come to us, we will come to the DM".

When the project of EMU entered the phase of realisation, any German government would have to convince the German people that the coming European currency would be as stable as the D-Mark. At that time this wish was common to all European partners. As a consequence, the Bundesbank played a leading role in the preparations for EMU while also bearing great responsibility going beyond its national role.

3. The Bundesbank and EMU

3.1. The rocky road to Maastricht

The regime of fixed but adjustable exchange rates established in Bretton Woods in 1944 collapsed in 1973. In a world of floating exchange rates, the member countries of the Common Market in Europe tried to limit the volatility of exchange rates between their currencies.[6] A decisive step was taken in 1979 when the European Monetary System (EMS) was created.[7] The plan was to arrange a system of fixed but adjustable exchange rates with the European Currency Unit, ECU, in the centre. However, the reality was different. As in the preceding arrangements of fixed exchange rates between European currencies, the D-Mark became the anchor of the system. De facto the EMS emerged as a D-Mark block. Those countries which did not or not fully join the Bundesbank's disinflation course were forced to devalue their currency. The stability-oriented monetary policy of the Bundesbank set the European standard. Politicians in France, for instance, claimed – or rather complained – "our monetary policy is now made in Frankfurt". The consequences for the Bundesbank were twofold. On the one hand, its role as the leading central bank in Europe was strengthened. On the other hand, it became obvious that in the end such an asymmetric arrangement was politically unsustainable. The moment that the Bundesbank's dominance reached its peak also marked the beginning of its end.

---

6   Szász, André, *The Road to European Monetary Union*, Houndmills, 1999.
7   Issing, Otmar, "The road to monetary union in Europe, Deutsche Bundesbank", *Auszüge aus Presseartikeln*, n. 72, 25 Oct. 1995.

Initiatives to take decisive steps towards EMU started in 1989. While continuing its policy to maintain price stability, the Bundesbank concentrated its activities on preparing the ground for the stability of a future European currency. President Karl Otto Pöhl played a prominent role as a member of the Delors Committee as well as in the Committee of Central Bank Governors.[8] The latter committee designed a draft statute for a future European Central Bank. In the negotiations leading up to Maastricht, the Bundesbank insisted time and again on the indispensable elements of the statute: priority for price stability and independence. It also made clear that the project of monetary union had consequences far beyond monetary policy. The Bundesbank always acknowledged the priority of politics in the decision to give up the D-Mark and join a common European currency. In February 1992 – preceded by a statement in October 1990 – the Central Bank Council declared:

The question of whether an EMU is to be established is a political decision. This decision is within the competence and responsibility of the government and Parliament. As part of its advisory function, the Bundesbank pointed out at an early stage that the implications of monetary policy pursued in a monetary union at Community level – in particular the implications for the value of money – will be crucially influenced by the economic and fiscal policies and by the behaviour of management and labour in all the participating countries. It also drew attention to the fact that a monetary union is 'an irrevocable joint and several community which, in the light of past experience, requires a more far-reaching association, in the form of a comprehensive political union, if it is to prove durable'.[9]

In its statement of 1990 (p. 44) the Bundesbank had stressed that the requirements listed are "indispensable [...] otherwise, considering the substantial risk involved, the favourable expectations associated with such a Union might well be disappointed".

3.2. The statute of the ECB

Approaching Maastricht, a broad consensus had emerged on the mandate of the future European System of Central Banks (ESCB) which found its legal basis in article 127 TFEU (1):

[...] the primary objective of the ESCB shall be to maintain price stability. Without prejudice to the objective of price stability, it shall support the general economic policies in the Community [...]

---

8   Issing, Otmar, *Entwicklungsgeschichte der Wirtschafts- und Währungsunion*.
9   Deutsche Bundesbank, *Statement by the Deutsche Bundesbank on the establishment of an Economic and Monetary Union in Europe*, Monthly Report, October (Published September 1990); see also Deutsche Bundesbank, Monthly Report, Feb. 1992.

This mandate is an almost literal translation of the mandate of the Bundesbank. However, the mandate of the ESCB is stricter. While "safeguarding the currency" initially also included the stability of the exchange rate – a "mission impossible" – the objective to maintain price stability is unambiguous. It is also legally on much safer ground, as any change would require a unanimous decision by governments and parliaments of all member states.

The proposal for independence of the European central bank, however, was debated. This is not surprising, since at the time of the negotiations no other national central bank in Europe enjoyed full independence, and some were even under strict control of the government. Resistance came in first place from France.[10] The success of the Bundesbank's monetary policy depended heavily on its independence. For Germany, this fundamental element of the mandate for the ECB was not negotiable – and in the end it was supported by all other partners.

The case in favour of endowing the ECB with the status of independence was also strengthened by convincing evidence from research. While the issue of independence for a long time played no role in the economic literature, this changed after the experience of the 1970s, which in the US were called the time of the great inflation. The overwhelming result of many empirical studies of many countries showed that the higher the degree of independence of a central bank, the lower the rate of inflation.

It was pure chance that the widely acknowledged result of research coincided with the negotiations on the Maastricht Treaty and complemented the message coming from the track record of the Bundesbank. Incidentally, most countries in the industrialised world decided in this period to endow their national central banks with the statute of independence.[11] It must be seen as an alarming signal that the independence of central banks has come under heavy pressure in the meantime.[12]

In the Committee of Central Bank Governors, the issue of voting was intensely debated. Should the governor of the Bundesbank, coming from the biggest economy, have the same voting power as the governor from the smallest country – at that time Luxemburg? Karl Otto Pöhl was finally convinced by the argument that the governors of the national central banks would be members of the Governing Council in a personal capacity, devoted to conducting monetary policy for the euro area as a whole – and not representing the interest of their respective country. The final consensus on the principle of one person, one vote can be seen as strong evidence for the European spirit which existed in the founding era of EMU.

---

10   Tietmeyer, Hans, *Herausforderung Euro*, München, 2005, p. 147.
11   Masciandaro, Donato and Davide Romelli, "Ups and Downs of Central Bank Independence from the Great Inflation to the Great Recession: Theory, Institutions and Empirics", *Financial History Review*, 2015.
12   Issing, Otmar, "The uncertain future of central bank independence", *Hawks and doves: deeds and words*, in Eijffinger, Sylvester and Donato Masciandaro (eds.), London: CEPR Press, 2018.

3.3. The need for fiscal rules

Fiscal policies can have very negative consequences for price developments. The task of the central bank to maintain price stability could be heavily impaired by fiscal policy. A central bank therefore has a strong interest in a fiscal policy which is consistent with its stability-oriented monetary policy – and vice versa. The Bundesbank highlighted this issue in its statement quoted above. To deal with this problem is a responsibility of governments. The German government was strengthened in the negotiations before Maastricht by the support of the Bundesbank. The German finance minister and the Bundesbank cooperated closely, based on a common understanding of the problem.

Chancellor Kohl was convinced that creating a monetary union without political union would be a fallacy. The Bundesbank, in its statement, declared the requirement of "a more far-reaching association, in the form of a comprehensive political union". But any initiative in this direction met insurmountable resistance.[13]

As a consequence, EMU became a unique institutional arrangement. The single monetary policy is conducted by a European central bank, while fiscal policy in principle remains in the hands of member states. It was (and still is) a tremendous challenge to both respect national sovereignty and to establish overall control of fiscal policies on the euro area level.

4. Conclusions

The Bundesbank, as the leading central bank in Europe with a track record of maintaining the D-Mark as one of the most stable currencies in the world, played a major role in the approach that finally led to EMU. Not only was there a common desire to make the euro a currency as stable as the D-Mark, the statute of the future ECB, in its fundamental components, reads like a copy of the law on the Bundesbank.

The successful start of EMU and the credibility which the ECB and the euro enjoyed from the beginning would not have been possible without the widely shared view that the new European central bank was modelled on the Bundesbank.[14] Nevertheless, it would be misleading to see the ECB as a clone of the Bundesbank. On this point, I made the following remark at the hearing preceding my appointment as member of the Board of the ECB before the European Parliament on 7 May 1998:

---

13 Szász, André, *op. cit.*, p. 222.
14 Issing, Otmar, *op. cit.*, 2008.

Concerning the connection between the Bundesbank and the ECB, you are absolutely right. They are two different things. I do not see the ECB as a Bundesbank clone. In the law it looks like it in many respects – independence, price stability, a central bank council – and yet they are in part completely different. The ECB Governing Council is composed of governors from countries with different tax systems, welfare systems and labour market conditions, so it is not directly comparable. The task is different. In working at the Bundesbank, I rested on the shoulders of the past, and lived off the reputation which that institution had built up over time. The ECB is a new institution that has yet to gain people's trust. It already enjoys the advance confidence of the markets; you can see that from long-term interest rates. But it then needs to justify that confidence through its policy. It needs to do that through transparency and through wise decisions. We all need to be aware that this is a difficult phase.[15]

---

15   *ibidem*, p. 42.

The Legacy of Banca d'Italia

Lorenzo Codogno[1]

1. Introduction

Assessing the legacy of Banca d'Italia when Italy entered monetary union is an overly ambitious task. Moreover, Banca d'Italia is alive and well, as part of the European System of Central Banks, and thus its legacy is an ongoing endeavour. Today, the bank continues to provide a precious and competent contribution to monetary policy in the Eurozone. Yet, this article tries to present some stylised considerations on how the experience and history of Banca d'Italia over the decades before monetary union helped it in the design and actual construction of the European Central Bank and in shaping how the monetary union has developed. The article focuses on those topics that are relevant for today's debate.

2. The early days: learning how to deal with the banking sector

Banca d'Italia was founded in 1893, meaning it is a relatively young institution among European central banks. Prior to the Bank's foundation, Italy was beset by problems relating to the fragmentation of the issuing banks that survived after the country's unification. The banking law that instituted Banca d'Italia defined banknote circulation and the link to gold, the central bank's limits for issuance, and the transition towards a single issuing institution. It also established its role of acting in the public interest as opposed to that of its shareholders. Nevertheless, Banca d'Italia remained a private company issuing banknotes under concession.

The situation gradually changed in the early part of the new century, under the leadership of Bonaldo Stringher. He was able to reconcile support to the economy with financial and exchange rate stability, amid profound transformation in the banking sector and fast industrialisation of the country. In 1907, Banca d'Italia prevented a financial crisis and strengthened its role as lender of last resort and guarantor of stability. Its reputation improved in the years leading up to World War I.

---

1 Lorenzo Codogno is a Visiting Professor in Practice at the London School of Economics and founder and economist of his consulting vehicle, LC-MA. In 2006-15 he was chief economist and director-general at the Italian Ministry of Economy and Finance.

With the end of the war, many financial institutions ran into problems with the conversion of many war-time industries to civilian use, and Banca d'Italia intervened massively to save the system. As part of the aim to return to monetary stability in the international financial system, Banca d'Italia supported the return to the gold standard after the war. At the same time, the government decided for a revaluation of the currency and deflated the economy. Stability was at the centre of the central bank strategy and, with this in mind, an in-depth institutional reform process started in earnest.

Banca d'Italia's institutional role became stronger, with the monopoly on banknote issuance and the management of clearing houses and payments. Capital requirements for banks were introduced as well as the protection of savings. Gold convertibility was re-established, with a new parity for the lira. The reform was completed in 1927-28 with a new Statute, and Banca d'Italia became a true central bank, responsible for setting the discount rate, although still reliant on government approval. The prioritisation of stability, inherited from these early years, remained a dominant feature during its coming of age as a modern central bank.

The Great Depression had severe repercussions for Italy's economic activity, and especially for its financial sector. Devaluation of other countries' currencies had a knock-on effect of lira revaluation, further exacerbating problems for the economy. It was the time when commercial banks had substantial equity holdings in the economy. The government and the central bank were forced to save the major commercial banks from collapse, set up a long-term financing institution and a new entity (IRI) to take controlling stakes in the major banks. Internal stability, especially that of the banking sector, had prevalence over the external value of the currency, although obviously the two are closely linked. These crises were lasting memories for the young central bank – a lesson never forgotten.

A new banking law was drafted in 1936, which is partly still in force today. The public interest role of Banca d'Italia as banker of banks was further expanded. At the end of 1936, a devaluation of the lira supported the economic recovery and improved the balance of payments. However, this was also the time in which the Fascist regime took full control of the Bank, abolishing all limits on State borrowing from the central bank by a simple ministerial decree.

As for many other central banks of the time, the struggle for a limited degree of autonomy continued, amid ongoing wars, political conflicts, and deep financial and economic crises. Nonetheless, giving independence to central banks was certainly not a primary concern of policymakers at the time, and most central banks enjoyed only limited autonomy.

3. From the ashes to the 'economic miracle', and from banking problems to currency/price stability

World War II inflicted substantial damage to the Italian economy. However, partly by virtue of the banking law introduced in 1936 that severed the equity link between commercial banks and private companies, the banking sector remained relatively stable, allowing it to play an essential role in the reconstruction. However, WWII also left the value of the lira at only one-third of its pre-war level, and this triggered runaway inflation.

Between 1945 and 1948, re-establishing stability was the main objective of Banca d'Italia, combined with the support to the economy. Banca d'Italia contributed significantly to attracting and managing the international aid programmes that helped the country to move out of the economic trough of the war and kick-start reconstruction while achieving financial stability and strengthening the currency. It laid the foundations for non-inflationary growth and the so-called 'economic miracle'.

In the post-war period, there was a de facto coordination between monetary and fiscal policy that allowed the country to recover, without jeopardising price stability or creating weakness in the lira. Banca d'Italia achieved this objective by introducing a compulsory reserve mechanism and monetary control. At the same time, Italy re-entered the international financial community by adhering to the Bretton Woods system. Later, in 1950, Italy participated into the European Payments Union.

A second important pillar was the re-establishment of certain limits to the monetary financing of the government. The overdraft on the Treasury's current account at the central bank was limited to 15% of the overall budget spending. Trade and foreign exchange began a liberalisation process. Banking supervision was re-organised under Banca d'Italia. The protection of savings was enshrined in the new constitution in 1948. In contrast to Germany, the policy debate was less about the separation of functions or giving full independence to the central bank, and more about ways to support the economic reconstruction of the country.

4. The '70s, '80s, and '90s: the search for independence and inflation-fighting credibility

In the 'economic boom' that followed the global conflict, Italy experienced rising productivity accompanied by an increase in inflation, compatible with continuing price competitiveness. The Italian lira enjoyed relative strength in the period 1947-1973. The situation reversed in the 20-year period that followed, amid important national and global phenomena such as the social unrest of the '70s and tensions in oil prices. On various occasions, weakness or depreciation of the currency was combined with an inflation rate higher than in other European countries. The question is whether this was an anomaly or the result of the institutional framework and macroeconomic policies pursued by the Italian government and Banca d'Italia.

The '70s and '80s were also characterised by the effort to attain stability. Still, Banca d'Italia had to face significant instability in the global economy, including repeated oil shocks and the end of the Bretton Woods system in August 1971. Moreover, it was a period of profound internal socio-cultural transformation for the country, political instability, insufficient competition in internal markets, and a rise in wages well in excess of productivity. Monetary policy alone was not enough to stabilise the system. An adjustment had to come from the 'real side' as well, by increasing flexibility and resilience in the economy, improving allocation efficiency and strengthening price transmission mechanisms. However, seriously undertaking reforms on the 'real' side was lacking as it proved politically incompatible, amid weak and unstable governments. Even Banca d'Italia came under attack, with the arrest of governor Paolo Baffi and deputy director-general Mario Sarcinelli on charges of misconduct. Although they were acquitted, Baffi, caught up in the political turbulence, decided to resign from his post in 1979. At the time, commentators attributed their arrest to the anger within the ruling Christian Democratic Party over Banca d'Italia's internal investigations into the misuse of cheap government credit for political ends. It was not an easy period for the relationship between the Bank and the various governments that came to power.

Fiscal policy appeared more inclined to accommodate political needs, ease tensions and maintain social peace, rather than promoting budgetary discipline and economic growth. The public net borrowing requirement exceeded 10% of GDP on multiple occasions, and the debt-to-GDP ratio rose sharply above 100%. Despite its strict monetary policy, Banca d'Italia was unable to counterbalance profligacy on the fiscal side, and at the same time maintain low inflation and a stable currency. Inflation rose from an average of 5.7% in 1970 to 11.4% in 1973 and 18.6% in 1974, reaching a peak of 25.7% in January 1975. It moved above 20% again in 1976-77, and once again in 1980, after the second oil shock. By introducing tight monetary policy, credit control and capital controls, Banca d'Italia managed to bring inflation down to 5.9% in 1986. However, to maintain price competitiveness, the Italian lira had to be devalued several times. In December 1978, Italy entered the Exchange Rate Mechanism (ERM) of the European Monetary System, although initially with a fluctuation band of +/- 6%, larger than the +/- 2.25% decided for the other countries. The band was then narrowed in 1990.

The real effective exchange rate based on consumer prices rose by 32.3% between October 1981 and August 1992, before the currency crisis that pushed the Italian lira out of the ERM. The Italian lira then depreciated against the deutschmark from 755.1 in August 1992 to 1250.7 in April 1995 – an almost 40% devaluation in less than three years – before moving back below 1000 by the end of 1996.

In February 1992, European leaders signed the Maastricht Treaty, which is at the root of the single currency and the European System of Central Banks. The '90s were the decade of economic convergence. Following the currency crisis in the summer of 1992, and especially since 1994, Banca d'Italia adopted a very tight stance, with the discount rate reaching 9% in 1995. In 1996, the policy interest rate started to decline gradually, still maintaining high real rates and favouring convergence in long-term interest rates. Despite the 1992 devaluation, inflation remained under control. It remained between 5.3% and 4.1% in the years 1992-1996 and fell to 2.0% in 1997 and 1998. Beginning in 1994, fiscal policy became equally tight to allow convergence toward the Maastricht criteria. The economy suffered because of the restrictive policy mix. Still, it was perceived as a necessary price to pay in the transition towards the shared policy objective of joining the monetary union with the first group of countries.

In the meantime, the institutional process was completed by allowing Banca d'Italia to set official interest rates without government approval. The Treasury account with Banca d'Italia was allowed to have only positive balances, and the central bank was no longer allowed to participate in government bond auctions. This completed the 'divorce' process to give independence to the central bank that had started in 1981. The referendum of 1985 began the abolition of the wage indexation mechanism, which was at the root of higher inflation, but it was not until 1992 that it was finally lifted. Most other structural reforms were still missing, however, making Italy ill-prepared for monetary union.

5. Taking stock of Banca d'Italia's experience

Over the years, Banca d'Italia severely criticised the conduct of economic and fiscal policy by the various governments, but the messages fell on deaf ears. The limited tools available to Banca d'Italia were not enough to counteract the loss in competitiveness. Thus, the Bank could only try to limit the rise in inflation and the depreciation of the lira but could not intervene to address its root causes. In fact, inflation had more to do with second-round effects of increases in oil prices produced by the wage indexation mechanisms and excessively expansionary fiscal policies. Moreover, even in the most acute phase of the crisis, Banca d'Italia was always careful not to 'rock the boat' with excessively tight policies which could have exacerbated the social unrest and amplified instability. When it was forced to do just this, it was heavily criticised. The economy, which had no safety valve other than currency depreciation, paid a high price for the lack of political and social consensus on stabilisation policies.

In Italy there has never been the same attachment to the central bank and the currency as in Germany, probably because Italy did not go through inflationary shocks as severe as those Germany experienced following the two world wars. Or perhaps it was because of other reasons, including that politicians have rarely listened to economists or dared to go for the far-reaching reforms needed. The revolutionary and disruptive changes between the wars and after WWII produced different institutional paths in Italy and Germany, although the struggle for stability was similar.

Over time, central banks have progressively increased their responsibilities and the complexities of their role. Central bank developments in Italy have partly shadowed those in other European countries, although with many Italian-specific characteristics. Probably the most notable difference compared to Germany was the de-facto limited independence of Banca d'Italia relative to the Deutsche Bundesbank. Independence came in 1981 – perhaps too late – and the process was completed only in the early '90s.

These developments raise a number of issues. In Italy the social and political backing of the role of the central bank has never been whole-hearted, and the institutional framework has tended to be incomplete. Was Banca d'Italia's performance defined by the deficiencies of the institutional framework? Or was the support for Banca d'Italia not sufficient to allow unpopular policies and a more independent position? Alternatively, was Banca d'Italia's institutional framework unable to ring-fence it enough from political pressure? What comes first: institutions and rules or consensus and behaviour? This is still an open issue, and the answer depends on the economic situation and the historical context.

6. A déjà-vu of policy issues?

Banca d'Italia has gone through many crises characterised by different driving factors in its short history, and it has always responded in a pragmatic and non-dogmatic way. This experience was part of Banca d'Italia's contribution to the European System of Central Banks. Although in a different context, these factors re-emerged in the monetary union. The European Central Bank had to deal with major banking and financial crises, some price and currency instability, and more recently, the complex relationship with fiscal and structural policies.

The newly created euro went through an almost 27% devaluation relative to the US dollar between January 1999 and November 2000, with a nearly 20.2% and 21.5% depreciation of its real effective exchange rate based on consumer prices and unit labour costs respectively. Moreover, the European Central Bank was heavily criticised for not meeting its inflation objective. In the first five and ten years since the launch of the euro, the Eurozone harmonised index of consumer prices was 2.0% and 2.2% on average, respectively. The experience was considered well above the defined parameters of price stability to the point that some criticised the European Central Bank for missing its target (for instance, Jordi Galí et al., 2004). In its second decade of operation, the European Central Bank delivered an average inflation rate of 1.3% that was well below its target. In Italy, inflation was 2.4% on average in the first decade and 1.3% in the second.

The model of governance envisaged by the Delors Report first and then implicitly confirmed by the Maastricht Treaty centred on monetary policy, while leaving other macroeconomic and structural policies mostly in national hands, notwithstanding a common EU fiscal framework and set of rules. At the outset of the monetary union, it was not politically feasible to go beyond that. In hindsight, this appears to have been a mistake. It was indeed too optimistic to expect that budgetary developments would be fully constrained by the framework and that the deeper integration of markets would give rise to broadly similar inflation trends. It was odd that the Eurozone had a central bank addressing only issues common to the Eurozone, while the Eurogroup was dealing almost exclusively with the position of individual countries, but not with the Eurozone's overall fiscal stance. Even the changes in governance that were introduced following the 2008-09 crisis fell short of significant steps towards real policy coordination, which is only gradually emerging nowadays. The aftermath of the 2008-09 and then the 2011-12 crises were indeed similar in some respect to post-war periods. The experiences of Banca d'Italia and other Eurozone central banks in managing post-war transformations evidenced the need for a close dialogue with the fiscal side. Regrettably, this experience was not sufficiently acted upon.

The need for an effective and coordinated policy mix has never been more pressing than today. Once the effective zero-lower-bound is reached, inevitably monetary policy has to accept a policy dialogue with fiscal policy in a sort of post-war way, in which both cooperate to achieve economic growth and stability. The current unprecedented scenario following the pandemic forces both monetary and fiscal policy to work in tandem even more forcefully. The situation is reminiscent of the post-war reconstruction in which Banca d'Italia acted pragmatically to promote growth while maintaining stability. Going back in history and learning from the layers of experience and the mistakes of the past may be beneficial for today's policies.

The issue of financial regulation and supervision in a unified currency area did not receive much attention before the launch of the euro. At the same time, Banca d'Italia perceived it as a problem (Padoa-Schioppa, 2004). Most European countries had set up Financial Supervisory Authorities separate from the central bank, as having everything under the same roof was perceived as potentially threatening the autonomy of monetary policy. Learning from its turbulent past, Banca d'Italia was among the few central banks in the Eurozone to maintain the supervisory function within the central bank. However, it was a minority view and not able to influence the new policy settings. Padoa-Schioppa warned against confusing central bank independence with loneliness, with even greater dangers to policy autonomy.

The 2008-09 crisis hit the Eurozone economy unevenly, and a typical balance of payments crisis within the Eurozone developed. Eventually, it led to a banking crisis and then a sovereign debt crisis. History repeats itself but in entirely different contexts. Banca d'Italia brought to the table the experience in dealing with a banking crisis, although its toolbox to deal with it did not prove entirely useful as demonstrated by various episodes of bank restructuring since the beginning of monetary union. The crisis amplified the degree of financial interdependence that had developed with the introduction of the euro. It eventually led to a centralisation in banking supervision.

7. Another legacy poorly absorbed in monetary union: the missing 'real side'

Was Italy unfit for monetary union? In the years that followed monetary union, inflation in Italy quickly converged to that of the Eurozone, which seems to support the view that institutions matter and economic agents react accordingly. Unfortunately, Italy's productivity differentials have widened since the beginning of monetary union, and, together with wage growth broadly in line with the rest of the Eurozone, this has resulted in a steady decline in price competitiveness. Companies were partly able to compensate by improving non-price competitiveness factors, but it was not enough. Price stability was not overly difficult to achieve, while the adjustment of the whole economy through increased flexibility and resilience was far more complicated. For that, Banca d'Italia had only soft institutional power compared to the various governments that instead were responsible for policy initiatives.

Nevertheless, the years of 'convergence' were characterised by very tight monetary policy by Banca d'Italia to prepare the economy for monetary union. Inflation and long-term interest rates declined. Since monetary union, Italy's inflation has broadly behaved in line with that of the Eurozone, notwithstanding all the scepticism in the wake of the launch of the single currency. It is evident that Banca d'Italia prepared price and wage setters appropriately for the new policy environment, but convergence on the inflation front was not enough, and that left other 'real' aspects unprepared.

The debate that preceded the launch of the single currency was about 'borrowing the inflation-fighting credibility of the Bundesbank', and having a seat at the table instead of being forced into policies decided elsewhere. German unification was a case in point. The tight policy decided by the Bundesbank at that time was not fit for most other European economies, and yet many central banks had no choice but to follow. As the leading economic powerhouse in Europe, Germany was able to drive monetary developments of other countries. Therefore, the deal was to accept the Bundesbank model to allow Germany to give up its beloved D-Mark while other countries got access to the policymaking table. All countries willingly accepted this implicit deal.

Banca d'Italia contributed with a different but equally profound history and experience, a shared drive for stability, plenty of technical expertise, while accepting the 'borrowing' of the Bundesbank's credibility. The combination of different backgrounds and experiences under the leadership of the Bundesbank worked reasonably well, but not without problems. Since then, the European Central Bank has been able to blend the different central banking cultures and backgrounds and develop its own distinct characteristics and culture over time. It has now moved away from the original Bundesbank-centred design of monetary policy strategy that prevailed in the early days of the monetary union in favour of a more eclectic approach.

The recent policy response by the European Central Bank, national fiscal policies and the pan-European investment plan, dubbed 'Next Generation EU', are encouraging. They can bring back the experience of the reconstruction after WWII, but that would not be enough. To make sure that the newly discovered coordination between monetary and fiscal policy works, the structural side also needs to make a substantial improvement, as Banca d'Italia reminded many times in the past, unfortunately without much success. Looking at structural issues, rather than just monetary or fiscal ones, is part of Banca d'Italia's legacy as well. This time, within the EU umbrella, there may be more chances to make it a success story. [2]

---

[2] Further works cited: Banca d'Italia, Annual Reports, various years; Ciocca, Pierluigi and Adalberto Ulizzi, "I tassi di cambio nominali e 'reali' dell'Italia dall'Unità nazionale al Sistema Monetario Europeo (1861-1979)", in *Ricerche per la storia della Banca d'Italia*, vol. 1, Rome-Bari: Laterza, 1990; Carli F., Pierluigi Ciocca (eds.), "La Banca d'Italia e l'economia. L'analisi dei Governatori", Turin: Aragno, 2019; Cipolla, Carlo, "Le avventure della lira", Bologna: il Mulino, 2001; Cotula, Franco, Marcello De Cecco, and Gianni Toniolo (eds.), *La Banca d'Italia. Sintesi della ricerca storica 1893-1960*, Rome-Bari: Laterza, 2003;

Lorenzo Codogno

Galí Jordi, Stefan Gerlach, Julio Rotemberg and Michael Woodford, *The Monetary Policy Strategy of the ECB Reconsidered: Monitoring the European Central Bank*, CEPR Report, 2004; Geneva Report on the World Economy, *It is all in the mix: how can monetary and fiscal policies work or fail together*, mimeo, 2020 ;International Monetary Fund, *Toward an integrated policy framework*, Sep. 2020; Padoa-Schioppa, Tommaso, *The Euro and Its Central Bank, Getting United After the Union*, MIT Press, 2004; Ricossa, Sergio and Ercole Tuccimei (eds.), *La Banca d'Italia e il risanamento post-bellico 1945- 1948*, Rome-Bari: Laterza, 1992; Rossi, Salvatore, *La politica economica italiana 1968-1998*, Rome-Bari: Laterza, 1998; Thygesen, Niels, *TPS and European Integration*, proceedings of the conference in memory of Tommaso Padoa-Schioppa, Dec. 2011.

Wrestling with Maastricht in France, Germany and Italy. The Role of the Intellectual Framework[1]

Daniel Gros[2]

The all-important fiscal criteria of the Maastricht Treaty were presaged by the Delors Report,[3] in which the (then 12) heads of the central banks recommended imposing 'binding guidelines' for fiscal policy. This resulted in the two key numbers, or reference values, of a maximum deficit of 3% of GDP and a debt ratio of 60% of GDP. These limits, fixed in the Maastricht Treaty, must be seen in the spirit of their time. Converging views on the desirability of imposing limits to national fiscal policy seemed fully justified, based on preceding decades' general experience of close association between large deficits, high inflation and financial instability.

Moreover, the only alternative to EMU that could still ensure some exchange rate stability in Europe seemed to be an asymmetric system in which the Bundesbank would de facto determine the monetary policy stance for the entire area. Even for those French and Italian policymakers who might have preferred more leeway to run deficits, Maastricht constituted the lesser evil.

---

1 This contribution draws heavily on Chapter 8 of Gros, Daniel and Niels Thygesen, *European Monetary Integraion*, London: Longman, 1998.

2 Daniel Gros is a Member of the Board and Distinguished Fellow at the Centre for European Policy Studies (CEPS). He joined CEPS in 1986 and has been the Director of CEPS from 2000 to 2020.

Prior to joining CEPS, Daniel worked at the IMF and at the European Commission as economic adviser to the Delors Committee that developed the plans for the euro.

Over the last decades, he has been a member of high-level advisory bodies to the French and Belgian governments and has provided advice to numerous central banks and governments, including Greece, the UK, and the US, at the highest political level.

He is currently also an adviser to the European Parliament and was a member of the Advisory Scientific Council (ASC) of the European Systemic Risk Board (ESRB) until June 2020. He held a Fulbright fellowship and was a visiting professor at the University of California at Berkeley in 2020.

He holds a Ph.D. in economics from the University of Chicago. He has published extensively on international economic affairs, including on issues related to monetary and fiscal policy, exchange rates, banking. He is the author of several books and editor of Economie Internationale and International Finance. He has taught at several leading European Universities and contributes a globally syndicated column on European economic issues to Project Syndicate.

3 Committee for the Study of Economic and Monetary Union, *Report on Economic and Monetary Union in the European Community* (the Delors Report), Luxembourg: EC Publications Office, 1989

Another important element at the time was a fundamental shift in the conception of fiscal policy. The Keynesian view of the 1960s had been that fiscal policy could be managed by a sort of 'benevolent' social planner, which would ensure that demand was always at the right level. This constituted the basis for the Werner Plan of 1969-70, which had recommended a complete centralisation of fiscal policy – and indeed all economic policy.[4]

By contrast, the view of the 1990s, derived from public choice theory, held that fiscal policy could not be trusted because fiscal policy is driven by special interest groups that are intent on maximising their own benefits. This view also held that the fiscal authorities are not always capable of ensuring that the outcome of interactions between these special interest groups, in terms of overall budgetary balance, corresponds to the national interest in demand management.[5] The entire excessive deficits procedure in the Maastricht Treaty implicitly adopts this view.

The profound change in the perception of fiscal policy explains the difference between the Werner Plan, with its vision of centralised decisions on economic policy, and the Delors Report, which left fiscal policy in national hands, subject only to upper limits on deficits. What were the arguments for limits on fiscal deficits and debt?

1. EMU could bring fiscal laxity and endanger price stability

The argument for binding guidelines grew from a concern that launching an EMU without any ceilings on deficits might encourage an excessively lax aggregate fiscal stance. In a monetary union the financing of external deficits becomes more automatic, and the potential effects of fiscal policy are more predictable and possibly larger within the borders of the initiating country.

It was thus expected that under EMU there would be less crowding out of fiscal expansion through higher interest rates at home and less need for concern about external imbalance. A policy adviser could well see reason to raise fiscal policy ambitions under EMU. A policymaker, no longer facing pressures on the currency or large reserve flows, might more readily act on this advice. This attitude, if widespread (and if consciously adopted by several member states), would indeed create a bias towards budgetary laxity.

---

[4] The Report called for a 'centre of decision for economic policy', independent of governments and placed under the democratic control of the European Parliament (to be elected by universal suffrage).

[5] Thygesen, Niels, "Should budgetary policies be coordinated further in EMU – and is that feasible?", *Banca Nazionale del Lavoro Quarterly Reviews*, Special Issue, Mar. 1996.

Given the starting point of large deficits during the 1980s and the possibility of further pressure due to the progressive ageing of the population, the fear that EMU would implicitly encourage laxity in budgetary policy seemed well founded at the time mainly, but not only, for policymakers in Germany.

The key issue was (and remains today) external effects. Why should the rest of the Union be concerned if any single member country (or several together) conduct an overly expansionary policy? The basic argument was that, if the deficit and/or debt becomes so large that it creates a liquidity or funding crisis for the country concerned, there will inevitably be pressures on the ECB to lower interest rates and conduct a looser monetary policy.

This leads to the next question: does the independence of the ECB not provide a sufficient guarantee that it will be able to withstand such pressures? The feeling then was that this might not be always the case. The problem is that the ECB will nevertheless have to weigh the costs of loosening its policy against the costs that arise for the EU economy if a member country experiences a public debt crisis, which could easily trigger a banking crisis. Once a crisis situation arises, even an independent ECB might be forced to cave in.

A related argument for binding guidelines relies on the same approach, which justifies the independence of central banks and their aim to achieve price stability. According to certain classes of models, only unexpected fiscal deficits can affect unemployment, so one might think the best policy is to keep the balance constant at a level that is sustainable. However, if the government cannot bind itself to such a policy, the public realises that each year it has an incentive to stimulate the economy with a larger than expected deficit. The public will anticipate this temptation and deficits might then be excessive (larger than optimal in the long run), but the economy would still not grow faster than average, and unemployment would not go down. In this view[6] the Maastricht limits could be seen as an attempt by governments to bind themselves to prudent fiscal behaviour and guarantee that they will not succumb to the temptation to stimulate the economy through deficit spending. Italian authors, among them Giavazzi and Pagano,[7] were very active in applying similar models to monetary policy, concluding that there might be advantages to tying one's hands.

---

[6] See Agell, Jonas, Lars Calmfors and Gunnar Jonsson, "Fiscal policy when monetary policy is tied to the mast", *European Economic Review*, 40, 1996, pp. 1413–40 and Beetsma, Roel and Harold Uhlig, "An analysis of the Stability Pact", *CEPR Discussion Paper*, no. 1669, 1997.

[7] Giavazzi, Francesco and Marco Pagano, "The advantage of tying one's hands: EMS discipline and Central Bank credibility", *European Economic Review*, vol. 32, issue 5, Jun. 1988, pp. 1055-1075.

Daniel Gros

2. Discipline through financial markets?

These arguments to limit deficits and debts would not be conclusive if alternative disciplining mechanisms were to emerge to prevent an excessively lax aggregate fiscal stance. Participation in EMU blocks the escape route of devaluation and surprise inflation that had occasionally been used to reduce the real value of public debt. The elimination of capital controls had already opened previously captive national markets for public debt, where governments were once able to finance deficits at below-market interest rates through high reserve requirements on bank deposits and compulsory minimum holdings of government debt. With these privileges for national debt creation gone, financial markets should be in a position to undertake a straight professional evaluation of the varying degrees of national governments' creditworthiness. Those persisting in rapidly increasing debt would face rising borrowing costs and some outright rationing of credit, possibly linked to a downgrading of their credit rating.

There is little evidence, however, that such mechanisms, even if they are allowed to develop fully, would provide adequate constraints on budgetary divergence. The experience within large federal states suggests that the sanction of an inferior credit rating is, outside periods of acute financial stress, of minor importance. Within Canada, where the divergence in budgetary stance and indebtedness is wider than in other federations, the range of borrowing costs spans less than 50 basis points. Within the United States, borrowing costs show a similar lack of sensitivity to state deficits, which tend to be fairly uniformly small anyway. Goldstein and Woglom[8] show, however, that in the USA the risk premium on states' debt increases at an increasing rate with the level of debt, and beyond a certain debt level credit might be cut off (as in the Stiglitz-Weiss model discussed below). At first, global financial markets had difficulty in properly assessing the credit risks attached to Developing Countries' sovereign debt, then in 1982 they reacted sharply and almost indiscriminately as the prospects for debtors worsened.

Even New York City, which almost went bankrupt in the mid-1970s, did not have to pay a very large premium until its credit was cut off almost completely. The cases of Mexico (and to some extent Italy) in 1995 show that financial markets can suddenly change mood and that there might be contagion effects, in the sense that difficulties in one country can lead markets to reassess the risk premium demanded for other countries. The US-led efforts to help Mexico overcome its financial crisis showed that the pressure

---

8 Goldstein, Morris and Geoffrey Woglom, "Market-based discipline in monetary unions: evidence from the US municipal bond market", in *Establishing a central bank: Issues in Europe and lessons from the US*, chapter 8, Cambridge University Press for the Centre for European Policy Studies, 1992, pp. 228–70.

for at least a partial bail-out exists, even without EMU. When the decisions about EMU were taken this was an open question. The experience with the Great Financial Crisis and its aftermath in the euro area has shown that the incentive for financial support to Member States is very strong. However, so far this has not affected the ability of the ECB to preserve price stability.

These episodes suggest that financial markets do not operate with smoothly increasing risk premia. The fundamental reason for this "modus operandi" of financial markets lies in the adverse selection effect of higher interest rates, as suggested by Stiglitz and Weiss.[9] The crucial point of this analysis is that borrowers always have better information than their lenders about their own financial position. Banks (or creditors in general) will therefore be reluctant to lend to borrowers who offer to pay very high interest rates, because only high-risk (bad) borrowers are likely to accept high interest rates. This is why credit (especially bank loan) markets are not characterised by smooth supply curves of credit that are only a function of the interest rate. The spread between bad and good borrowers is usually rather low, and beyond a certain interest rate, credit is just cut off. Financial markets might therefore exercise very little discipline until a certain threshold has been reached. Beyond this point the unavailability of any further funds would precipitate at least a liquidity crisis for the government concerned. Sudden changes in the perception of risk can also lead to a sudden re-rating of the debt of certain countries, precipitating a financial crisis.

Stiglitz and Weiss (1981) also show that a small reduction in the quantity of credit available can in some cases cause extensive credit rationing. A small tightening of credit conditions by the ECB could thus, at times, push a member country into a liquidity crisis. Knowing this the ECB might hesitate to tighten policy when this would be needed from the point of view of the average of the euro area. The absence of a more graduated discipline means, therefore, that a funding crisis could undermine a tight monetary stance.

3. Incentives to engage in excessive deficits

Another reason for limiting deficits, and hence limiting the build-up of public debt, is provided by the link between public debt and macroeconomic stability implicit in many of the prevalent macroeconomic models of the time. The standard macroeconomic models of the 1980s imply that it can be in the interest of society to

---

9 Stiglitz, Joseph and Andrew Weiss, "Credit rationing in markets with imperfect information", *American Economic Review*, 71, 1981, 3, pp. 393–410.

appoint an independent 'conservative' central banker.[10] A similar type of model can be applied to the market for public debt, where a trade-off exists between the distortions caused by taxes and the real *ex post* interest rate that the government pays on its debt.[11] The higher inflation is, the lower the real *ex post* debt service burden for the economy, at given nominal interest rates (and hence inflationary expectations). This implies that a central bank that cares for social welfare has an incentive to produce surprise inflation.

The importance of this effect obviously depends on the debt-to-GDP ratio. A higher debt ratio is equivalent to a less 'conservative' central banker. This approach implies not only that inflation will be higher with a higher debt level, but also that above a certain threshold level of debt/GDP ratio a stabilisation crisis could make it very costly, even for a determined central bank, to maintain price stability.[12] This is another argument for limits on public debt in the defence of price stability.

Why would governments engage in excessive deficits and debt that are against the interests of the country? The public choice literature on this issue illustrates that policy in this area is subject to a sort of 'prisoners' dilemma': in most fields of fiscal policy the beneficiaries of the expenditure decisions are few and can therefore organise themselves more easily to exert pressure on the government. The remainder of the population, which has to pay, is far more numerous, facing much greater difficulties in organising opposition against spending decisions[13]. If the entire population consists of many pressure groups, the outcome of this struggle will be a deficit that is larger than socially optimal. The various facets of this problem are analysed in von Hagen and Harden,[14] who conclude that a proper budgetary process can mitigate the problem. The literature on political business cycles[15] shows another reason why deficits tend to be larger than optimal. This does not imply that all deficits are always due to these factors, but few would deny that the large debt accumulated in countries, such as Belgium and Italy, were not in the interest of those countries.

---

10   Rogoff, Kenneth, "The optimal degree of commitment to an intermediate monetary target", *Quarterly Journal of Economics*, 100, 1985, pp. 1169–90.

11   Gros, Daniel, "Towards economic and monetary union: problems and prospects", *CEPS Paper*, n. 65, CEPS, 1996.

12   Gros, Daniel, "Self-Fulfilling Public Debt Crises", *Working Document*, no. 102, Brussels, Centre for European Policy Studies, CEPS, Jul. 1996.

13   Buchanan, James, *Democracy in Deficit: The Political Legacy of Lord Keynes*, Academic Press, New York, 1997.

14   Von Hagen, Jürgen and Ian Harden, "National budget processes and fiscal performance", *European Economy Reports and Studies*, 1994, 3, pp. 310–418.

15   Rogoff, Kenneth, "Equilibrium Political Budget Cycles", *American Economic Review*. 1990, 80, pp. 21-36.

4. Crowding out

Another line of argument for ceilings on excessive deficits and debt comes from the idea that, at least in a full-employment economy, public spending crowds out investment because it absorbs domestic savings. This implies that, (independently of EMU) a lower deficit would be beneficial in the medium to long run. This is a point of view that was often overlooked in the European debate on EMU, but it was important in the US debate[16] about the costs of fiscal deficits when the latter started during the early 1980s (although these deficits were almost always below 3% of GDP and the US federal debt had not yet exceeded the 60% Maastricht norm).

One reason why countries, like Italy and some others, opposed the Maastricht criteria was that they would necessitate a reduction in deficits by between three and five percentage points of GDP, if one uses the long-term average as the starting point. With full crowding in, this should lead to an increase in the investment rate, which should in turn increase income and output by several percentage points. Increases in output are not equivalent to increases in welfare, but even if one concentrates on purely welfare-theory considerations, Romer[17] shows that even relatively small deficits, like the ones in the US, could have very large social costs. One could thus argue that the fiscal adjustment required for EMU membership would be in the interest of the country concerned – but not necessarily in the interest of the policy maker who has to implement it because reducing a fiscal deficit carries a high political cost.

To the extent that increased national savings in the EU are not invested domestically (i.e., to the extent that the current account does change), output produced at home will not grow faster, but investment in the rest of the world will yield a return. Moreover, with the prospect of a greying EU population, it seems entirely appropriate for the EU to export capital in order to finance at least part of its consumption at retirement by the returns from these investments.

More evidence on the costs of fiscal laxity is provided by simulations undertaken by the staff of the IMF using its macroeconomic model.[18] These simulations illustrate that a lower public debt level tends to lead to lower interest rates and hence to higher investment. The simulations ask what would happen if all the industrialised countries were to reduce their debt/GDP ratio by 20 percentage points. The outcome, according to the IMF's model, would be, in the long run, a drop in real interest rates of one

---

16 See Romer, David, "What are the costs of excessive deficits?", *Macroeconomics Annual*, 3, National Bureau of Economic Research, 1988, pp. 63–98.
17 Romer, David, *op. cit.*
18 IMF, Washington, DC: World Economic Outlook, 1995.

full percentage point, which would stimulate investment to such an extent that the capital stock would increase by about 10% and world output and consumption would go up by about 3%. Simulations reported in IMF[19] then show what might happen if some countries were to undertake such a policy. All industrialised countries together essentially constitute a closed economy, but in this case one can take into account the fact that, if only one country reduces public dis-savings, the current account will be affected. The IMF did not simulate a 'Maastricht'-inspired reduction in the public debt of EU member countries from 80% to 60% of GDP. But the simulations it provides for the USA (which is of similar size to the EU) suggest that the impact would still be substantial: real GDP would increase by less (only 0.6 per cent), but consumption could still increase by over 2% because of the accumulation of external assets through the current account.

These arguments suggest that rules that force EU governments to save more might actually be in the interest of their own countries in the long run.

5. Concluding remarks

The discussion about budgetary rules in an EMU should not be viewed as a discussion between Germany on the one side, and France and Italy on the other. Political leaders in the latter two countries indeed wanted to preserve the freedom to run larger deficits. However, they lost out in the debate because the underlying intellectual framework of the time saw little value in discretionary fiscal policy and emphasised the importance of 'rules versus discretion'.[20] This intellectual framework was largely imported from the United States, where it had been developed to explain the 'stagflation' of the 1970-80s. Many economists in Italy were quick to apply this framework to the European experience, thus implicitly justifying restrictions on discretionary fiscal policy; an approach which was widely shared in the central banking community, even in the Latin countries. This broader intellectual background constitutes one of the reasons why the German position was, in the end, widely accepted.

---

19 IMF, Washington, DC: World Economic Outlook, 1996.
20 Kydland, Finn E. and Edward C. Prescott, "Rules Rather than Discretion: The Inconsistency of Optimal Plans", Journal of Political Economy, vol. 85, 1977, n. 3, pp. 473-492.

The Turbulent Period around the Time of Maastricht

André Sapir[1]

The long and winding history of the birth of the single currency, starting from the publication of the Werner Report on Economic and Monetary Union in October 1970 and ending with the launch of the euro in January 1999, is well known to the readers of this volume. One of the decisive episodes in this history was the Treaty of Maastricht, signed in February 1992 and entered into force in November 1993, which committed European Community (EC) members (with the exception of Denmark and the United Kingdom) to prepare for and eventually adopt the single currency.

Under the Bretton Woods system, European currencies were fixed or quasi-fixed. When the system started to unravel in 1970-71, the G10 countries sought to limit fluctuations among their currencies.[2] The December 1971 Smithsonian Agreement set bands of ±2.25% for currencies to move against the US dollar. This provided a "tunnel" with bands of ±4.5% within which European currencies could trade. Such bands were viewed as excessive by the EC countries who agreed in October 1972 to begin implementing the Werner Plan by establishing a "snake in the tunnel" with bilateral margins between their currencies limited to 2.25%. The "tunnel" collapsed in 1973 when the United States decided to let the dollar float freely. Soon afterwards, the "snake" became unsustainable, with several currencies leaving the system, including the Italian lira (in 1973) and the French franc (in 1974, but re-joining in 1975 and leaving again in 1976). By 1977 the system had become a Deutsche Mark (DM) zone with just the Belgian and Luxembourg francs, the Dutch guilder and the Danish krone tracking it. The Werner Plan was abandoned.

Although EMU was temporarily shelved when the Werner Plan was discarded, the goal of exchange rate stability in Europe was not. It was rekindled in March 1979, with the creation of the European Monetary System (EMS) and the establishment of the Exchange Rate Mechanism (ERM) with a band of ±2.25% among

---

1   André Sapir is Professor at Université Libre de Bruxelles and Senior Fellow of Bruegel. He was Economic Advisor to European Commission President Romano Prodi in 2001-4. He has written extensively on European economic integration, including EMU.
2   The G10 includes the United States, the United Kingdom, Japan, Canada, Sweden and five of the original six EC countries. Luxembourg does not belong to the G10 because it did not have an autonomous currency when the G10 was created in 1962, nor later.

seven of the then nine EC countries (EC9).[3] Italy also belonged to the ERM since its creation, but with a wider band of ±6% that it finally abandoned in January 1990 in favour of the normal band. The United Kingdom stayed outside the ERM but eventually joined in October 1990, with a band of ±6%. By then all EC9 countries, plus Spain, belonged to the ERM.[4]

It was not a coincidence that the decisions by the United Kingdom to join the ERM and by Italy to enter the ERM's narrow band both took place in 1990. These two decisions can be traced back to the 1986 Single European Act, which committed EC member states to complete the Single Market by 1993 and confirmed the objective of progressive realization of Economic and Monetary Union enshrined in the Werner Plan. In June 1988, European leaders mandated a committee chaired by Jacques Delors, the then President of the European Commission, to study and propose concrete stages leading to EMU. The resulting Delors Report proposed a three-stage process timed to begin on 1 July 1990, the day when the Single Market legislation for the full liberalization of capital movements was due to come into force.

As recommended by the Delors Report, the first stage of EMU started on 1 July 1990. The aim of this first step was two-fold: to achieve greater convergence of economic performance through the strengthening of economic and monetary policy coordination; and to prepare and ratify the necessary changes to the Treaty of Rome, as amended by the Single European Act. Preparation for the new treaty was undertaken swiftly and an agreement among EC leaders was reached in Maastricht in December 1991, paving the road for the signature of the Maastricht Treaty in February 1992 and its entry into force in November 1993, after ratification by all EC12 countries.

While the political and institutional dimensions of stage one proved remarkably successful, the economic and financial dimensions were much more turbulent. A few months after the signature of the Treaty of Maastricht, the EC plunged into the 1992-93 EMS crisis.

During the period from March 1979 to January 1987, there had been frequent (eleven in total) realignments of currencies inside the ERM, mainly the Italian lira (eight realignments against the Deutsche Mark resulting in a nominal depreciation of nearly 40%) and the French franc (six realignments against the Deutsche Mark resulting in a

---

3   Formally, the EMS and the ERM are distinct from one another, the latter referring only to the exchange rate arrangement within a system that also includes other features, like credit facilities. In practice, however, the terms EMS and the ERM are often used interchangeably. I will follow this practice here.
4   Portugal and Spain joined the EU in 1986. Spain joined the ERM in 1989 and Portugal in 1992. Greece, which became an EU member in 1981, only joined the ERM in 1998.

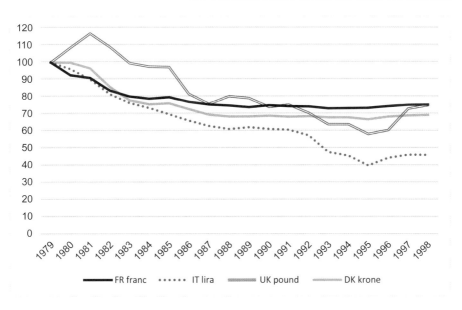

Fig. 1: Nominal exchange rates against the Deutsche Mark, 1979=100.
Note: values below (above) 100 indicate a depreciation (appreciation) of a currency against the Deutsche Mark relative to the situation in 1979.
Source: Own computation based on AMECO database.

depreciation of around 30%) (see Fig. 1). After January 1987, there was no realignment until 1992.[5] There were, however, several factors that undermined the long-term stability of the ERM during this period.

One was the divergence of fiscal and monetary policies in several countries, especially in Italy and the United Kingdom, compared to the situation in Germany, the de facto anchor of the EMS. A second factor was the liberalisation of capital movements (in July 1990), which made such divergence both attractive and susceptible to speculative attacks. The last factor was German reunification (in October 1990), which profoundly affected the country's fiscal and monetary policies during the 1990s, and consequently the other EMS countries.[6]

---

5   Except for a small devaluation of the lira in January 1990, when it narrowed its bands.
6   See, for instance, Cobham, David, "Causes and Effects of the European Monetary Crises 1992-93", *Journal of Common Market Studies*, n. 34, 1996, pp. 585-604.

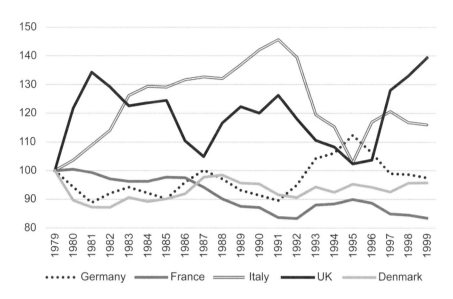

Fig 2. Real effective exchange rates, based on unit labour costs, 1979=100
Note: values below (above) 100 indicate a gain (loss) in competitiveness of a country against its EU partners relative to the situation in 1979.
Source: Own computation based on AMECO database.

Besides these internal factors, the literature has discussed the possibility that events outside Europe may also have contributed to the 1992-93 EMS crisis.[7] Specifically, it has been argued that this period coincided with a weak dollar leading to a strong Deutsche Mark and tensions on intra-ERM parities. This hypothesis has recently received empirical confirmation by Eichengreen and Naef,[8] who found that the dollar's depreciation in 1991-92 was a major factor in the 1992-93 the EMS crisis.

It did not take long for this explosive cocktail of internal and external factors to come to a head in the two countries that had accumulated severe losses of competitiveness, Italy and the UK, where the real exchange rate had appreciated by respectively 45 and 25% since 1979 (see Fig. 2). Market pressures led to the exit of the British pound and the Italian lira from the ERM in September 1992.

---

7   See, for instance, Gros, Daniel "The EMS Crisis of the 1990s: Parallels with the Present Crisis?", *CEPS Working Document*, n. 393, Brussels: Centre for European Policy Studies, 2014.
8   Eichengreen, Barry and Alain Naef, "Imported or Home Grown? The 1992-3 EMS Crisis", *CEPR Discussion Paper Series*, n. 15340, London: Centre for European Policy Research, 2020.

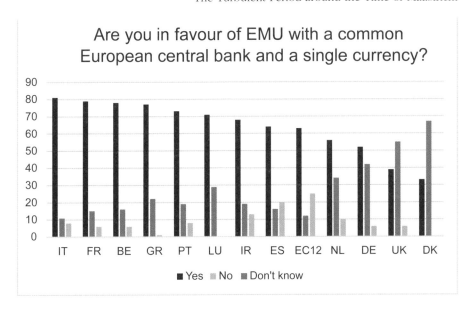

Fig. 3. Attitudes towards EMU in May 1991
Source: Own computation based on *Flash Eurobarometer*, n. 5, 22-29 May 1991.

Realignments of the remaining currencies failed to calm markets until it was decided, in August 1993, to widen the ERM fluctuation bands to ±15% for all ERM participants. The widening of the bands permitted the rapid depreciation of the French franc and the Danish krone against the Deutsche Mark, but these currencies rapidly recovered and made up all their losses by January 1994.[9] The underlying reason for this rapid return to the pre-crisis parities of these two currencies was that France and Denmark had avoided losses in competitiveness after joining the ERM in 1979 (see Fig. 2) and therefore did not need a correction of their exchange rates.

Besides the three economic factors listed above, political choices, including those made at Maastricht, played an important role in the ERM crisis. I will illustrate this point by examining two pairs of countries, with highly contrasting attitudes of their citizens towards EMU in May 1991, a few months before the conclusion of the Maastricht negotiations (see Fig. 3). The first pair is Denmark and the United Kingdom, the two EC12 countries where opponents of the single currency outnumbered those in favour in 1991, eventually resulting in their obtaining an opt-out from the single currency in the Maastricht Treaty and not joining it at its creation in 1999 or later. The second pair is France and Italy, the two EC12 countries where those

---

9   The Belgian franc had the same evolution.

in favour of the single currency outnumbered its opponents by the largest margin in 1991, and which eventually joined the euro in 1999. Yet, when the ERM crisis erupted in September 1992, the main contrast was not between but within the two pairs, with the UK and Italy leaving the ERM, and Denmark and France remaining inside the mechanism.

Denmark and the UK had both joined the EC (together with Ireland) in 1973. When the EMS was launched in 1979, Denmark immediately joined the ERM. After several realignments during the early days, the krone essentially shadowed the Deutsche Mark (and later the euro) starting in 1983. By contrast, the UK only joined the ERM in 1990, after much hesitation and political battles within the government, and exited in September 1992. The two countries adopted very different positions during the Maastricht negotiations, despite their electorates sharing the same opposition to the single currency.

The UK government sought and obtained an opt-out clause already in the original text of the treaty, which leaders signed at Maastricht in February 1992. It was not entirely a surprise, therefore, that speculation against the British pound remaining in the ERM occurred a few months later and was successful on Black Wednesday (16 September 1992) in forcing the pound to leave the ERM. Markets had correctly anticipated that the UK government was not committed to joining the single currency, or even to defend a fixed but adjustable peg within the ERM, which required aligning its macroeconomic policies more closely with those of Germany.

The position of the Danish government was completely different. During the Maastricht negotiations, it showed commitment to joining the single currency and did not therefore demand an opt-out clause. It was only after Danish voters rejected (by 50.7%) the Maastricht treaty in a referendum held in June 1992 that the Danish government sought such a clause, which it obtained from its partners in December 1992. It was no surprise, therefore, that the Danish krone managed to resist against speculative attacks in September 1992 since Danish authorities had clearly communicated their determination to maintain the krone inside the ERM. The evolution of nominal (see Fig. 1) and real (see Fig. 2) exchange rates was proof of this commitment.

The difference between Denmark and the UK in their commitment towards fixed parities with European partners was obviously not just political. It was also a reflection of the relative importance of Germany as a trading partner for the two countries. In 1990, Germany accounted for 22% of Danish total (exports plus imports, and intra- plus extra-EU) trade in goods, but for only 14% of British trade.

The comparison between France and Italy is equally instructive. The two countries had a broadly similar record inside the ERM prior to the Maastricht negotiation, with, respectively, six and eight realignments of their currencies against the Deutsche Mark. The chronic weakness of the French franc and the Italian lira was probably an important factor behind the overwhelming support in favour of the single currency in the Eurobarometer survey of May 1991 (see Fig. 3).

Despite strong popular support in the two countries, political and monetary authorities had more divergent attitudes. In France, support for the ERM as a means to achieve monetary stability and for EMU as an important political step towards European integration was always strong, at least during the presidencies of Valéry Giscard d'Estaing (the co-architect of the EMS together with German Chancellor Helmut Schmidt) and of François Mitterrand (the main European political engineer of the Maastricht treaty together with Chancellor Helmut Kohl). During this period, the successive governors of the Banque de France were equally supportive of the ERM and EMU initiatives. This unity helped France to play a leading role during the Maastricht negotiations.

In Italy, the situation was somewhat different. As Maes and Quaglia[10] explain, there were two schools of thought on the EMS inside the government and within the Banca d'Italia. The main dividing line concerned the ability and desirability for Italy to tie its hands on monetary policy by joining the European exchange rate mechanism, but there were obviously also geopolitical factors that entered into the question, since Italy may have been the only original EC6 outside the EMS. The compromise was to join the EMS at its creation in 1979, but with a wider fluctuation band of ±6%. Unfortunately, this compromise proved to be unsatisfactory. It did not prevent frequent realignments of the lira nor were such realignments sufficient to correct the country's gradual loss of competitiveness between 1979 and 1992. Internal divisions continued during the Maastricht negotiations, which weakened Italy's hand, except when it worked together with France.

Although France and Italy had different internal dynamics, they defended the same approach to monetary integration during the Maastricht negotiation. The two countries were the main proponents of the "monetarist school", which held that nominal convergence was not indispensable as a precondition for monetary union and that the credibility of the new common central bank would achieve the objective of price stability regardless of past economic performance by the members of the monetary union. By contrast the "economist school", sponsored mainly by Germany and the Netherlands, insisted that monetary union could only come as the final 'coronation' after a successful process of economic convergence, which would guarantee price stability.

---

10   Maes, Ivo and Lucia Quaglia, "The Process of European Monetary Integration: a Comparison of the Belgian and Italian Approaches", *Working Paper Research,* No. 40, Brussels: National Bank of Belgium, 2003.

The Maastricht agreement was a compromise between the monetarist position, which obtained a strict timetable for the introduction of the single currency,[11] and the economist position, which obtained that countries would have to meet strict convergence criteria before adopting the single currency.

The 1992-93 EMS crisis was interpreted as a vindication by the two sides. France, Italy, and other monetarists came out reinforced in their position that the only way to maintain exchange rate stability in Europe was by completing the transition to the single currency as fast as possible, and certainly no later than the deadline agreed at Maastricht. Germany, the Netherlands and other economist countries came out equally reinforced in their view that exchange rate stability was possible inside the ERM provided that countries adopted the right policies, and that it was necessary to achieve convergence in economic policies and exchange rate stability before moving to the single currency.

---

11   On the eve of the December 1991 Maastricht summit, President Mitterrand and Italian Prime Minister Giulio Andreotti came up with a plan which was accepted at Maastricht. It proposed making the introduction of the single currency compulsory by no later than 1999 for all countries fulfilling the prescribed conditions.

Beyond the Clash of Cultures

Gertrude Tumpel-Gugerell[1]

> If you pro-Europeans [...] you people in Brussels [...] propose a 100 per cent monetary union with a European Central Bank, with a treaty, I can accept it. What I do not accept are provisions which are not really clear in their legal foundation and which do not offer a clear indication of the direction that is being taken.
>
> Karl Otto Pöhl, conversation with Tommaso Padoa-Schioppa, 1982, quoted in Marshall, Matt.[2]

The Euro was introduced as a coin with two sides – the European, common side as a symbol to achieve stability and to advance European integration, the other side representing national symbols, the wish of the founding members to shape the new currency. Germany and Italy approached the project with different expectations.

The Euro was not the dream of central bankers nor was the European Monetary System. The EMS was presented by Chancellor Helmut Schmidt and President Giscard D'Estaing to stabilise exchange rates after the turbulences of the Post-Bretton Woods era and required primarily an assessment of exchange rates and their adequacy in the macroeconomic context.

The Werner Plan in 1970 proposed the coordination of economic, monetary and credit policy and the liberalisation of capital flows. It addressed structural and regional problems, and a harmonisation of taxes was foreseen as a first step. In retrospect, it was a more comprehensive script than the design of the Euro at its creation would be.

The Euro was advanced as a political project, complementing the single market and a vehicle to advance political union. *L'Europe se fera par la monnaie ou ne se fera pas*[3] is a famous quote which can be interpreted in two ways: either Europe can succeed on the monetary project or it will not succeed at all. Or, as it was later interpreted, monetary integration requires political integration to follow. The Bundesbank took an opposing position. It was widely understood amongst economists in Germany that political union should come first, which was then to be followed by a single currency.

---

1   G. Tumpel-Gugerell, Board Member of the ECB (2003-2011), Vice-Governor (OeNB, 1998-2003), EFC-Member during €-preparation, Expert Group of the EC on Eurobills (Chair, 2014). Evaluator of the ESM, (2017). Non-Executive Director at Commerzbank, OMV,VIG and AT&S.
2   Marshall, Matt, *The Bank*, Random House Business Books, 1999, p. 343.
3   Rueff, Jacques, "L'Europe se fera par la monnaie ou ne se fera pas", *Commentaire*, no. 3, 1978, pp. 386-388.

These different approaches became more visible during the Euro crisis, which has a number of explanatory factors. What shall be investigated in the following is the influence on events of different lines of economic thinking, economic policy concepts and attitudes towards a common currency.

Lower growth than expected

Growth expectations were at 3% p.a. when the euro was introduced in 1999. Actual rates remained below that after the bursting of the dot.com bubble and after the convergence dividend had run its course. Following the closer integration of money and capital markets, the financial sector boomed and doubled its size within a decade. Deregulation and financial innovation enabled banks to do business with an equity capital ratio as low as 2% and cross border financial flows took place in unprecedent amounts. Access to financing was easy due to the euro bonus in the form of low interest rates and the assumption, prevailing among market participants, that issuers of public debt would be bailed out when in trouble, contrary to the legal framework of the single currency.

While the script for monetary policy had been prepared in detail in the Delors report, developed by the Committee of Governors, as well as in numerous working groups in the newly created European Monetary Institute and the ECB, fiscal policy coordination remained in a laboratory stage. In 2003, some countries decided not to follow the rules of the Stability and Growth Pact, and a number of other countries willingly followed this example, after the Court of Justice had confirmed the right of member countries not to follow the recommendations issued by the European Commission. This policy line, taken during a relatively benign period in financial markets, aggravated the dimension of the following crises. Yet, it was not the cause, but rather the consequence of an institutional setup with a single monetary policy and sovereign national fiscal policies.

Adjustments to the structural features of a currency union and macroeconomic alignment did not take place, while the financial sector was underregulated. The use of own risk models and business outside the balance sheet led to an understatement of the risks banks took and eventually created a systemic risk.

New rules of the game

While in the framework of the European Monetary System fiscal adjustments were supposed to take the place of exchange rate adjustments and were demanded through political pressure or moral suasion from other participants in the system, everybody seemed to be equal in EMU and could in effect only be persuaded to change a problematic policy course. Yet the framework was not really tested until the Financial Crisis.

Thanks to swift policy action (public guarantees, low interest rates and abundant liquidity as well as countercyclical measures and recapitalisation of the banking sector with public money) the euro zone, like the global economy, recovered relatively quickly in early 2009. Central banks were aligned globally and acted in close coordination with governments. When, in late 2009, it was revealed that the fiscal position of Greece was much worse than previously notified, the message from Europe was that Greece should try to address the issue on its own.

In the meantime, speculation against Greece took hold, spreads between Greek and German sovereign bond yields rose and the impact on other countries intensified during the first months of 2010. The flash crash in New York on May 5th added to the general uncertainty. It became clear that Greece would need external support.

Additionally, the dollar-market for some European banks dried up. Despite financial support for Greece in the form of an IMF-type stand-by agreement and by EMU partner countries, the situation remained tense: governments had neither institutions nor instruments available to defend the cohesion of the Euro area. The ECB's announcement on May 10 to purchase government bonds came unexpectedly. Government bond purchases had been used as an open market instrument by many central banks in the past. However, now government bond purchases were a novelty for the euro area as they were not a classical open market operation. Instead, it was seen as the task of governments (of Germany and other countries) – and not the ECB – to step in when an EMU country was in trouble.

This first clash of cultures, namely the question of who has to defend EMU, lasts until today. While the public debate in Germany sees the central bank overstepping its mandate to support highly indebted countries, the expectation in other countries is that the ECB will continue to shield them against default and higher interest rates.

The first attempt to reinforce voluntary fiscal policy coordination in a monetary union of sovereign states was the Stability and Growth Pact (later modified and extended by the Fiscal Compact and the European Semester). Would the euro area be able to counter bets against its cohesion, visible in the widening of bond yield spreads for Italy, Portugal, Spain and Ireland in the spring of 2010?

The difference of opinion related primarily to the role of the central bank – should it intervene to keep market access, e.g. for Greece, or should governments take action to stabilise government finances in the euro zone? While the ECB acted as a bridge until the creation of the European Financial Stability Facility – which was later replaced by the European Stability Mechanism (ESM) – the role of the central bank changed from thereon. A detailed description of these decisive weeks in the history of the Euro is given by Bastasin.[4]

The policy response to the euro crisis against the contagion of rising interest rates from country to country, started as a bilateral stabilisation effort: governments were lending to governments. The ESM was created as a hybrid institution; intergovernmental in decision-making, but with a common European objective, namely system stability. Apart from providing emergency funding assistance, the role of the ESM is the permanent and systematic monitoring of public debt markets, giving an analytical underpinning to the support between countries and acting as interlocutor between debtors and creditors.

The second clash of cultures – where does Europe's fiscal capacity end, what can countries do on their own, and when is the European shield necessary – is still present and will remain for the foreseeable future.

Supervisor without power – ECB as a financial watchdog

In the preparation of the Euro-framework, the task as a supervisor for the financial system of the new currency was not allocated to the ECB but remained at the national level, mostly with Central Banks or with separate supervisory institutions in charge. This arrangement was the understanding of the Bundesbank – the central bank should be independent, also from tasks which could bring the institution close to politics and compromise its independence. Moreover, in view of the strong role of the Bank of England and later the Financial Service Authority in regulatory matters, the UK, as a non-member country of EMU, was not keen on having supervision centralised at the ECB in Frankfurt.

The third clash of cultures emerged: was it the responsibility of a central bank to stabilise the financial system or was this a task for bank creditors and shareholders, and eventually the governments of the respective country? While the Great Financial Crisis of 2007/08 had been mastered in close coordination between governments and central banks, the ECB took on a new role in the context of the euro crisis: It cooperated with the European Commission and the IMF in the design and execution of adjustment programmes. The ECB had to take a view on the financial state of banks and to provide emergency liquidity on a large scale.

The opposition to the first bond purchase program of the ECB in May 2020 (called Securities Markets Programme) may have resulted from this different interpretation of

---

4   Bastasin, Carlo, *Saving Europe*, Brookings Institution Press, 2012, p. 189.

the role of a central bank, influenced in some parts of EMU by the experience of monetary financing as a precursor to hyperinflation in Germany in 1923. Only with the creation of Banking Union in 2014 did the ECB become the single supervisor and therefore was in a much better position to assess the stability of the banking sector.

Central banks and macroeconomic stabilisation

The authors of the ECB statute wanted to create a stable currency, keep inflation under control and let the central bank act without political interference. While the history of central banking in the 17th century was about the role of central banks as stabiliser of the financial system (Sweden, UK), the fight against inflation was the only mandate of the Bundesbank. The fourth clash of cultures was more than the responsibility for supervision – it referred to the wider responsibility for macroeconomic stabilisation.

While the Maastricht Treaty was a far-reaching achievement in developing a common understanding for monetary policy actions, at the time of its signing in the early 1990s the challenges ahead could not be anticipated. For most of the second half of the 20th century the fight against inflation was the primary challenge. Now the opposite problem, inflation below the medium-term objective as a consequence of shocks to economic activity, required new policy concepts and the jury is still out on the right measures to be taken. While the path of monetary policy was relatively uncontroversial during the first decade of the euro, the different roles of a central bank, with or without responsibility for financial sector stabilisation, became more visible during the crisis. Even further apart were the different roles central banks had played in pre-euro times.

While the Bundesbank had a clear framework without responsibility for supervision and macroeconomic stability, low growth was not a concern when the Bundesbank Law was decided in 1957. Economic growth was included in the objectives, if it carried no prejudice to price stability. Keynesianism was practised temporarily in the late 1960s in Germany, but it was no longer an option after the change in government in the early 1980s. Monetarism and ordo-liberalism shaped monetary policy and teaching at German Universities.

In the 1960s and 1970s Italy was fighting high inflation and used devaluations as a tool to regain international competitiveness; the Banca d'Italia was the financial watchdog with a strong hold on the banking sector. Franco Modigliani in his memoir *Adventures of an economist*[5] describes his years of advice to the Banca d'Italia, his impact reinforced from the fact that a number of leading economists working at the bank (Fazio, Padoa-Schioppa, Draghi etc) had studied at

---

5   Modigliani, Franco, *Adventures of an Economist*, Texere, 2001, p. 175.

the MIT. It was a period when Keynesianism had a certain influence on economic thinking, on econometric modelling and the design of policy responses. The Banca d'Italia was linked closely to the Treasury as bank for the State and intervening in the government bond market.

Did these different roles and experiences play a role in the Euro crisis?

Despite early intervention by the ECB and a preliminary stabilisation of government debt markets, at least on the surface, the difficulties of rebalancing the fiscal situation and restructuring the financial system continued. After the announcement of a debt restructuring for Greece, Italy was under international pressure due to its fiscal position and political uncertainty. The concerns about Europe were rising and a deep mistrust against European banks culminated in mid 2012.

Only after the announcement of Banking Union and a far-reaching declaration by the ECB ("to do whatever it takes") in July 2012, did the worst seem to be over. A new debate about Europe's future institutional set up had started. Difficulties to reach an agreement with Greece lasted until the summer of 2015, but the cohesion of the system was not put into question again.

Conclusion

I have described four cultural clashes in the European Monetary Union. They occurred over the following question:

1. Should central banks intervene in government debt markets?

2. Is it a country's responsibility to rebalance its fiscal position and when should it get support from European partners and European Institutions?

3. Should central banks stabilise the financial sector or is this the role of bank creditors and shareholders, customers, and eventually governments?

4. Should central banks stabilise aggregate demand or restrict themselves to price stability, interest rate policy and liquidity provision?

Differences in view about these questions may have contributed to the length and depth of the crisis and they will remain alive to a certain extent for the foreseeable future. The Euro crisis has transformed the eurozone and steps towards a political union have been taken. Understanding and bridging the cultural differences becomes more important than ever.

The Euro Crisis: Clash of Cultures?

Harold James[1]

The European debt crisis led both to the outbreak of a war of ideas in the European continent and to a seismic shift of power within Europe.[2] It produced a debate about the desirability of rules, but also about who should formulate the rules and how they should be enforced. The clash is often treated as if it is a war of ideas fought out across the river Rhine, between France and Germany. Italy played an ambiguous role in respect to the central issues in this battle of ideas: the country was divided between multiple intellectual traditions, with a north that looks intellectually and economically more like Germany, and a south with more sympathy for French style theories. Italy also has a particular – and very old – tradition of thinking about how policy needs to be embedded in consensus in order to achieve legitimacy. Unfortunately, Italian politics are highly polarized and contentious, so that consensus about basics appears as a remote dream.

The basic elements of the contrasting German and French philosophies can be delineated quite simply. The northern vision is about rules, the southern emphasizes discretion. Specific policy preferences follow from the general orientation: the rule-based approach worries a great deal about avoiding bailouts that will set a bad example and encourage inadequate behavior among other actors (economists call this the moral hazard problem). In contrast, the discretionary approach sees many economic issues as temporary liquidity problems that can be solved easily with an injection of new lending. From this point of view, the provision of liquidity is costless: there is no bailout, no incurred loss, and in fact the knock-on effects make everyone better off. There are, in this vision, multiple possible states of the world, multiple equilibria, and the benign action of government and monetary authorities can shift the whole polity from a bad situation into a good one. The ECB should do more and more. To this, the adherents of the moral hazard view point out the costs that will pile up in the future from the bad example that has just been set: the ECB's activism is destroying Europe.

---

1   Harold James, the Claude and Lore Kelly Professor in European Studies at Princeton University, is Professor of History and International Affairs at the Woodrow Wilson School, and official historian of the International Monetary Fund.

2   See Brunnermeier, Markus Konrad, Harold James and Jean-Pierre Landau, *The Euro and the Battle of Economic Ideas*, Princeton University Press, 2016.

The economic culture clash flared up at the turning points of the euro crisis. First, in regard to the Greek crisis in May 2010. Then the issue at stake was what sort of rules were needed to prevent the rescue operation constituting a moral hazard issue that would invite more countries to further fiscal misbehaviour. Divisions resurfaced again in thinking about the appropriate central bank (ECB) response to the threat of Eurozone disintegration in the summer of 2012. Then it looked as if Europe was tipping into something worse than a regular "bad equilibrium" but had embarked on a spiral of collapse, with ever-widening contagion. Germany yielded, the Chancellor abandoned her moral hazard concern, and encouraged the ECB to break the spiral. But many Germans continued to worry about the long-term moral hazard implications of the action. A further revival of the clash of ideas occurred in 2015, in respect to a renewed uncertainty about the Greek program, when Greek negotiators tried to present their case as a generalized act of southern resistance to the German vision.

Fiscal and Monetary Interactions

A central feature of debates about German and Italian economic policy – and about the appropriate response to the Eurozone debt crisis – was the relationship between monetary and fiscal policy. That involved a different type of clash, about who made and enforced rules. The political culture clash moved in parallel with the economic culture clash.

The German debate was conditioned by the long and complex history of the German response to inflation. The post-First World War hyperinflation constituted a national trauma, and German policymakers were concerned to avoid a repetition. The driving force of 1920s inflation had been the policy of the German government and the German central bank. Both were highly sensitive to political considerations. Both worried that rising unemployment might destabilize the precarious political order. So, they were willing to do anything in fiscal and monetary policy to counteract any kind of economic slowdown. The government ran large budget deficits as it tried to keep up employment in the state-owned railroad and postal systems, and also to generate more purchasing power. It kept on looking for new and ingenious ways to administer repeated fiscal stimuli. Equally significantly, the President of the central bank, an elderly Prussian bureaucrat called Rudolf Havenstein, boasted about his success in getting new printing plants, printing plate manufacturers and paper factories to meet the enormous demand for new money. He found more and more ingenious ways of stimulating bank lending to large businesses on ever more dubious securities. And he kept on explaining that keeping the money presses rolling was a patriotic duty. There was in short what would now be

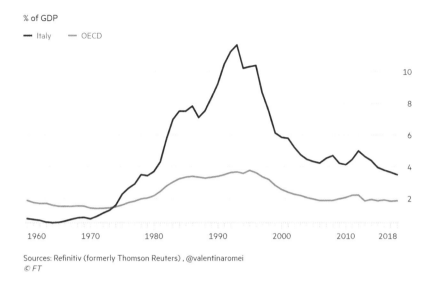

Fig. 1: Italian and OECD Countries Interest Payments as Share of GDP

called a "Havenstein put" in which the central bank would keep its interest rate at levels sufficiently low so that German business could continue to expand.

The post-inflation stabilization relied on a new central bank law (1924) which set a quantitative ceiling on the amount of government paper the central bank could lend against. These provisions were echoed in the 1957 law establishing the Deutsche Bundesbank, which imposed a limit on central bank lending to the government, and on the Treasury bills the bank might buy. These limits were quite low, respectively 3 and 4 billion Deutsche Marks, or 2.7 and 3.6 percent of German GDP in 1957. The German response to the historical legacy involved putting constraints on monetization of fiscal deficits in order to protect the political process from being over-burdened by distributive clashes.

The German experience also showed how desirable restraints came from the outside. That was the case in the 1924 bank law, which was embedded in the international reparations and stabilization plan imposed at the London Conference: it was a treaty and hence could not easily or unilaterally be changed by Germans. The external constraint was also the main feature of the post-1945 central bank legislation, which came from the US military and was initially opposed by the German experts.[3] The remarkably successful stabilization after 1948 bred a preference for externally generated solutions as a way of establishing systems of rules.

---

3   See Buchheim, Christoph, "Die Unabhängigkeit der Bundesbank: Folge eine amerikanischen Oktrois",*Vierteljahrshefte für Zeitgeschichte*, 49/1, 2000.

Precisely this issue about how rules originate figured very heavily in the Italian debate. Italy at the beginning of the 1990s had a very high level of government debt (it doubled in the course of the 1980s). Servicing the government debt was a major element of the budget. The attraction of the move to the currency union was that it would bring down interest levels, and thus reduce government spending. A famous analogy developed by Italian economists was that credibility was constructed by "tying hands". There were constraints here but applied not so much in order to save politics from being over-burdened, but to increase the opportunities open to politicians by reducing the cost of servicing debt. The classic model of this operation was the English "financial revolution" of the 1690s, including the founding of the Bank of England, which had made government debt more credible and hence – in the long term – government borrowing cheaper. The commitment to monetary integration, and the rules laid out in the Maastricht Treaty, reduced Italian interest rates, and payments on debt thus halved from 12 to 6 percent of GDP over the course of the 1990s, and fell further to below 4 percent on the eve of the debt crisis.

The credibility argument was not really new to the political economy of the late twentieth century. The basic argument was well known to late medieval Italian city states. Institutions – most famously the Casa di San Giorgio in Genoa – that aligned the interests of creditors and public authorities reduced the cost of public borrowing. The Casa was widely celebrated, with Machiavelli delivering a famous encomium.[4] The principles were taken up in late seventeenth century England, including in a pamphlet by William Paterson, and provided the basis for the Bank of England and modern central banking.[5] The – very old – Italian model is how an institutionalized commitment to solidarity can build civic prosperity. In the European debt crisis, Italian governments sought to avoid the imposition of external constraints – conditionality – with the argument that the constraints were more effective if they were internally generated, with domestic support. In particular, Mario Monti as Prime Minister consistently rejected the idea of an IMF or troika-imposed program.

---

4   Machiavelli, Niccolò, *History of Florence and Other Selections*, Myron P. Gilmore (ed.), Judith A. Rawson (transl.), New York: Washington Square Press, 1970, p. 304: "This is a truly unique example and one never found in the real or imaginary republics of the philosophers: liberty and tyranny, citizenship and debauchery, justice and license side by side within the same circle of walls and among the same citizens. It is that institution alone that keeps the city true to its ancient and venerable traditions".

5   Paterson, William, *A brief account of the intended Bank of England*, London: Randal Taylor, 1694, p. 11: "And as to the Security of the Bank, for such as may intrust their Effects therein, it will be clear and visible, and every way equal to, if not exceeding the best in Christendom; for the other Funds or Banks in the Christian World, at best have only Effects to answer, without pretending to have anything over: Nor are they Corroborated by the Interests, Property and Estates of Private Men, that of Genua only excepted".

The Euro Crisis: Clash of Cultures?

Observing rules brought clear gains, in both the German and Italian models. But in a crisis, it is always tempting temporarily to ignore the rules. Following them exactly would push the economy into further contraction. The essence of crisis response lies in working out short term solutions that do not create longer term violations of the basic commitments, to democracy and to civic solidarity. Crises require a leap of faith, but there were two contrasting diagnoses. One (German) version presented the necessary leap as an embrace of austerity, in order to make fundamental reforms. Another (Italian and French) version saw the need for growth, in order to break a cycle of contraction in which debt becomes unsustainable and the debt to GDP ratio soars because of the contraction of the denominator (GDP).

The actions of the ECB, especially after 2012, set up a new situation and a new clash of interpretations. German commentators frequently uttered the suspicion that the new measures were designed by Mario Draghi, the President of the ECB from November 2011, to help Italian banks and the Italian government, and thus amounted to fiscal support. This belief provided the basis for challenging the ECB's monetary policy in the German Constitutional Court: the case was settled in June 2020 by a ruling that stated that the 2015 bond buying program, the Public Sector Purchase Program (PSPP), had not been adequately scrutinized by the German government and parliament. From an early stage in the crisis, there had been arguments – initially from the parties of the left and then increasingly from populist right critics – that the European rescue mechanisms were undemocratic, and that the German lower (Bundestag) and upper (Bundesrat) parliamentary houses had not been consulted. The complaint argued that the ECB program put market participants in a position to buy without risk, and that it "removes the incentive of issuing states to pursue a sound fiscal policy". The ECB countered that this was simply the normal operation of monetary policy. But it was clear that the normal operation of monetary policy affected the interest rate, and hence calculations about debt sustainability.

The new normal will last as long as there is no inflationary surge. Post-Covid 19 however, monetary aggregates are rising in Europe (as in the UK and the US). Deflationary and inflationary signals make for uncertainty. The collapse of demand has unsurprisingly led to major price falls for a range of consumer goods, including textiles and automobiles. On the other hand, the collapse of supply chains and a politically driven reversal of globalization is likely to make many goods more expensive, including many food products. There is likely to be a rapid increase in "perceived inflation" in that trips to the supermarket are already becoming much more expensive. Asset prices already look as if they are being driven by a monetary overhang, and increased savings rates, as the initial post-COVID 19 losses were reversed. Influential commentators such as Martin Wolf spoke about a possibility of a recurrence of 1970s run-away inflation, and a likely combination of inflation and stagnation (stagflation).[6] For at least a few months, or even a very few years, however, the tug of war between inflation and deflation may be unresolved, and policy uncertainty will prevail.

If and when the inflationary scenario materializes, there will be a rapid move away from fixed yield instruments, and government financing will become much more expensive. That outcome would see a return to the euro debt crisis of the early 2010s. But, this time already highly inflated central bank balance sheets and more indebted governments would magnify the risk. The economic and political environment surrounding the EU is likely also to be more unstable, as a return to inflation fears is likely to occur earlier and faster there.

If this scenario is realistic, it changes the policy incentives, and creates in particular a great attractiveness to fund as much debt as possible quickly, including very long term maturities, or even, as suggested by Francesco Giavazzi and Guido Tabellini (very prominent Italian advocates of a rules-based approach), non-maturing permanent debt. This could be modelled on the very successful British "consols" (British government consolidated stock) launched in the eighteenth century (which were themselves based on a Dutch model from the middle of the seventeenth century, when the instrument was used to finance dike construction).[7]

Such long-term instruments can however only be issued by very secure borrowers. They put the emphasis back on credibility and rules: if there is any doubt as to the credibility, they would not be likely to find much of a market. The ECB without an adequate long-term fiscal arrangement would simply look like a version of the post-World War I German Reichsbank. Small European countries, or emerging markets, will not be able to access this type of instrument. The proposal thus depends on a very radical move to some form of debt mutualization in Europe, a move for which there is perhaps no political appetite. The European Commission project for €750 billions borrowing relies on an idea of only going quite gradually to the market and launching a tax that would deliver a funding stream only by 2027.[8]

---

6 Wolf, Martin, "Why Inflation may Follow the Pandemic", *Financial Times*, 19 May, 2020, https://www.ft.com/content/cdae43be-9901-11ea-adb1-529f96d8a00b. See also Charles Goodhart and Manoj Pradhan, *The Great Demographic Reversal: Ageing Societies, Waning Inequality, and an Inflation Revival*, London: Palgrave Macmillan, 2020, which considers longer time changes, most notably demographic changes, that will shift a structural balance to higher inflation.
7 https://voxeu.org/article/covid-perpetual-eurobonds.
8 https://www.ft.com/content/b9ff37b1-29b4-40ea-8b01-b4b82acc8ccf.

We are currently at a moment when this move would have a very powerful rationale. If the conclusion about the likelihood of the short-lived gap before the onset of inflation is correct, Europe may well be about to give up a very substantial free lunch. As advertisers like to say, this is an offer that cannot and will not be repeated. Higher levels of debt are for the moment sustainable – including in the contentious case of Greece. The debate will be increasingly about the character of fiscal policy: is spending oriented toward increasing productivity, fostering innovative technology?

A risk to government debt is also a risk of reviving the "doom loop" that gripped Europe in the Eurozone debt crisis. The doom loop had two components, one fiscal and another macro-economic. The first was that banks held large amounts of government debt as assets, so that a collapse in debt prices eroded their solvency and ultimately required recapitalization by the government (adding to the fiscal strain). Second, other assets of the banks suffered as the economy shrank; but the likelihood of a higher fiscal burden in the future to deal with the cost of bank recapitalization also weighed on economic growth. Fiscal and monetary measures are needed to avoid a new shock of the kind that became evident in the notorious press conference when ECB President Christine Lagarde explained (correctly, from a legal perspective) that the central bank was "not here to close spreads" between the borrowing costs of member states. She rapidly needed to walk back that statement.

Lessons about Conditionality

The euro crisis was a profound shock to European self-understanding. Europe could not work out its own rescue mechanism, and the European leaders brought in the IMF less as a source of financial resources than as a provider of professionalism and an outside vision of how to accomplish economic reform. Jean Tirole some time ago described the IMF and other international institutions as "delegated monitors".[9] A European mechanism, the European Stability Mechanism, was designed to develop into a European version of the IMF, managing conditionality. But the monitors were often used as part of a mechanism of blame transference, and their political capital began to erode. And then, perhaps unsurprisingly, Europeans became frustrated with the outcome.

The course of the crisis destroyed a good deal of all the participants' credibility. The euro is divisive because it looks like a straitjacket. And the problem with the imposition of external constraints is that it establishes a psychological mechanism of blame trans-

---

9   Tirole, Jean, *Financial crises, liquidity, and the international monetary system*, Princeton: Princeton University Press, 2002.

ference. When the policy that results from those external constraints does not produce growth, then the euro is reinterpreted as a trap. What was once a dream has become a nightmare of entrapment. When wage growth occurred despite the external constraint, and growth faltered, there was no way out. The euro thus is responsible for trapping southern Europe into a low competitiveness scenario.

In Germany and many northern and eastern European countries, journalists, politicians and voters blamed southern European profligacy; in Greece and Italy, but also in Ireland, many turned against what they saw as a new bid for German hegemony, imposed through a cruel fiscal diktat designed to undermine and destroy Germany's rivals. In both cases, the response was described as populism. Some German commentators – including rather oddly Finance Minister Wolfgang Schäuble – claimed that a significant part (Schäuble said half but offered no evidence to underpin the statistic) of the vote for the radical right AfD (Alternative für Deutschland) was a protest of German savers against the low interest rate regime of the ECB.

A great deal of political capital was invested in the euro rescue, as leaders insisted over and over again that rescuing the euro was vital for the survival of the European Union. As a financial maneuver, the strategy worked. Market bets that the area would collapse were effectively countered. But over time Europe's political capital – the foundation of credibility – was substantially eroded. Ten years after the outbreak of the European debt crisis, the European Union looked more vulnerable. The corona virus pandemic raised many of the issues that had been left unresolved in the European debt crisis: the fiscal capacity of member states of the European Union, the extent that a severe problem in one or more large countries could lead to the questioning of the Union, the limits of monetary policy responses, and the desirability of a European-level fiscal stabilizer. It left a revulsion against the principle of conditionality. As Spanish Prime Minister Pedro Sánchez put it, countries did not want the troika or "men in black" anymore. The center-right Greek prime minister Kyriakos Mitsotakis similarly warned that strict conditionality is "politically unacceptable". And Italian Prime Minister Giuseppe Conte called the ESM an "absolutely inadequate instrument" in tackling Italy's fiscal problems.[10] That backlash raises once more the question central to the Italian tradition and Machiavelli: how to build consensus and civil community.

---

10   https://www.elespanol.com/espana/politica/20200516/escabulle-sanchez-no-preguntaria-alega-obviando-espanol/490451392_0.html ; https://www.ft.com/content/13c622ad-9b1b-44ca-8054-206841c77a18 ; https://euranetplus-inside.eu/euranet-plus-panorama-covid-19-special-cracking-up/.

Chapter IV

The Way Forward

Monetary, Fiscal and Financial Policy Interactions – Conceptual and Policy Considerations[1]

Klaus Masuch[2]

1. Introduction

> When central banks have to use balance sheet policies extensively, there is an inevitable strengthening of the interplay between monetary and fiscal policies. […] But if monetary and fiscal policies are interacting more closely, it also raises important questions […]. These include how to set policy in a world of possibly permanently higher levels of public debt, and the appropriate design of Europe's fiscal framework […].[3]

This article discusses the importance of an enhanced monetary-fiscal policy interaction, against the current background of low inflation, low interest rates and high corporate and sovereign debt. The article raises conceptual issues and questions on *possible* longer-term challenges and risks, which enhanced policy interactions can mitigate. It mainly focuses on risks of persistently too low inflation, as central banks always have the possibility to counteract too high inflation by raising policy rates. It discusses conceptual issues relevant for advanced economies in general (only the last section specifically addresses euro area issues). Given the current challenging situation and high uncertainty, the discussion of options for policy interaction going forward is inherently very complex and speculative. With this in mind, the following lists the main issues discussed in this article.

---

1 This article should not be reported as representing the views of the European Central Bank (ECB). The views expressed are my own and do not necessarily reflect those of the ECB. I benefitted a lot from general discussions with, and / or very helpful comments received on a previous version from Martin Bijsterbosch, Olivier Blanchard, Markus Brunnermeier, John Cochrane, Cristina Checherita-Westphal, Ettore Dorrucci, John Fell, Federic Holm-Hadulla, Marien Ferdianduisse, Otmar Issing, Christophe Kamps, Wolfgang Lemke, Thomas Mayer, Francesco Papadia, Huw Pill, Beatrice Pierluigi, Sebastian Schmidt, Ralph Setzer, Frank Smets, Ludwig Straub, Isabel Vansteenkiste, Thomas Vlassopulous and Andreas Westphal. Needless to say, all views and arguments are my own and not necessarily shared by those who provided comments. The article does not discuss legal issues but assumes that fiscal and monetary policy measures are consistent with the relevant primary laws or constitutions.

2 Klaus Masuch is Principal Adviser to the DG Economics of the European Central Bank. He coordinates ECB work on monetary and fiscal policy interactions and EU country surveillance. Prior assignments include heading the divisions Monetary Policy Strategy (2000-06) and EU Countries (2007-13) and crisis related country missions (2009-15).

3 Lagarde, Christine, *The monetary policy strategy review: some preliminary considerations*. Speech at the "ECB and Its Watchers XXI" conference, Frankfurt am Main, 30 Sep. 2020.

Under current circumstances, monetary and fiscal policies need to work "hand in hand". Expansionary and effective fiscal policies, supported by accommodative monetary policies, are indispensable to lift trend inflation towards the inflation target.

Monetary and fiscal policies are closely linked through the intertemporal public sector budget (Section 2). Since the global financial crisis of 2007–2009, central banks of advanced economies such as the Federal Reserve, the European Central Bank and the Bank of England adopted unconventional monetary policy measures (UMP), as traditional monetary policies were increasingly constrained by the effective lower bound on nominal interest rates (ELB).[4]

In particular balance sheet expansions have proven to be very effective in counteracting severe financial stress and the associated worsening of financing conditions. They also helped to support financing conditions and real growth. This notwithstanding, balance sheet expansions (and expectations of their future use) can provide a public subsidy to financial firms and investors relative to pre-existing market prices and shift risks to the public sector ("risk shifting" UMP).

Such risk shifting can be desirable, e.g. if it mitigates risks that stem from self-fulfilling runs or other externalities and inefficiencies in market dynamics. However, the costs and benefits of that subsidy should – in principle – be included into the fiscal accounts via the consolidation of the central bank's balance sheet. This can help to assess the net social benefits or costs of alternative designs of the overall policy mix. One question may be whether, absorbing a given amount of public resources, the government, e.g. via targeted loan guarantees and transfers, could have an overall more desirable impact on both inflation and broader political objectives than the central bank via further balance sheet expansions (Section 3).

The expectation of a favourable future growth-interest rate differential (g-r) – other things equal – provides more leeway for public debt financing.[5] Monetary accommodation improves financing conditions, thereby increasing the capacity of the government to finance additional transfers and productive public investment. "High quality" fiscal, structural and financial (government) policies are needed to support (i) the effectiveness of monetary policy close to the lower bound[6] and (ii) sustainable long-term growth, thereby improving debt sustainability and increasing fiscal space (Section 4).

---

[4] The Bank of Japan had used UMP already for many years before the global financial crisis.

[5] In this article I assume that real growth will be below real interest rates in the longer run (g<r). This does not exclude that for some years to come real growth can be above the real interest rate. Importantly, the relevant growth rate from the government perspective is the growth rate of taxable output or income. Higher growth helps in terms of debt sustainability, insofar as it increases (expected or potential) tax revenues.

[6] See e. g. Masuch, Klaus, Robert Anderton, Ralph Setzer and Nicholai Benalal (eds.), Structural policies in the euro area, ECB OP, No. 210, June 2018.

The remainder of the article does not focus on the desirable effects of balance sheet policies on which there is a lot of empirical evidence. The main focus is on possible unintended future side effects and tail risks related to the monetary-fiscal policy interaction. To assess whether risk shifting UMP are optimal in general equilibrium also requires looking at possible adverse side effects, which may be related to various market imperfections, heterogeneity and constraints of other policy makers (Section 5). For example, fiscal or regulatory authorities may not be able to appropriately counteract some negative side effects. In such a second-best world (with policy failure), certain risk shifting UMP might give rise to unwelcome changes in behaviour of private agents and policy makers, leading to undesirable longer-term net effects on various public policy objectives.

The possibility of private or public default risks can make monetary-fiscal interaction quite complex, also as it may be difficult to distinguish between a liquidity crisis and a genuine solvency crisis (Section 6).

Sections 7 asks whether specific risk shifting UMP might at some point risk contributing towards lower instead of higher inflation (expectations), possibly related to interaction with fiscal and financial policies. A well known example is the possibility of a reversal rate.[7] Another less widely discussed question is whether there could potentially also be an undesirability of balance sheet expansion beyond a certain threshold – so to speak a "reversal quantity". Much of the public discussion seems to take the former as a fact, whereas quantitative easing is seen as unambiguously having a monotonic stimulative effect.

Finally, Section 8 takes a different perspective and discusses selected post pandemic challenges for the euro area.

2. *The intertemporal budget constraint of the public sector and monetary-fiscal policy interactions*

One important channel of monetary-fiscal policy interaction is the intertemporal budget constraint of the consolidated public sector. The key conventional instrument of monetary policy are policy interest rate changes which have a direct impact on current and expected *risk-free* interest rates, and thereby yields of debt instruments along the yield curve. Lower risk-free yield curves will, ceteris paribus reduce future borrowing

---

[7] Brunnermeier, Markus and Yann Koby, *The reversal interest rate*, NBER WP, 2018. For a recent discussion see Darracq Pariès, Matthieu, Christoffer Kok and Matthias Rottner, *Reversal interest rate and macroprudential policy*, ECB WPS, n. 2487, Nov. 2020. Their framework suggests that the "reversal interest rate is located in negative territory of around −1% per annum".

costs of the government and private firms. At the same time, increases in fiscal deficits and debt levels will, ceteris paribus, stimulate aggregate demand thereby supporting monetary policy in case of too low inflation.

Most New Keynesian models, which have been increasingly employed over the recent decades by central banks, imply that monetary policy is effective and alone can control inflation. This conclusion is however based on an important assumption: fiscal policy will over time always stabilise debt such that sovereign default or credit risk premia are ruled out by assumption. In other words, in response to a monetary policy tightening, fiscal policy will automatically also tighten its stance, by increasing the present value of future primary surpluses.[8] Such a fiscal behaviour is a necessary, but not always sufficient, condition for monetary policy controlling inflation (monetary dominance).

Importantly, this kind of automatic fiscal policy support is also necessary for the success of monetary policy, when inflation is below the objective and the central bank engages in expansionary policies. In this case, the necessary fiscal support requires that the government eventually lowers taxes or increases primary expenditures, creating a lower primary surplus in reaction to the lower interest rates.[9] In other words, if inflation is too low, additional monetary easing and expansionary fiscal policies need to go hand in hand and complement each other.[10]

The fiscal authority may choose to initially use lower interest rates for building fiscal buffers (i.e. reducing debt or slowing down its accumulation instead of lowering the primary surplus). This can be appropriate from a longer-term debt sustainability perspective. While it may delay the achievement of the inflation target, the higher fiscal buffers could be important for successful stabilisation of output and inflation in a future recession. However, monetary policy might also be confronted with an overly restrictive fiscal policy. For example, depressed long-term growth perspectives and too little buffers may at some point require strong fiscal consolidation to address credibility problems and ensure inter-temporal solvency. In such a case, while monetary policy may be criticised for undershooting its objective, it may indeed be pro-cyclical fiscal policies and a lack of growth enhancing structural polices which are, at

---

8 This feature of NK models is stressed by proponents of the fiscal theory of the price level (FTPL). See e.g. Leeper, Eric and Campbell Leith, "Understanding Inflation as a Joint Monetary Fiscal Phenomenon", in Taylor, John. B. and Harald Uhlig Elsevier (eds.), *Handbook of Macroeconomics*, vol. 2, Elsevier, 2016; Woodford, Michael, "Fiscal Requirements for Price Stability", *Journal of Money, Credit and Banking*, vol. 33, n. 3, Aug. 2001, pp. 669–728.
9 See Sims, Chris, *Fiscal policy, monetary policy and central bank independence*. Speech in Jackson Hole, Aug. 2016.
10 "Indeed, one explanation for the superior inflation performance of the United States relative to the euro area in recent times is that monetary and fiscal policies were more aligned". Lagarde, Christine, *op. cit.*

least in part, responsible for this outcome. Paradoxically, such fiscal and structural policies, by contributing to lower than previously expected inflation, may create debt-deflation-type costs, also worsening the fiscal situation by increasing the real value of outstanding public debt.

Over the recent decade nominal policy rates approached the lower bound on nominal rates, which is below zero. Already when rates come closer to the lower bound, the expected effectiveness of the conventional policy tool – lowering policy rates and thereby risk-free market rates in response to negative aggregate demand shocks – is severely constrained.

3. Central Bank (CB) balance sheet expansion, taking out risk from the market – implications for fiscal policy

During the global financial crisis, and especially after the Lehman collapse, central banks increasingly made use of UMP to lower financing cost. To analyse monetary-fiscal interactions it appears useful to distinguish two broad categories of expansionary UMP. Risk neutral UMP lower the risk free yield curve, in particular via negative policy rates and explicit communication about the central bank's policy plans (forward guidance). In contrast, risk shifting UMP improve financing conditions by lowering risk premia in bond and loan markets mainly via balance sheet policies (e.g. taking out duration or credit risks from the private investors) in the form of large scale asset purchases or via credit easing, i.e. (large scale) liquidity provision to banks, usually at favourable conditions, i.e. interest rates (well) below market rates. Risk shifting UMP can be important to stabilise financial markets, e.g. in case of self-fulling runs where they help to reduce overall risks in the economy[11]. They have proven to be very effective in counteracting a collapse of the interbank market during the global financial crisis, or in addressing a panic and large liquidity premia in certain segments of financial markets (e.g. at the beginning of the Covid-19 crisis in March 2020), effectively counteracting deflation risks. The announcement of outright monetary transactions by the ECB in 2012 counteracted re-denomination risks in sovereign bonds, even without any actual purchases becoming necessary.[12]

---

11 The term "risk neutral" UMP describes that such instruments initially (or on impact) mainly affect the risk-free yield curve, not directly risk premia. In general equilibrium such policies may however impact on (financial stability) risks. Similarly, the term "risk shifting" (or "subsidisation") just describes what happens on impact – e.g. the central bank takes out duration risks (or provides subsidies to banks) and shifts the associated risks (and cost) onto its own balance sheet. This does not exclude that such policies may lower overall risks (or have an overall positive benefit-cost balance) in general equilibrium.

12 This can be seen as supporting the view that this policy effectively addressed a self-fulfilling run, rather than fundamentally justified risk premia.

Balance sheet policies tend to benefit or subsidise banks or financial investors relative to market prices which would prevail with no such CB intervention.[13] Both forms of UMP can lower future funding costs of the sovereign. However, the cost of the subsidy implied by risk shifting UMP should – in principle – be included into the fiscal accounts via the consolidation of the CB balance sheet with the government balance sheet in constructing the public sector accounts. If the CB incurs losses on its subsidisation of credit (e.g. as it does not demand a sufficient risk premium, is financing at below fundamentally justified market rates, etc.), then this may lead towards additional fiscal consolidation becoming necessary. From this perspective, the subsidy element can be evaluated on traditional public finance criteria (e.g. are the costs implicit in the subsidies justified by externalities, public goods or social policy objectives?). An important argument is that all UMP normally help to reduce unemployment. Such an effect would need to be included in an overall comparative cost-benefit analysis.

A comprehensive general equilibrium analysis also should take into account monetary-fiscal interactions via the consolidated public sector balance sheet. This helps to assess alternative combinations of monetary-fiscal policy interactions. From this perspective, a key question is whether the government or the monetary authority will make a socially more efficient use of any given amount of public money or resources. For example, the government might use such resources for loan gurantees, lower effective taxes on new investment and/ or more generous unemployment insurance and thereby might have an overall more desirable impact on both price stability and broader social welfare (e.g. employment or distributional objectives) than the CB via balance sheet policies.[14]

---

13 "[…] if there were no subsidies, then nobody would take up the TLTROs". Draghi, Mario, ECB Press Conference, 7 Mar. 2019. This was part of a reply to a question by a journalist who had asked: "The TLTROs are also kind of subsidies for banks, especially for weak banks. A lot of these banks are paying dividends to their shareholders and bonuses to their senior managers. Do you think this fits together with the subsidies?" Mario Draghi also said: "[…] the issue is not whether there is a subsidy or not; there is a subsidy. […] The issue is whether the TLTRO fulfils monetary policy objectives and helps the transmission of monetary policy. We believe it has always done that, it's been very effective, as a matter of fact, in reactivating the banking sector in the eurozone and in transmitting […] the better lending conditions to firms and households, to the private sector in the economy. I think that's the yardstick of successful TLTRO […]"

14 An important difference is that fiscal policy can restrict its support to new loans or new investment project (e.g. via targeted guarantees or lower taxes etc.), while asset purchases on impact normally also make every investor holding relevant outstanding (legacy) debt richer, in order to achieve its key aim to support future financing conditions of new loans or newly issued bonds. It would be interesting to have a model simulation that can compare both policies with respect to their impact via distributional effects on outstanding debt and on future, new lending and investment decisions, assuming that both policies use the same amount of subsidies or transfers and accept the same amount of risks on the public sector balance sheet for their respective measures.

4. The enhanced importance of fiscal policy at the effective lower bound (ELB)

In spite of substantial balance sheet expansions implemented by monetary policies since the global financial crisis, inflation outcomes in Japan, the euro area and, somewhat less so, in the US, fell persistently short of inflation expectations and targets. This may reflect that government policies failed to provide sufficient support.

In recent years, even before the Covid-19 crisis, a growing number of academics argued that fiscal policy has become much more effective when monetary policy is close to the ELB and keeps risk free rates low for an extended period. Accordingly, monetary policy, even with far-reaching UMP, will likely not be effective enough to increase trend inflation back to target without strong support from fiscal policy. Moreover, many observers argue that with the real interest rates in most advanced economies likely remaining around, or possibly below, the real GDP growth rate for some time, debt sustainability can also be ensured with higher debt levels and so the capacity for debt financing has increased. Most governments therefore have the scope for supporting aggregate demand in a low inflation and interest rate environment.

> Through negative policy rates and quantitative easing (QE), monetary policy [in Japan] has done everything it could, but it could not do enough on its own. [...] In an environment of very low neutral rates, fiscal policy has an essential macroeconomic role to play, even if monetary policy is no longer at the ELB.[15]

Also the Fed Chair Powell has raised implications of the ELB on nominal interest rates:

> [...] The Fed has less scope to support the economy during an economic downturn by simply cutting the federal funds rate. The result can be worse economic outcomes in terms of both employment and price stability, with the costs of such outcomes likely falling hardest on those least able to bear them.[16]

Some academics argue that in a situation of inflation below target, low interest rates and weak demand dynamics, effective support would require that fiscal authorities explicitly aim at higher inflation and make this clear to the general public.[17] The

---

15 Blanchard, Olivier and Takeshi Tashiro, *Fiscal Policy Options for Japan*, Peterson Institute for International Economics, May 2019. See also Eichenbaum, Martin, Rethinking Fiscal Policy in an era of low interest rates. Monetary Authority of Singapore, Macroeconomic Review, Apr. 2019.

16 Powell, Jerome H. *Economic Challenges and the Fed's Monetary Policy Review*, Speech at the symposium sponsored by the Federal Reserve Bank of Kansas City, 27 Aug. 2020.

17 See for example Sims, Chris, *op. cit.* Cochrane, John, *Fiscal theory of monetary policy with partially-repaid long-term debt*, NBER WP 26745, 2020.

government should communicate that budget plans are based on inflation in line with the inflation target, rather than with current (too low) inflation expectations. In this view, which is in particular supported by advocates of the fiscal theory of the price level (FTPL), fiscal policy would announce lower taxes and/or higher social transfers (more precisely a lower present value of future primary surpluses), assuming that higher inflation will at least in part substitute for a higher primary surplus, ensuring debt sustainability. The chances of success seem higher if fiscal authorities (i) in particular use transfers to low/middle income households and the unemployed (with high marginal propensity to consume – MPC) and (ii) can convince the public that this will push wage growth, employment etc. higher (implying that consumption increases and inflation will move higher to the inflation target), credibly ruling out higher future tax rates or spending cuts. While appropriate fiscal support is important, this particular strategy of a temporary unbacked fiscal expansion is not without risks. For example, at some point g-r might fall,[18] leading to higher solvency risks. The government may then re-optimise and prefer high inflation to lower the real burden of public debt and continue with unbacked fiscal expansion. Of course, the CB can raise real policy rates to bring inflation back to target. However, such a "confrontational" policy mix – too expansionary fiscal policy counteracted by tight monetary policy – comes with high economic and social costs.[19]

To minimise that risk, it appears important that the government makes a credible commitment to support the inflation target and implement well targeted and efficient spending programmes that, in addition to supporting demand, enhance sustainable trend growth. A key question of course is how to ensure that such policies are time consistent and thus credible. A step in this direction could be a fiscal framework and clear government communication which makes the inflation target (say 2%) an objective also of fiscal authorities, at least for periods where monetary policy is close to the ELB.[20] Finally, governments with debt sustainability concerns could address too low inflation also with measures that do not increase deficits or debt levels, such as a pre-announced

---

18   A decline in g-r could be due to various developments, for example, (i) a slowdown in trend growth which is not 1-to-1 reflected in lower real rates, (ii) a larger supply of additional global safe assets (due to high deficits in the US, Japan and the EU) may raise the real natural rate, and (iii) trend inflation may increase above the target and the CB may have to increase real policy rates to ensure that price stability is maintained.

19   Bianchi, Francesco and Leonardo Melosi, "The dire effects of the lack of monetary and fiscal coordination", *Journal of Monetary Economics*, 104, 2019, pp. 1-22.

20   This might for example be supported by public sector transfers and wages being automatically increased by 2% every year, also in periods where inflation outturns fall short of the target of 2%. To the extent that recessions or crises are correlated with disinflation or deflation, such a scheme would act as an additional automatic stabiliser, which in particular provides social insurance to low income and vulnerable people with high marginal propensity to consume (MPC), reinforcing the credibility of the inflation target in bad economic times when monetary policy is constrained by the ELB.

gradual increase of consumption or carbon taxes.[21] A gradual increase in carbon taxes would of course be designed to address climate change. Lifting inflation towards the target would be a beneficial side-effect, which could be supported by using carbon tax revenues in particular to lower labour taxes or increase transfers to households with relatively low income and wealth.

Close to the ELB, monetary and fiscal policy interaction may need to investigate whether more fiscal policy support for aggregate demand may in certain circumstances be preferable relative to CB balance sheet extensions (or vice versa). In some cases, when the CB assumes large risks on its balance sheet, there might be adverse longer-term spill-overs to public finances. For example, the government may suffer from lower CB dividends, or in case of a severe shock may even have to recapitalise the CB.[22]

Compared to some UMP with subsidisation elements, fiscal instruments may be more efficient and better targeted, socially fairer, and more directly support demand and inflation. For example, social transfers are usually aimed at vulnerable or low-income workers and families, who often have a higher MPC than financial investors directly benefiting from risk shifting UMP via lower risk premia on outstanding long-term credit claims or bonds.[23] While fiscal transfers increase aggregate demand

---

21   For example, Farhi, Emmanuel, Isabel Correia, Juan Pablo Nicolini and Pedro Teles, "Unconventional Fiscal Policy at the Zero Bound", *American Economic Review*, 103, 4, 2013, pp. 1172-1211, study the liquidity trap in the context of a standard New Keynesian model and characterize jointly optimal monetary and fiscal policy. They propose a specific unconventional design of fiscal policies (including consumption taxes to increase inflation), which does not use unbacked fiscal expansions and thus can avoid the risk of a debt overhang. They show that even if lump sum taxes cannot be raised, such "unconventional fiscal policy can perfectly replicate the effects of negative nominal interest rates at the second-best. […] Our main result is to demonstrate how distortionary taxes can be used to replicate the effects of negative nominal interest rates and completely circumvent the zero bound problem".

22   Consider the example of a CB after a long period with large asset purchases, associated with insufficient fiscal support and too low inflation expectations. The balance sheet of this CB may reach a very large size with a substantial maturity mismatch and exposure to inflation and interest rate risks. Assume at that point a policy change (or an exogenous "shock") shifts trend inflation and long-term inflation expectations persistently upwards to above the target, such that policy rates (including rates paid on CB reserves) would need to normalise. This could cause large balance sheet losses for the CB, in particular in case higher real policy rates would be associated also with default related losses on the asset side (e.g. corporate bonds). At the same time, digital currencies and other developments may limit the future demand for (physical) banknotes, eroding the NPV of future seigniorage income. Such developments together might risk undermining the financial independence of the CB.

23   A household with long-term fixed rate debt may see the net present value (NPV) of its loan liability increase. However, when rolling over this loan in the future, the household will benefit, if rates at that point are still at the lower level.

by making poor and low-income people better off, asset purchases on impact first increase asset prices (thereby lowering yields) and thus the wealth of financial investors and subsequently may impact on growth and employment, inter alia, via the portfolio rebalancing channel. Even in the case where both policies have the same long-term effects on employment, targeted fiscal measures might not only be more efficient than risk shifting UMP, but also more conducive to (perceived) social fairness.[24] This is especially relevant in case of a shock, which has a very asymmetric impact, such as Covid-19, that has particularly negative impact on many low and middle income families and owners of small businesses in certain sectors, while financial investors holding bonds, shares of large firms and real estate in many cases (e.g. in the autumn of 2020) even enjoy an increase of their financial wealth relative to the previous year.

5. Monetary-fiscal-financial sector policy interactions and adverse side-effects

Some UMP measures may have adverse side-effects on efficient allocation, distributional objectives or financial stability. Governments (incl. via transfers, tax policies and financial sector policies) may not always be able to fully undo or correct such adverse side-effects.[25] They may face constraints which are unavoidable in a democracy, such as those embedded in laws, constitutions or political economy dynamics. Also, international capital flows, tax havens, and / or weak administrative capacities may impose constraints, for example on the aim of the government or parliament to correct rising inequality and to achieve both social fairness and higher aggregate demand via fair and effective taxation of capital or wealth. However, if fiscal authorities cannot easily undo the socially undesirable side effects of some risk-shifting UMP, this may make such

---

24   For example, assume two alternative policies to address a recession – e.g. corporate bond purchases versus targeted fiscal policies (e.g. a combination of lower labour taxes, higher social transfers and subsides on new investments physical capital and education). Assume both these policies are calibrated such that they are associated with the same positive impact on employment and new investment. It may well be the case that the corporate bond purchases lead to relatively higher wealth of owners of legacy bonds and shares, while financial investors profit less from the fiscal package, which however has a more positive impact on expected net wages (and thus human capital relative to financial capital) and equality.

25   See e.g. Smets, Frank, 2014, "Financial Stability and Monetary Policy: How Closely Interlinked?", *International Journal of Central Banking*, June 2014: "In a crisis situation, liquidity policies by the central bank may avoid a collapse of the banking sector, but also reduce the incentive for banks to recapitalize and restructure and promote the evergreening of non-performing loans and regulatory forbearance by supervisors. In principle, well-targeted macroprudential policies can offset the side effects of these monetary policies, but in practice there may be limits".

policies less desirable from a social welfare point of view.²⁶ To the extent that this could be the case, monetary-fiscal policy interaction may need to be very concrete, discussing whether and how concretely the government can or cannot correct potential unwelcome allocative and distributive implications of UMP measures that take out market risk or provide other forms of subsidisation.

Unwelcome spill-overs across policy areas can of course also be caused by fiscal (and financial sector) policies or regulations that may limit the effectiveness of monetary policy, for example if bank regulation fails to ensure a sufficiently high capital buffer for banks.²⁷ Another example is given by government policies or regulations which weaken the efficiency of insolvency procedures and of the judicial system to deal with bad debt (NPLs), or which provide tax or other incentives (e.g. via implicit bail-out guarantees) that bias decision making of firms and their banks in favour of debt rather than equity financing and /or increase doom-loop risks²⁸. In the above cases, suboptimal fiscal, structural or financial sector policies may weaken the effectiveness of the monetary policy transmission mechanism, in particular following adverse shocks. However, once fiscal and financial policies have allowed leverage to get higher than socially optimal, some policies supporting credit growth might no longer be unambiguously advisable, as they may push private sector leverage further in the wrong direction, increasing risks of future deleveraging pressures or higher aggregate savings.²⁹ High private leverage and the associated risks of deleveraging pressures need to be primarily addressed by banks and governments. Monetary policy can reduce roll-over costs for firms by keeping risk free interest rates low and thus

---

26 It also needs to be assessed whether such constraints on government policies can make certain UMP less effective in achieving the inflation target over the medium term. This might be the case, for example, if a Fed-Put creates large financial stability risk, due to constraints on regulation (incl. a proper regulation of non-banks) and as a financial crisis can create deflation risks.

27 "We show that macroprudential policy in the form of a countercyclical capital buffer, which prescribes the build-up of buffers in good times, can mitigate substantially the probability of encountering the reversal rate, improves welfare and reduces economic fluctuations". Matthieu Darracq Pariès et. al. , *op. cit.*

28 "[…] When banks can count on bailouts by the Sovereign, they optimally diversify as little as supervision allows them to, so as to enjoy the maximal put on taxpayer money. […] In an economy with no cost of default and no financial intermediaries, Bulow and Rogoff (1988, 1991) show that debt buybacks are a giveaway to legacy foreign creditors and reduce the country's welfare. The banks' purchase of domestic bonds resembles a buyback. […] when the buyback is operated through financial intermediaries that may require a bailout by the Sovereign, the Bulow–Rogoff result is reinstated". Farhi, Emmanuel, and Jean Tirole, "Deadly Embrace: Sovereign and Financial Balance Sheets Doom Loops", *Review of Economic Studies*, 85, 3, pp. 1781-1823, 2018.

29 See also Mian, Atif R., Straub, Ludwig and Sufi, Amir, "Indebted Demand" *NBER Working Paper* n. 26940, April 2020. https://scholar.harvard.edu/files/straub/files/mss_indebteddemand.pdf.

financing conditions favourable, however, it cannot address the underlying fundamental reason for high leverage and credit risk premia.[30]

In case of insufficiently capitalised, but viable banks, the government or regulator should ideally ask shareholders to swiftly recapitalise them. If private investors do not want to provide new capital as demanded by the regulators, legacy shareholders will lose their capital and the public sector will provide new capital (in the form of state aid). However, the government may hesitate to act, possibly under pressures from the financial sector and legacy shareholders (and bond holders). The government might also misinterpret that exceptional CB liquidity provision to banks is allowing it to procrastinate. This is a case for intensified monetary-fiscal interaction, also with the view to avoiding the social costs of financial dominance.[31] In such a discussion it could be made clear that using public resources in the form of equity injections by the government may in the longer run be more supportive of aggregate demand and equality, compared to the same amount of resources given to the banks via a central bank lending facility at subsidised rates. In the first case, after the fiscal authority measure, the taxpayer holds an equity claim (participating in the upside potential) in (hopefully) viable banks and the shareholder has been bailed in, while in the second case the taxpayer has effectively provided a transfer/gift to legacy shareholders, hoping that the latter will use part of this support not to pay higher dividends, but to provide new net loans to the real economy at reduced interest rates. The swift recapitalisation of the banks by the private sector or the state could help to make monetary policy measures more effective, thereby providing an additional social benefit in the form of enhanced macro stabilisation.

---

[30] Viable but over indebted firms require debt relief from banks and other creditors and equity injections by private investors. They would benefit from improved structural and financial sector policies, more efficient procedures for private sector debt relief and enhanced insolvency procedures, which are relevant for non-viable competitors.

[31] Brunnermeier defines "financial dominance [...] as the ex-ante behavior of the financial sector, which out of fear that losses will be pushed onto it, purposely stays (or even becomes) undercapitalized. This behavior increases volatility and might force fiscal or monetary authority to absorb losses". [...] This implies a risk for the CB: "Under financial dominance [...] the financial sector [...] might be needed to be bailed out. A second game of chicken between the fiscal or monetary authority might arise of who has to bail out the financial sector". This "hostage strategy is like a doubling up strategy. That is, the government gambles for resurrection: if the initial crisis is followed by a good shock the low interest rate helps to grow out of the problems (provided that the diabolic effects are not too large), but if it is followed by another adverse shock, things will look really dire [...]" Brunnermeier, Markus, *Financial Dominance*, Paolo Baffi Lecture, 2016.

6. High debt, default risk and monetary-fiscal interactions

In models which allow for default risk, the policy interactions and macro-dynamics become more complicated. For example, if legacy debt is high and there is uncertainty about the credibility of policy makers, credit risk premia can increase, undermining aggregate demand, especially, if higher risk premia are large and persistent and yields on private loan contracts increase with sovereign yields.

The possibility of private or public default also raises issues about the proper reaction of monetary policy to rising risk premia. Here it is important to distinguish between a liquidity crisis and genuine solvency problems, which in reality and in real time is often very difficult to do. In the case of a liquidity crisis or a self-fulfilling run, the literature generally sees a strong case for monetary policy to actively support the fiscal authority (e.g. via purchases of debt instruments financed by the issuance of central bank reserves). In the case of solvency problems caused by weak fundamentals, rather than a fundamentally unjustified self-fulfilling run, central bank interventions to keep such risk premia low can however be problematic. They may be perceived as socially unfair and undermine demand, if the compression of solvency premia shifts wealth from taxpayers and recipients of social transfers to financial investors.

A debt overhang can pose problems for monetary policy, in particular in case adverse shocks increase debt and/or lower expected income growth relative to ex ante real interest rates. Two types of adverse scenarios might be considered – persistently high inflation above the target and persistently too low inflation (see Section 7).

The first adverse scenario describes a currently rather remote tail risk, which could be mitigated by enhanced monetary-fiscal cooperation. Without that, it might start when deep solvency problems have been allowed to emerge, and no other solutions such as gradual fiscal consolidation, a comprehensive one-off wealth tax or an orderly welfare enhancing sovereign debt restructuring (SDR), are politically or technically feasible. In this case, pressures on the CB could emerge to engage in large scale and extended policies to keep public debt sustainable. For example, markets and governments may argue that the CB should step up public debt purchases, as this would be needed to raise inflation towards the target and counteract fundamentally unjustified credit premia. Extended asset purchases might however also lower solvency risk premia, allowing (i) financial investors to benefit from capital gains and shift risks to the public sector, and (ii) politicians to hide the problem of debt overhangs for longer. A further worsening of the fiscal situation (e.g. associated with lower future g-r) could increase the risks of a non-cooperative and socially costly monetary fiscal interaction.

An independent CB will of course resist attempts by financial markets and fiscal players to dominate it by joining forces.[32] This has been made very clear, for example, by the former ECB President, Mario Draghi, when explaining the purpose and design of the ECB's outright monetary transactions (OMTs) in a speech in 2013:

> By way of drawing a parallel between OMTs and our standard liquidity operations: as the credit provided to banking counterparties cannot be, and must not be, interpreted as an injection of capital into failing banks; in the same vein, under OMTs, in compressing the premium for the risk of "redenomination", the ECB cannot and does not intend to provide financial support to governments which reinstate solvency conditions which have not already been approved ex ante.[33]

7. A Reversal quantity? – Can balance sheet expansions and taking out market risks go too far and eventually undermine aggregate demand?

> [...] imperfectly targeted support to distressed institutions makes private leverage choices strategic complements. When everyone engages in maturity mismatch, authorities have little choice but intervening, creating both current and deferred (sowing the seeds of the next crisis) social costs. In turn, it is profitable to adopt a risky balance sheet. [...] One of the many striking features of the recent financial crisis is the extreme exposure of economically and politically sensitive actors to liquidity needs and market conditions. [...] The overall picture is one of a wide-scale maturity mismatch [...] of substantial systematic-risk exposure, [...] this wide-scale transformation is closely related to the unprecedented intervention by central banks and treasuries.[34]

Balance sheet policies have supported financing conditions and demand by mitigating risks that stem from self-fulfilling runs or other externalities and inefficiencies in market dynamics. They can be very effective in particular in times of financial panic and severe liquidity crises, counteracting a deeper recession and deflation risks. However, accumulating large amounts of nominal long-term debt instruments over many years (i. e. also outside such episodes of market dislocation) might at some point have non-linear effects and might even bring the CB into a weak position relative to fiscal policy or the financial industry. In other words, a kind of reversal quantity in terms of CB balance sheet size and maturity mismatch

---

32 On various aspects of financial dominance see Brunnermeier, Markus, 2016, *op. cit.*, as well as Farhi, Emmanuel, and Jean Tirole, "Leverage and the Central Banker's Put". *American Economic Review, Papers and Proceedings*, 2, 2009, pp. 589-593.

33 Draghi, Mario, *The euro, monetary policy and reforms*, Speech delivered at LUISS "Guido Carli" University, Rome, 6 May 2013.

34 Farhi, Emmanuel, and Jean Tirole. 2012. "Collective Moral Hazard, Maturity Mismatch and Systemic Bailouts", *American Economic Review*, 102 (1), 1, 2012, pp. 60-93.

might exist. Beyond that level, further risk shifting balance sheet policies (this does not include policy rate changes or forward guidance) may no longer be effective in stabilizing inflation around the target, and the probability of a persistent low inflation trap, or, in the longer-run, volatile high inflation may result, in particular in case of an insufficient interaction on the policy mix. Which of the two adverse scenarios could be more likely depends on many factors, e.g. the concrete nature of adverse shocks, the fiscal constitution and reaction function, size and maturity of debt, doom-loop and other financial instability risks and not least the mandate and independence of the CB. Importantly, for political economy reasons, insufficient fiscal policy expansion and thus persistent low inflation seems more likely, if the relative political power of banks, other creditors and financial investors is stronger compared to debtors, taxpayers and the young. In the following the case of persistently too low inflation is discussed, also as it currently seems to be the most relevant risk over the coming years. Several transmission channels might be relevant in this context.

Firstly, extensive use of balance sheet policies over time may strenghten expectations in financial markets that the CB would also in the future likely avoid: (i) a collapse of asset prices or (ii) losses of large financial firms. Such a costless implicit public insurance for high risk portfolio strategies could give rise to increased leverage both of financial and non-financial firms, risky carry-trades, search for yield, weak bank capital buffers etc. Already in 2009, two independent academics, Emanuel Farhi and Jean Tirole, have pointed to such risks in their paper *Leverage and the Central Banker's Put*. Expectations of such a Fed-Put may increase with market experiencing balance sheet expansions associated with a strong direct or indirect support for asset prices and financial firms (possibly in conjunction with related implicit guarantees by the government). At some size of the CB balance sheet the general public may expect that this, together with the Fed-Put, can shift future losses and bail-out costs onto taxpayers and recipients of public transfers, at least, once an adverse scenario materialises. This may lower aggregate demand, also as financial investors have already profited in the past (being better informed about such complex issues than the general public) and anyhow may have lower marginal propensity to consume as those who will bear the bulk of the costs.

Secondly, at some point, large CB balance sheets may reduce the net social benefits of a SDR, eventually effectively eliminating this option for governments. Anticipating this, markets will lower default risk premia and firms and households may anticipate more consolidation, undermining aggregate demand. Thirdly, similarly a large CB balance sheet with duration mismatch may remove the net benefits of surprise inflation as a potential (partial) "solution" to a large debt overhang. Once the broader public expects this, inflation expectations will rise and aggregate demand may fall.[35]

---

35   See also Bianchi, Francesco and Leonardo Melosi, "Escaping the Great recession", *American Economic Review*, 107, 4, 2017, pp. 1030-1058.

The reason for the second and the third channel is that the stock of long-term public debt held by the CB reduces the "tax base" of both a SDR haircut (reflecting the default free nature of CB reserves) and a surprise and persistent increase of inflation (reflecting the maturity mismatch). A haircut on CB holdings of sovereign bonds has a zero-sum effect for the whole public sector, which is obvious from the consolidated public sector balance sheet. The higher the share of public bonds held by the CB, the less efficient a given haircut or surprise inflation will be in terms of lowering the real burden of public debt. With given positive costs of these two strategies, the net social benefits of SDR and of surprise and persistent increase in inflation may become negative, even in case of a large sovereign debt overhang. In this case, the only option left in the case of a severe shock to public debt (or of a major decline in expected g-r) may be more fiscal consolidation. Paradoxically, the reversal quantity in this case could in part be the consequence of two elements which initially supported the effectiveness of balance sheet extensions: the fact that there is no default risk on CB reserves and the strategy of taking out duration risk.

A counterargument is that the monetary policy can always step up asset purchases which support financing conditions and thereby public and private spending. However, close to the ELB, further substantial reduction in yields may no longer be achievable, such that the counteracting forces discussed above may at some point dominate the intended substitution effect induced by additional balance sheet expansions.

8. Post pandemic challenges for the euro area policy mix

Both the substantial fiscal measures and expansions in reaction to the Covid-19 pandemic and very accommodative monetary policy have been necessary and helped to avoid much larger output and employment losses. Looking forward, a key question for the euro area is how to deal with both the lasting legacy of the global financial crisis and the economic fallout from the pandemic, not least in view of large economic heterogeneity across countries. In order to address the challenges and avoid the risks associated with the current environment of low inflation and low interest rates discussed above, several possible policy options might be considered.

First, the pandemic shock had a very asymmetric impact across sectors, countries, professions, and types of households or workers. This will, for years to come, require specific and targeted fiscal and regulatory measures and instruments (e.g. social insurance, public investment) to support aggregate demand, the reallocation of resources, equity financing, education etc. and thereby sustainable growth prospects. Monetary policy cannot use such instruments.[36] In a democracy, transfers, subsidies, social insurance etc. are clearly the responsibility of governments and parliaments. Monetary policy provides its important contribution by keeping financing conditions favourable.

Second, additional challenges stem from pre-existing vulnerabilities and cross-country heterogeneity in terms of economic and institutional structures and policy approaches (e.g. fiscal reaction functions). Without effective and strong fiscal policy support, the overall policy-mix may not sufficiently enhance aggregate demand and trend inflation, notwithstanding UMP. The large heterogeneity of public sector debt levels could make it more difficult for fiscal authorities to achieve a well-coordinated expansion.

Third, a substantial and ideally one-off comprehensive wealth or capital income tax implemented after the pandemic[37] could be one element of a package that would contribute substantially towards a credible solution to high sovereign debt. Basic principles could be agreed between euro area member states, and all countries could be invited to participate in the initiative. The wealth tax could be complemented by cross-country fiscal insurance allowing for fiscal transfers to countries hit by exogenous, asymmetric shocks.

To be effective, the wealth tax may need to be sizeable, but one-off in nature, falling mainly on the existing capital stock and currently outstanding financial assets. This would help to mitigate disincentives for future investments. A sufficiently large tax-exempt amount per taxpayer could support broad public acceptance. The revenues from this tax may be used for several purposes. First, they could finance social transfers and insurance for unemployed persons, low/middle income or wealth households, including owners of SMEs which are hit hard by the pandemic, and possibly cuts in labour taxes (incl. social security contributions) for workers. Second, it would in part be used to ensure a gradual decline of the debt level over the coming years. The wealth tax would shift resources from international and domestic investors (with mostly low marginal propensity to consume in the euro area) to relatively poorer (high MPC) domestic households and consumers. Compared to an extended conventional fiscal consolidation process, a one-off wealth tax would tend to have advantages from an economic and distributional perspective. Such a wealth tax

---

36 Michael Woodford, "Effective Demand Failures and the Limits of Monetary Stabilization Policy", *NBER*, 2020: "The COVID-19 pandemic presents a challenge for stabilization policy […] In such a situation, economic activity in many sectors of the economy can be much lower than would maximize welfare […] and interest-rate policy cannot eliminate the distortions […] Fiscal transfers are instead well-suited to addressing the fundamental problem, and can under certain circumstances achieve a first-best allocation of resources without any need for a monetary policy response".
37 See for example Camille Landais, Emmanuel Saez, Gabriel Zucman, *A progressive European wealth tax to fund the European COVID response*, 3 Apr. 2020, VoxEU.

would, over the medium term, support aggregate demand and inflation in the euro area. If large enough, and thus not expected to be repeated, a one-off wealth tax could help reduce expectations and uncertainty about higher future taxes, also thereby supporting aggregate demand. However, a wealth tax usually faces strong resistance from the financial industry, powerful lobbies, and well-connected vested interest.

Needless to say, as with any other tax, there are various difficulties of implementing a fair and largely non-distortionary wealth tax. One problem is that financial assets (or their returns) are very difficult to tax effectively. This is due to international profit-shifting to tax havens, weak and insufficient capital income and corporate taxation laws, which are difficult to change. Moreover, a one-off wealth tax – to be fair and efficient – should be comprehensive, which raises the issue of how to value assets which are not traded in liquid markets.

Finally, there are several options to make the monetary union institutionally more complete. If done in an efficient manner that also convincingly addresses time consistency and moral hazard problems, this would make monetary policy more effective. Different options and elements of a package to enhance the institutional completeness of a monetary union are discussed in the literature. Some examples are: (i) a central fiscal capacity which has the means to counteract asymmetric shocks and provide cross-country public risk sharing for the stabilization of asymmetric shocks, (ii) credible fiscal rules that ensure sound and countercyclical national economic policies, (iii) regulations which limit sovereign-doom loop risks, complemented by a common sovereign safe asset that helps to address cross-border fragmentation, (iv) a complete banking and capital market union which enhances cross-border private risk sharing and reduce fragmentation risks, (v) an efficient mechanism for an orderly SDR. Finally, (vi) the independence of the central bank may need ex ante fiscal support in the form of a strong capital position of the CB (or an explicit state guarantees to cover specific risks and losses associated with some UMP). A substantial and efficient package along these lines, could allow for a better policy-mix via an improved monetary-fiscal policy interaction. However, over the coming years, it seems rather unlikely that member states will agree on a substantial regime change and implement the necessary Treaty changes. Monetary-fiscal policy interaction may therefore need to be enhanced and intensified, without assuming that the main challenges will in part be addressed by substantial progress towards a swiftly established and well-designed fiscal, banking and capital market union.

"Haus, Casa or Maison". The Perfect Opening for Talking about EMU Architecture

Giulio Tremonti[1]

A currency has never, at any time in history, been merely a "technical" entity, a monad removed from life and politics. It has always been a structural element of a given political architecture. Except that, at a time of crisis such as the present one, I would add "Hütte, Rifugio" to "Haus, Casa or Maison"! What I intend to argue here, in particular, is that in our current dramatic crisis, politics alone can breathe (new) life into the euro. I shall be following the thread of history to argue my point. In fact, we do not even need that much history in this case. We need less than a century, a mere 77 years: a timespan which, for simplicity's sake, I shall split into three parts: the age of peace (1943–89); the age of globalisation (1992–2007); and the age of crisis (2008–20).

The Age of Peace (1943–89)

It is no mere coincidence that it was Jean Monnet, whom President Roosevelt had appointed as his personal representative, who caused the notion of a political Europe to prevail over the English idea of a purely mercantile Europe in Algiers in 1943. Algiers was followed by other venues, Italian venues this time. First, Messina in 1952 with the coal and steel conference (Italy at the time had neither coal nor steel, of course, but what it wanted was Europe), then Rome in 1957 with the *Treaty of Rome*, possibly the loftiest moment in our history.

The Treaty entailed handing over to Brussels all those areas of legislative and administrative authority required to set up the EEC, while leaving all other areas of authority with national governments. This was a deliberate political choice, because, while the people at the time had confidence in their leaders' actions, the leaders themselves did not forget the principle that underpins the very root of democracy: "no taxation without representation". The finest passage in the Treaty is Adenauer's: "The forest cannot be so thick that it prevents us from seeing the trees". The EEC gave Europe three decades of prosperity and civilization.

---

[1] Giulio Tremonti, Professor of law, admitted to the Supreme Court, President of Aspen Institute Italia. He was Senator, Deputy Prime Minister, Minister of Economy and Finance and Vice President of the Chamber of Deputies. He is author of various publications.

Giulio Tremonti

The Age of Globalisation (1992–2007)

With the fall of the Wall, the Maastricht era was embodied in two new signs: €, ▽. The sign of the new currency and a drawing of an inverted pyramid. Both marked the start of the construction of a new and revolutionary political entity in Europe. In the post-war era, the EEC had been a model for the rest of the world, showing how economic integration was possible even among countries that had been at each other's throats for centuries. In the same way, it was now thought that what was emerging in Europe was the best possible political model in the context of the mercantile and democratic geography that was pushing the world toward integration.

That is not exactly the way things turned out, however. While the euro was an outstanding success, we cannot say the same of Europe. Rather than Europe entering globalisation – exporting and imposing its winning political model on the world at large – globalisation entered Europe and found it unprepared and bemused. A great deal of that could have been avoided, if Brussels' acquisition of too many areas of authority had been avoided (the inverted pyramid). It would have helped if there had been less hubris and more political depth at the heart of Europe's governance.

Below is a summary of (Italian) ideas and initiatives which first a Chancellor and then a British prime minister (not a Conservative) amiably called "proto-populist". These ideas might well have improved Europe's architecture, making it a little more efficient and a little more popular (rather than populist):

- no. 1   Objection to the unilateral – repeat, unilateral – decision, applied only in Europe (not on any other continent), to remove import duty radically rather than gradually.

- no.2   The idea that European regulations were as excessive (normally 10 km's worth of European Official Gazette were published every year) as they were pervasive. It was clear that this was likely to trigger a dual negative effect: (i) It pulled the carpet from under the feet of Europe's businesses – especially its small and medium-sized ones – by forcing them to vie on the world's markets with competitors unhampered by regulations. In particular, it is not the replacement of the lira by the euro but the removal of import duty and the excess of European regulations that made Italy's industry (not as technologically advanced as Germany's) less competitive in the globalized world. (ii) It alienated Europe from people's hearts with regulations too often written with the best of intentions yet whose effect was to pry too much into the lives of others!

The Perfect Opening for Talking about EMU Architecture

- no. 3   A warning that democracy is not a product for export (not even through enlargement) but a process that needs to be built over time and with patience in order to avoid counter-effects (witness today's Visegrad group). In any event, some of the European Court of Justice's verdicts really do seem to be too advanced, particularly in the sphere of morals... the kind of thing that would shock even the decadent Emperor Heliogabalus.

- no. 4   The idea of using VAT also as a kind of "de-tax" to fund development in Africa, not just to mitigate the impact of migration on Europe but also to forestall the effects of the dramatic void that emigration would generate (is generating) in Africa. Presented not only at the *Ecofin* but also in *Le Monde* (on 11 September 2001), the idea was rejected by the Prodi Commission on the grounds that migration was the solution to our demographic problems.

- no. 5   The idea (admittedly a little far-fetched yet certainly not tainted with Euroscepticism) of printing a "1 euro note" to lend the euro a global outreach... a bit like the 1 dollar bill. In any event, we shall soon be seeing a "one euro bitcoin"!

- no. 6   The idea of issuing eurobonds, introduced in the Italian presidency's agenda in 2003 pursuant to the "Delors plan" of 1994, to fund European infrastructure but also, in addition, to fund the European defence industry. The plan was rejected... by everyone.

- no. 7   The Italian presidency's opposition to sanctions being levied on Germany and France – sanctions demanded by the Commission and by the ECB for countries that were already under infringement procedure but that were not intentionally deviating from the European parameters, a case in which the *Pact* explicitly rules out sanctions. It is interesting to note that, just a few days later, those calling for sanctions said that the *Pact* was stupid!

- no. 8   An obsession from the outset, an obsession right up to 2008: the idea that private debt is good, or at least less dangerous than public debt. We should note the downward trend in Italy's public debt in 2008, when it was moving toward 100% of GDP.

- no. 9   It was, in fact, fairly easy to see the risks inherent in the global world, a world that had shifted in one fell swoop from the era of "Liberté, Égalité, Fraternité" to the era of "Globalité, Marché, Monnaie"; in other words, to a world in which the only rule was that there were no rules.

Italy, on the other hand, vainly argued – and not only in a European context – that it did not have to be that way. Italians pointed out that there was also a dark side to globalisation: "The spectre of poverty" (1995), "Europe, lethal risks" (2005), "Fear and hope. The looming global crisis and how to overcome it" (2007); "Wikileaks" (message from Rome to Washington): 30 October 2008: "Italy has gone farther, advocating radical reform of international finance […] expressing deep suspicions about the benefits of globalisation and a rather eclectic economic philosophy" (it is worth noting that orthodox economic philosophy – i.e. the Lehman Brothers' philosophy – had just collapsed).

The Age of Crisis (2008–20)

The crisis triggered by globalisation hit Europe totally out of the blue, taking it completely by surprise, in the fall of 2008. In the summer of 2008, the Eurogroup and Ecofin were still planning to levy sanctions on the United Kingdom for unauthorised government subsidies to Northern Rock. It was only after the summer that what would have been an exception demanding punishment became a broadly applied rule: public budgets were no longer being seen as a sickness but as a medicine.

In that connection, it is worth considering a letter that Italy addressed to the French presidency on 29 September 2008, a letter in which the idea of setting up a "European fund" was put forward for the very first time. Speaking in double-entry terms today, we can see that the positive actions adopted to manage the crisis were also accompanied by certain negative actions.

No support was forthcoming for (Italy's) idea of shifting from "free trade" to "fair trade", as proposed when drafting the multilateral treaty known as the Global Legal Standard. This treaty was approved by the OECD Assembly in 2010 but it certainly was not backed by those (including Europe) who thought, on the contrary, that the right choice was the purely financial choice of setting up a "Financial Stability Board". Allow me here to remind you that in the Global Legal Standard, in connection with rules governing fair trade, Article 4 talks about: "environmental and hygiene regulations"!

Then there was the unfortunate walk on the pier of Deauville, in the fall of 2010, when the message that governments can go bankrupt just like market entities was issued! See the rejected idea of Eurobonds[2].

---

2   Juncker, Jean-Claude and Giulio Tremonti, "E-bonds would end the crisis", *Financial Times*, 5 Dec. 2010.

The Trichet-Draghi letter to Prime Minister Berlusconi was dated 5 August 2011, i.e. after the June European Council had officially approved the Italian budget, calling on Italy to bring forward its balanced budget, thus crank-starting the soft "coup d'état" that was to be finalised with regard to Italy the following November. Omissis on the "Troika" in Greece.

"Whatever it takes": not the first-aid it was supposed to be but a long spell in hospital lasting fully eight years with a triple negative impact: (i) The disappearance of politics: not one of the reforms still being called for has been implemented in Europe since then… why bother? After all, we have the ECB. (ii) The political sceptre has been transferred from governments and from the EU to the money market. (iii) Thus, with zero or sub-zero interest rates and with the replacement of billions by trillions, we now face the risk of an uncontrollable and therefore devastating financial crisis in the near future (and the crisis will not only be financial, either).

The bank union cobbled together focused chiefly on Non-Performing Loans rather than – or at least also – on "derivatives". Most recently, Brexit, a bilateral error of judgment is manifesting itself. On the British side, an excess of swashbuckling and of nostalgic rhetoric; on the European side, an excess of bureaucracy, from the (draft) directive on "toilet flushing" to one on "Health and safety measures to stop hairdressers wearing high-heel shoes". Perhaps today we should remember what Nietzsche said: Europe does not exist without England. Perhaps today we should remember that in the middle of the financial crisis, in 2009, the City was crucial for Europe. In any case, we've missed the boat (and it cannot be replaced by the Balkans).

The Right Side of History

The Bible is a goldmine of myths and legends: "Paradise Lost", the "Flood", the "Tower of Babel". The latter may well be the legend that most closely reflects both our present and our future. In *Genesis*, mankind challenges the deity by erecting a tower to heaven. God's reaction takes the shape of our loss of a "single language". If we replace "single language" by "single thought", that is exactly what has happened and is still happening. The pandemic is in fact not as disruptive for its impact on health as it is for its impact on the system: this collapse of the global mental construction has driven the world for the past thirty years. This collapse is having – and will continue to have – a massive effect of discontinuity; the geopolitical, political, social and economic consequences are massive.

Europe's response this year has been outstanding, timely and positive ("ex malo bonum"), ranging from the suspension of the "Treaty" where it talks about "parameters" and its "ban on government aid" right up to the "Recovery and Resiliency Facility". But even so, that is not going to be enough. For instance, the idea that it is possible to make a distinction within the public debt between bad debt and good debt is insufficient! In general terms, it is not going to be enough just to stick to the financial aspect.

In particular, the euro in itself is not enough. In the dramatic times we are living through, there cannot be – or at least there cannot be for too long – an excessively marked separation between currency and politics: politics without a currency, a currency without politics.

This is true not only for the euro but for every kind of currency, because what is currently or potentially in a critical condition is the currency's very raison d'être. Why is the superstition of gold making such a forceful comeback? What limits are there in central banks' endless digital output of growing quantities of monetary symbols (trillions)? What is the relationship between the actions of the ECB and inflation, which no longer appears to be either a ceiling or a target, in a world in which, in the West, there are no longer any working masses with their wage demands, in a world in which we have e-commerce? What technical role is (going to be) played by the currency in a world that is dominated by e-commerce today but that is going to develop in the future on platforms which, "Libra-style", will tend in the end to bypass conventional currency? What limits are there on the growth of the debt, be it public or private?

It is for all these reasons that what is needed in the growing vacuum forming around the euro is politics. Today, this can (and, I believe, must) be justified, driven and symbolised precisely by the notion of the defence of our common house ("Haus, Casa or Maison"), and thus by a common European commitment to, and investment in, defence and security. In these terms and on that basis, a European policy which, while tailored to reflect the spirit of our age, is as intense as the policy devised in 1957, is necessary and may even be sufficient.

A democratic test: if you go into a pub and talk about the need to bolster the banking union or to introduce a European finance minister, they probably will not know what you're talking about; but if you talk about European defence and security they are highly likely to buy you a drink.

Is the ECB Ready for the Next 20 Years of Monetary Union?

Pier Carlo Padoan[1]

Introduction

It is not obvious what the question embedded in the title really means. Clearly the answer depends on what the next 20 years will look like in term of economic policy challenges. In this respect one major challenge for the ECB will lie in the possibility, or the appropriateness, of returning to a "conventional" monetary policy stance, i.e. to what extent, if at all, the existing unconventional monetary policy, activated as a response to the great financial crisis and the Coronavirus crisis, will eventually be dismantled and we will return to a conventional framework (possibly revised with respect to the pre-crisis one). In particular to what extent can this be obtained without hurting long term growth while achieving a reasonable inflation target. My conclusion is that the effectiveness of monetary policy, over the longer run, will depend, inter alia, on the effectiveness of fiscal and structural policies in the EZ (Eurozone). While such a conclusion leaves out many key questions about the way the ECB operates, it highlights issues largely neglected in the debate.

The debate on the future of the Eurozone before the Coronavirus crisis has followed a clear pattern of priorities. High priority has been devoted to completing Banking Union. Increasing attention has been devoted to Capital Markets Union, and to the reform of the EU budget. Some attention has been devoted to issues related to progress towards fiscal union. Limited (but growing) attention has been devoted to issues related to adjustment, convergence, and stabilisation mechanisms. In the public debate, discussion about the role of monetary policy has largely been devoted to the merits and limits of unconventional monetary policy and to the, sometimes implicit, view that monetary policy can do little to support long term growth directly.

---

1 Pier Carlo Padoan, School of European Political Economy, LUISS Rome. This paper draws on Padoan, Pier Carlo "Growth in Europe. Notes for a Policy Agenda", *Credit and Capital Markets*, vol 53, Jan. 2020.

Pier Carlo Padoan

Growth and imbalances in the EZ

Indeed, growth in Europe has been weakening over the past decades, already before the arrival of the Coronavirus, suggesting explanations related to long term factors as well as to the large negative shock represented by the Great Financial Crisis. Growth can hardly be explained by single factors, rather it is the result of the interaction of macroeconomic, microeconomic, and structural dynamics and related policies (monetary, fiscal, financial, and structural). It is useful to summarise some of the desirable features of the growth mechanism in the EZ and connect them to the role of monetary policy.

In terms of convergence, it would be desirable that structural differences between countries and regions narrow down or are eliminated. In terms of stabilisation it would be desirable for macroeconomic fluctuations to be minimised and that adjustment of imbalances be obtained at minimum costs. More generally one would expect that the EZ be characterised by strong and sustainable growth and that both cyclical and structural factors contribute to achieving this. The ECB monetary policy should be geared to this long-term objective, while taking into account preservation of monetary stability. Growth is sustained if imbalances are adjusted, i.e. there is no persistence and accumulation of imbalances. If imbalances persist and grow larger, they eventually break out into a crisis and weaken growth.

What do we know about adjustment mechanisms within the EZ? We can distinguish phases in the functioning of the EZ since its inception. 1) The period from the introduction of the euro until the breakout of the "sovereign debt crisis" (starting with the Greek crisis). 2) The crisis and the institutional response. 3) The post financial crisis period. 4) The impact of the Coronavirus crisis.

The initial stage has been characterised by significant interest rate convergence, suggesting that, thanks to the single currency, country risk was gradually erased. At the same time, current account imbalances have widened reflecting, to a large extent, growing savings-investment gaps. This mechanism was generating destabilising dynamics. In surplus countries imbalances fueled capital outflows. In deficit countries, capital inflows were invested largely in non-tradable sectors (notably real estate), fueling structural divergence and real exchange rate appreciation.[2] All in all, in the initial stage monetary union has been characterised by real divergence. As events showed such a path was unsustainable and a crisis broke out.

---

2   Buti, Marco and Alessandro Turrini, "Three Ways of Convergence", *VoxEU*, 17 Apr. 2015.

Crisis and response

The crisis triggered a broad policy response based on major institutional changes, including the introduction of unconventional monetary policy measures. The crisis also highlighted the lack of appropriate instruments for crisis management as well as the need for a new institutional architecture to complement Monetary Union with a Banking Union and a Capital Markets Union. The crisis sparked a broad policy debate over the mechanisms required for a well-functioning EZ. The debate concentrated on the bank/sovereign nexus as a major source of fragility that needed to be addressed. Banking Union was launched. The ESM was launched. Capital Markets Union, on the contrary, has lagged behind.

As the EZ slowly (and painfully) exited the crisis, a new pattern of adjustment, convergence and stabilisation emerged. Interest rate convergence was replaced by divergence as markets began to price country risk. Current account adjustment remained asymmetric with pressure concentrated on deficit countries. This aspect highlighted that, in a monetary union, adjustment of current accounts requires changes in competitiveness (real exchange rates), which in turn requires lower inflation in deficit countries, and higher inflation in surplus countries. Clearly a pattern not confirmed by facts. At the same time, in high debt countries the need to adjust current account deficits may conflict with the need of higher nominal growth to maintain debt on a declining path – the more so, if the country displays a positive difference between the interest rate and the (nominal) growth rate. A condition which, other things being equal, implies that debt is sustainable only if the country runs an offsetting primary surplus. Clearly, the monetary policy stance could provide a fundamental input in determining the interest rate dynamics. But what about supporting growth?

While it emerged that the internal adjustment mechanism in the EZ was in a very limited way supportive of growth, it became clear that current account imbalances also reflect structural factors and therefore adjustment also requires structural change. In the EZ and elsewhere, labour market dynamics became increasingly blurred, for instance, as wages hardly reflected labour demand pressure. This has weakened the effectiveness of monetary policy. How could wage adjustment be improved? Could more wage coordination better address imbalances? Do we need more wage centralisation or decentralisation, possibly better reflecting productivity? Lacking wage adjustment, imbalances will be more persistent and fiscal response more deflationary with further implications for growth.

Imbalances and structural factors

Persistent saving/investment imbalances, to the extent that they reflect structural factors, require structural reforms (SR) to boost investment in surplus countries and wage flexibility in deficit countries. Both actions would support growth. This, in turn, requires looking more in depth at how structural reforms impact on the economy and help strengthen symmetry, and how monetary policy can contribute to adjustment of imbalances.

First, for a given set of structural measures, the cyclical stance impacts on SR effectiveness.[3] This depends on both fiscal and monetary stimuli. Evidence shows that such an impact is stronger in an upswing at least for two reasons: first, as the cycle gains strength, the propensity to invest is stronger and investment is the vehicle through which reforms impact the economy. Think of, e.g. new capital spending taking place as a consequence of a more favorable business environment, or a more innovation intensive capital stock reflecting better innovation incentives or more effective human capital formation. There is a complementarity between the structural, the microeconomic and the macro dimensions in the adjustment process. Monetary policy has an impact on all these dimensions.

Second, the Structural Reform cycle may be very long. By this I refer to the sequence of steps that are needed to fully implement a reform measure. The cycle evolves from the moment in which new legislation is introduced and approved by Parliament, to be followed by the adoption of administrative measures, their actual implementation and possible revision. And the "final stage" that involves the impact on behavior (of firms and households) reflecting the change in incentives, which the reform (should) produce. Finally, one should not forget the perception (by firms and households) that the reforms have improved individual welfare. Possibly (but not necessarily) such a perception may lead to an increase in approval and political support for the Government that is recognised as responsible for the improvement.

The duration of the reform cycle may differ significantly across the reform portfolio and across countries. For instance, education reforms are usually credited with the largest impact on long term growth, but they also carry the longest implementation cycles. Other reforms such as product market liberalisation require shorter cycles and may produce an impact on behavior also through expectations, if the announcement of their introduction is credible enough.

---

3 Boone, Laurence and Marco Buti, "Right Here, Right now and the Quest for a More Balanced Policy", *VoxEu*, 18 Oct. 2019.

However, also due to the duration of the reform cycle, introducing reforms may not be rewarding for incumbents as eventual benefits of reforms may be recognised too late (with respect to a possible vote in favour of the reforming Government). This is a particular severe problem given that the costs of reforms are usually concentrated on limited segments of the population, while benefits are delayed and distributed over larger population groups. This opens the opportunity to introduce instruments to provide compensation measures for those segments of the population that are negatively impacted by the reform process.

The main message in this respect is that the impact of monetary policy is enhanced by reforms that improve the way markets operate, i.e. reforms that improve the transmission mechanism of monetary policy. However, while structural reforms are essential to support growth, the incentive to introduce them may be too weak to spark reform. This is reverberated on persistent imbalances and lower growth. Conversely, given the need for a lengthy horizon for reforms to deliver results, a contribution from monetary policy comes from a credible long-term monetary policy stance.

Over the longer term, structural aspects gain more prominence. One structural aspect that has been important in the debate is Secular Stagnation. Symptoms of Secular Stagnation in Europe include the persistent decline in productivity growth, the associated decline in profitability, and the decline in the natural rate of interest. Evidence also shows a structural shift in the long-term growth rate with respect to the growth trend which would have prevailed in the absence of the financial crisis, and more so after the Coronavirus crisis. This latter aspect is particularly evident in periphery countries.

What can policy do? The debate on Secular Stagnation has concentrated on a dilemma: is Secular Stagnation a demand or a supply phenomenon? Both demand (investment) and supply (productivity factors) play a role. Demand factors relate to lack of investment, supply factors relate to lack of structural reforms and hence productivity enhancement. Structural reforms in turn require investment to be implemented. Investment is needed to "introduce" structural reforms, and hence drive structural change, in the economy. Investments need profitability to be activated, and profitability depends on structural reforms. So, both sides of the coin must interact to react to stagnation pressures.

One implication of the above is that, also because of risks of Secular Stagnation, supporting long term growth in the EU requires more investment, both public and private. In this respect, it is at times argued that monetary policy can do little against Secular Stagnation. The debate about the effectiveness of monetary policy in a zero bound environment is well known. I would argue that monetary policy, by supporting investment (directly and indirectly) can support reforms and long-term growth.

Pier Carlo Padoan

The new policy agenda after the great financial crisis

After the great financial crisis and before the Coronavirus crisis broke out the debate shifted. It became increasingly clear that monetary policy alone cannot bear the burden of supporting the EZ economy. ECB action must be complemented with fiscal and structural policies. Progress in the structural reform agenda[4] improves the effectiveness of monetary policy, while the national fiscal policy framework (Stability and Growth Pact) must be adjusted.

Beyond changes in national fiscal rules, an EZ fiscal capacity is needed. The EU budget would be the instrument to deal with convergence and structural adjustment. Its impact would be enhanced by operating in coordination with the structural agenda. Budget resources should provide buffers favoring structural adjustment costs of transition. On the other hand, a stabilisation instrument is needed, for instance, an unemployment insurance mechanism. Such a mechanism could improve labour market adjustment, prevent hysteresis and avoid the possibility that cyclical unemployment turns structural, while avoiding a transfer union.[5] A fiscal capacity should be developed to support both stabilisation and adjustment of imbalances, but also efficient allocation of resources and therefore an impact on long term growth.

The impact of the Coronavirus crisis

The outbreak of the Coronavirus crisis has strongly accelerated both the debate and the policy reaction to the crisis, including that of monetary policy. Many of the policy issues discussed before the arrival of the virus have been taken up thereafter. The impact of Covid-19 on the EZ and other advanced economies following the lockdown has been a huge supply shock and demand shock consequences, which have been described, in the more optimistic scenarios, as V shaped. The V shaped scenario implies a strong and determined policy response by both fiscal and monetary policy. The ECB has responded quickly and significantly, inter alia by enhancing its asset purchase programs, thus moving further away from a conventional framework. One question for the long term is therefore to what extent such a shift represents a permanent feature.[6]

---

[4] Masuch, Klaus, Robert Anderton, Ralph Setzer and Nicholai Benalal (eds). "Structural policies in the euro area", *ECB Occasional Papers* Series, n. 210, Jun. 2018 https://www.ecb.europa.eu/pub/pdf/scpops/ecb.op210.en.pdf; OECD, *Going for growth*, 2018; http://www.oecd.org/economy/going-for-growth/.

[5] Giammusso Federico and Pier Carlo Padoan, *Un Rainy Day Fund europeo a sostegno dell'occupazione*, Mimeo ASTRID, May 2019.

[6] Benigno, Pierpaolo, Paolo Canofari, Giovanni Di Bartolomeo and Marcello Messori. "Theory, Evidence, and Risks of the ECB's APP", *Working Paper 5*, Sep. 2020.

The impact of the Coronavirus crisis on the effectiveness of the monetary policy response depends on two variables: the increase in uncertainty and the related significant increase in the propensity to save. The extent to which they persist beyond the short term will impact on the longer term behaviour of the ECB. The pandemic has triggered an unprecedented increase in uncertainty about the duration and effectiveness of containment measures and their impact on economic activity and employment; the speed of the recovery once containment measures are eased; and the extent to which the pandemic will permanently impact consumption, investment and the growth potential.

In addition to the direct effects, heightened uncertainty is likely to dampen activity via a number of channels. First, as investment and employment decisions may be costly to revert or irreversible, it might be preferable for a company to postpone a decision until further information has become available or uncertainty about the future economic outlook has diminished. Second, high uncertainty may dampen activity through increasing risk premia and the rising costs of debt financing, as reduced predictability is generally associated with higher risk aversion. Third, high uncertainty could lead households to increase their precautionary savings, which would reduce current private consumption and further dampen growth. Fourth, episodes of very high uncertainty might cause permanent changes in the behavior of households and businesses, especially if they occur frequently. Finally, high uncertainty could make an economy less sensitive to monetary and fiscal policy actions. "Liquidity preference" may prevail for a long time. This picture is confirmed by the fact that the propensity of households to save during the Coronavirus crisis has also reached unprecedented levels

While uncertainty may abate over time as the impact of the Coronavirus fades away, its initial impact may be strong in the short term and remain persistent over the medium term. So monetary policy could further weaken its impact with respect to the pre-Coronavirus environment. Indeed, this has prompted the acceleration of unconventional measures and pushed back in time the return towards more conventional frameworks. However, the policy response and notably the Next Generation EU (NGEU) dramatically changes the policy scenario in all its main dimensions: fiscal, financial, structural and, indirectly, monetary.

A fiscal policy boost comes from the large amount of loans and grants that, through the EU budget, are channeled towards countries, while the suspension of the Stability and Growth Pact boosts domestic fiscal space. The financial space is diversified and strengthened by the issuance of "European bonds" targeted at financing specific EU investment and reform projects. The structural policy space is crucial as the funds will be disbursed only after checking the progress in the structural reforms and public investment projects carried out by member states.

Progress in the structural agenda should improve the impact of monetary policy on growth and sustainability. In addition, the issuance of European bonds, also by the SURE facility to support labour market adjustment, paves the way for the introduction of an EU safe assets which could strengthen monetary stability.

All in all, the extent to which policies implemented under the Next Generation EU framework are effective will increase confidence in the new economic policy framework, and possibly uncertainty will decrease. In a less uncertain scenario monetary policy will be more effective also thanks to a better (more efficient) structural framework once reforms are implemented. At this stage, the ECB may be in the position to revert to a more conventional policy environment (although this may take some time to materialise).

Conclusions

The ECB will be ready for the next two decades of monetary union also to the extent that the contribution of policies other than monetary policy will take on a larger role than in the past in the support to growth and stability. Reacting to the Great Financial Crisis and the Coronavirus crisis, monetary policy has taken on a major burden, and in so doing it has moved away from conventional policies. The capacity of the ECB to "reinvent itself" is a welcome feature that has been key in responding to the crisis. However, further moving in uncharted territory has limits, and the need to unwind or reconsider such policies is becoming more pressing. How can the ECB unwind, rather than expand, unconventional policies without hurting the recovery from the crisis, today and possibly in dealing with future crises? A smooth exit will be more likely if structural policies are implemented so as to enhance potential growth and improve the transmission of monetary policy, and to the extent to which there is tangible progress towards fiscal union to complement monetary policy in sustaining demand and contributing to macroeconomic stabilisation. The response to the Coronavirus crisis, most notably NGEU, will prove effective also by allowing monetary policy to operate more efficiently while establishing a process towards the unwinding of unconventional policies.

The ECB is not Ready for the Next 20 Years of Monetary Union

Gunther Schnabl[1]

1. Introduction

When, in the early 1990s, the Maastricht Treaty set the stage for a common European currency, there were two models of central banks in Europe.[2] The Anglo-French model foresaw a central bank which was dependent on the ministry of finance and contributed to the financing of government expenditure. Inflation rates were high and the currencies continued to depreciate against the Deutsche Mark in countries following this model. The Deutsche Bundesbank model was an independent central bank with a strong focus on price stability. Inflation rates were low and the Deutsche Mark appreciated against other European currencies.

The appreciation of the Deutsche Mark forced German export enterprises to continuously adjust their competitiveness. This led to high productivity gains, which could be used to lift real wages and to expand the German social security system.[3] Parts of these productivity gains were redistributed mostly to the Southern European countries via the common European institutions and exchange rate depreciation of the Southern European and some other currencies.[4] Thus, the pre-euro currency competition in Europe – with the German central bank being an anchor for monetary stability – constituted an important source of growth and welfare, which came along with a high degree of acceptance of the European integration process among the European citizens.

---

1   Prof. Dr. Gunther Schnabl is a professor for International Economics and Economic Policy at Leipzig University. He is a Senior Research Fellow at Flossbach von Storch Research Institute.
2   De Grauwe, Paul, *The Economics of Monetary Union*, Oxford: Oxford University Press, 2012.
3   Müller, Sebastian and Gunther Schnabl, "The Brexit as a Forerunner: Monetary Policy, Economic Order and Divergence Forces in the European Union". *Economists' Voice* 16, 1, 2019.
4   A depreciation increases the competitiveness of an economy shifting employment from the neighbouring country to the country that is depreciating its currency (beggar-thy-neighbour). Usually, the neighbour responds by depreciating its currency as well, thereby reversing the process. This leads to competitive depreciations, which destabilise both economies, as for instance observed during the 1930s. In Europe since the 1970s, the focus of the German central bank on price stability prevented such destabilising competitive depreciations. The resulting appreciation of the Deutsche Mark forced the German enterprises into strong productivity gains and thereby welfare gains, which were partially shifted to Southern Europe via the depreciation of the Southern European currencies. In return, this enhanced in Southern Europe the demand for German products.

The Maastricht Treaty tried to forge these two central bank models together to build the institutional foundation of the common European currency. As the Germans remained reluctant to give up the dominant role of the Deutsche Mark in the European monetary system, Germany had the bargaining power to model the European Central Bank after the blueprint of the Deutsche Bundesbank.[5] In Art. 127 (1) of the Treaty on the Functioning of European Union (TFEU) it is stated that "The primary objective of the ESCB shall be to maintain price stability". In Article 126 (1) TFEU it is written that "Member States shall avoid excessive deficits". to isolate the European Central Bank (ECB) from political pressure to finance government expenditure.

2. The Gradual Transformation of European Monetary Policy

However, during more than 20 years since euro introduction, the common central bank was gradually transformed from a German-type into a French-Italian-type central bank model. Originally, the European Central Bank had aimed to keep consumer price inflation below 2% along with a reference value for money supply growth (4.5%). In 2003, the objective was defined to be a rate of inflation lower than but close to 2% over the medium term, which was later reinterpreted as a 2%-point target. The reference value for money supply growth was dropped.[6]

Given that globally the transmission of monetary policy has shifted from affecting consumer prices to influencing asset prices since the mid 1980s,[7] the reinterpretation of the inflation target as a point target in combination with a low inflation environment has allowed the ECB to take an increasingly active role in business cycle stabilisation. Whereas during crises the key interest rates were strongly cut, interest rates were not lifted to the same degree during the recoveries after the crises. Thus, key interest rates fell towards and below zero, where they remain stuck now (Fig. 1).

Since the outbreak of the European financial and debt crisis, the inflation rate remained mostly below 2%, and asset purchases, in particular government bond purchases, could gain a prominent role in monetary policy making. Up to the present (end November 2020), the ECB has purchased (inter alia) government bonds

---

5   De Grauwe, Paul, *op. cit.*, p. 153
6   Stark, Jürgen, Thomas Mayer and Gunther Schnabl: "Ultra Vires: The Transformation of European Monetary Policy". *The International Economy*, Summer 2020.
7   Schnabl, Gunther: "The Failure of ECB Monetary Policy from a Mises/Hayek Perspective". In Godart-van der Kroon, Annette and Patril Vonlanthen (eds.): *Banking and Monetary Policy from the Perspective of Austrian Economics*, Springer, Berlin, 2018, pp. 127-152.

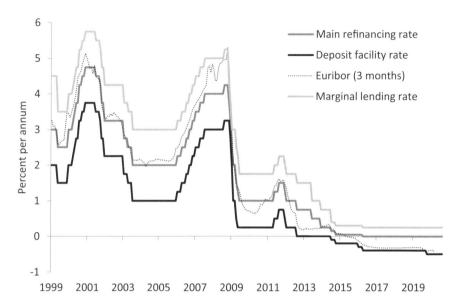

Fig. 1: ECB Key Interest Rates and Euribor
Source: ECB.

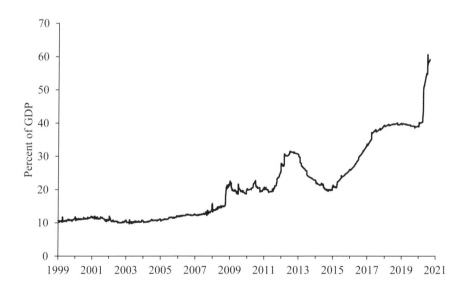

Fig. 2: ECB Balance Sheet as Percent of GDP
Source: ECB and IMF 2020 own calculation based on the assumption of a nominal growth rate of -13.3% in the second quarter 2020.

equivalent to 3.0 trillion euros The borderline between monetary and fiscal policy has become increasingly blurred. With the Coronavirus crisis (inter alia) additional purchases of government and corporate bonds equivalent of 1.85 trillion euros (in the Pandemic Emergency Purchase Progamme) and an expansion of (Targeted) Longer-term Refinancing Operations up to 3 trillion euros, at strongly eased collateral conditions, were announced.[8]

Thus, the balance sheet of the ECB has been inflated from about 10% of euro area GDP in January 1999 to roughly 60% by mid 2020 (Figure 2). The ECB now also pursues other economic policy goals, such as stabilising the financial system, safeguarding the euro and even protecting the climate.[9] An important guideline seems to be to do "whatever it takes", as announced by ECB president Mario Draghi at the peak of the European financial and debt crisis.[10] Thus, the ECB has become one of the most important players in the European capital markets, both as a market participant and as a regulator. With the recent Coronavirus crisis, expectations that the ultra-loose monetary policy will persist for a long time have strengthened.

3. Burdens for the Future of the European Monetary Union

This has created four major burdens for the future of the European Monetary Union. First, with a high probability of asymmetric shocks, the European Monetary Union continues to miss the characteristics of an optimum currency area as defined by Mundell.[11] The hope that EMU would be transformed into a monetary union with business cycles synchronised via intensified trade, thanks to lower transaction costs for trade due to a common currency,[12] was not fulfilled. Furthermore, from the very beginning, business cycles in EMU were not only idiosyncratic but further amplified by uncoordinated fiscal policies.[13]

---

8   European Central Bank, *ECB Announces Package of Temporary Collateral Easing Measures*, Press Release, 7 Apr. 2020.
9   Stark, Jurgen et al., *op. cit.*
10 Draghi, Mario, *Verbatim of the remarks made by Mario Draghi*, Speech by Mario Draghi, President of the European Central Bank at the Global Investment Conference in London, 26 Jul. 2012.
11 Mundell, Robert: "Optimum Currency Areas", *American Economic Review* 51, 1961, pp. 657-665.
12 Frankel, Jeffrey and Andrew Rose, "The Endogeneity of the Optimum Currency Criteria", *Economic Journal*, no. 108, 1998, pp. 1009-1025.
13 Schnabl, Gunther, *op. cit.*

The idiosyncratic business cycles not only undermined the effectiveness of the ECB's monetary policy, but turned it into a major reason for severe crises. Between 2003 and 2008, following the ECB interest rate cuts in response to the bursting dot com bubble, the interest rate was too high for the stagnating north. It was too low for the booming south and therefore contributed to the financial exuberance, which finally led to the European financial and debt crisis. Between 2010 and 2020, interest rates were too low for the north. This led to exuberance in the German stock and real estate markets, which amplified the slump during the Coronavirus crisis.

Second, the euro constitutes a straitjacket, which – given rigid labour markets in most euro member states – impedes the southern euro area countries in adjusting their competitiveness by exchange rate depreciation, as it was the case before euro introduction. Although the Coronavirus crisis was in the first phase understood as a symmetric shock affecting all euro area countries equally, the southern euro area economies were hit harder, as they rely more on tourism as a source of income and economic growth. With euro area membership, exchange rate adjustment to restore competitiveness is impossible. Attempts by the European Union to support the southern and other euro area countries by transfers are likely to perpetuate the structural rigidities in the public and private sectors. A sustained economic recovery of the southern European countries is therefore not in sight.

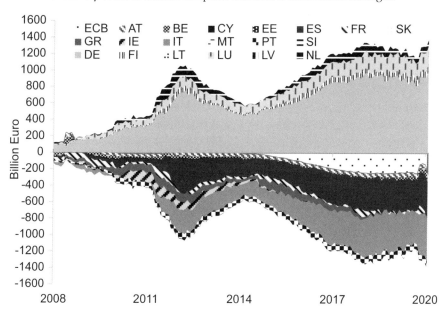

Fig. 3: TARGET2-Imbalances in the European System of Central Banks
Source: ECB.

Third, the structural rigidities in the southern euro area alongside increasingly low growth perspectives in the northern euro area, including Germany, will constitute a major burden for the governments in the future. A further rise of the euro area debt far beyond the Maastricht limit of 60% of GDP seems inevitable. The need to keep euro area government debt sustainable will further enhance the pressure on the ECB to buy bonds of the national governments as well as – to a growing degree – of European institutions, including the European Union. The ECB will have to yield to the pressure, although government financing via the central bank is prohibited in Art. 123 and Art. 310 of TFEU (Treaty on the Functioning of the European Union), and the bending of the Treaty will weaken the credibility of the EU. The further expansion of government bond purchases by the ECB will continue to undermine the credibility of the euro as a safe nominal asset, and this will further drive up the prices of real assets such as stocks, real estate and gold.

Fourth, the perpetuation and further expansion of the corporate bond purchases of the European Central Bank as well as the Targeted Longer-term Refinancing Operations will sustain easy liquidity conditions for enterprises in the euro area. This "quasi soft budget constraint"[14] will continue to undermine incentives for innovation and efficiency increases in the euro area. Productivity gains, which have already converged towards zero before the Coronavirus crisis, are likely to turn into losses, with a respective negative impact on growth. The resulting downward pressure on real wages is likely to be stronger for new entrants into the labour market, i.e. young people, than for older employees and pensioners, who constitute an important part of the electorate in the ageing European societies.

4. The Impact on the Credibility of the ECB and the EU

The upshot is that the euro has contributed to growing divisions within the euro area and the European Union. One is between the north and the south with respect to income levels and economic dynamics. The north will be forced to provide increasing transfers to prevent the south from falling even more behind. The most prominent indicator for the growing split in the euro area are the imbalances within the TARGET2 payments system of the European System of Central Banks (see Fig. 3), which has assumed the role of a quasi-unlimited, interest rate-free, intra-euro area credit mechanism.[15] The claims of the Deutsche Bundesbank on the

---

14 Kornai, János, "The Soft Budget Constraint", *Kyklos* 39, 1, 1986, pp. 3-30.
15 Sinn, Hans-Werner and Timo Wollmershäuser, "Target Loans, Current Account Balances and Capital Flows: the ECB's Rescue Facility", *International Tax and Public Finance*, 19, 2012, pp. 468-508.

Eurosystem in the TARGET2 payment system have exceeded one trillion euros. They may have to be written off in total or in part, if countries leave the euro area or the system ceases to exist.

Growing divisions also run through the societies of every single euro area member state due to the distribution effects of the persistently and increasingly loose monetary policy. Whereas rich people tend to profit from rising asset prices, the European middle class, who tends to save more in bank deposits,[16] suffers an erosion of their savings. Young people who enter the labour markets are faced with a decline of real wages compared to previous generations. In many regions across Europe, the strong rise in real estate prices has made it difficult for young people to acquire their own house or apartment.

Given gloomy growth perspectives and growing inequality in the euro area, distrust in the ECB is growing despite more efforts of the ECB to oppose this trend. The new ECB president Christine Lagarde has launched the campaign "ECB Listens", which allows the citizens to communicate their opinions in the course of the ECB's

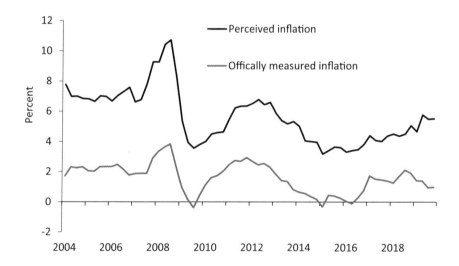

Fig. 4: Officially Measured and Perceived Inflation in the Euro Area
Source: European Commission.

---

16 Deposits are more important as form of savings in the former low-inflation countries, as pressure was weaker to hedge against inflation. In contrast, in many southern countries – possibly due to the former high-inflation experience – more people have owner-occupied housing.

monetary policy strategy review process. The new German ECB board member Schnabel[17] is trying to convince the German public that criticism of the monetary policy of the ECB is simply a misunderstanding, while at the same time this view is opposed by other ECB board members.[18]

Distrust in the ECB is growing in two regards. As shown in Fig. 4, inflation perceptions on average are far higher than inflation officially measured by Eurostat. This can be due to the fact that people tend to perceive increasing prices stronger than falling prices. An alternative interpretation is that quality improvements are one-sidedly used to downscale official inflation figures and that rising asset prices and rising costs of public goods are not included in official inflation measures.[19]

In addition, the direct trust in the ECB is fading. Net trust in the ECB – i.e. the difference between the percentage of interviewed people who tend to trust the ECB minus the percentage of people who tend not to trust the ECB – has substantially deteriorated since euro introduction and has in many cases become negative. Fig. 5 reveals – despite fluctuations linked to the business cycle – a downward trend. This distrust is – with the exception of Portugal – even stronger in southern euro area countries such as Italy, France and Spain, than in Germany. While the trust in the ECB recovered during the boom years until 2019, it is likely to turn more negative again with the current crisis.

All this implies that ECB is anything but ready for the next 20 years of monetary union. With a growing number of people in Europe missing the positive welfare gains of the pre-euro integration process, more people are likely to become euro-sceptic and/or EU-sceptic, as it is already observed in most EU countries. More European citizens are likely to drift towards more extreme political parties, with political instability in Europe further growing, as it can be observed best in Italy. Therefore, to make sure the euro survives for another 20 years, decisive measures are necessary.

---

17 Schnabel, Isabel, *Narratives about the ECB's Monetary Policy – Reality or Fiction?* Speech by Isabel Schnabel, Member of the Executive Board of the ECB at the Juristische Studiengesellschaft, 11 Feb. 2020.

18 Mersch, Yves, *Asset price inflation and monetary policy*. Keynote speech by Yves Mersch, Member of the Executive Board of the ECB and Vice-Chair of the Supervisory Board of the ECB, at the celebration of INVESTAS' 60th anniversary, 27 Jan. 2020.

19 Israel, Karl and Gunther Schnabl, "Alternative Measures of Price Inflation in Germany since 1999" *CESifo Working Paper* 8583, 2020.

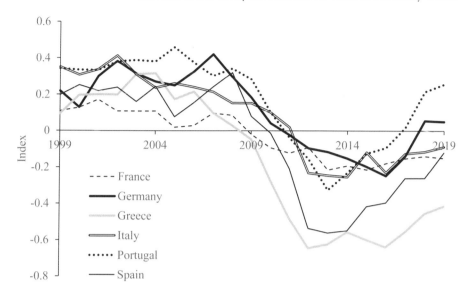

Fig. 5: Trust in European Central Bank
Source: European Commission.

5. What has to be done to get ready for another 20 years

The 750 billion Next Generation EU Fund, which was announced as 'a magnificent signal of solidarity and willingness to reform'[20] aims to cure the structural problems of the euro area by even more central-bank financed government expenditure, now also at the level of the European Union. This process is likely to come along with a gradual centralisation of fiscal policy at the European level, which is seen to help absorb asymmetric shocks, possibly via the establishment of a transfer system. Whilst this approach will help to conserve the euro area in the short term, it is likely to further hinder growth and increase inequality. This will in the longer term further destabilise the European Monetary Union and European Union.

A break-up of the euro area would help to adjust the competitiveness of southern European countries as one of the most important burdens of the European Monetary Union. It would help a return to the pre-euro currency competition, which would foster growth and welfare in Europe. A resolution of structural rigidities would lead to productivity gains, which would help to boost the income levels of all European citizens. The downside is that an uncontrolled break-up would be accompanied by strong turbulences in financial markets and therefore growing political uncertainty.

---

20   European Commission, *op. cit.*

An intermediate solution could be the introduction of parallel currencies, either in the southern or the northern part of the euro area.[21] This step would help the euro to persist, while at the same time allowing for an adjustment of competitiveness between the northern and the southern euro area. Any euro area member state would have the freedom to make its own decision concerning euro area membership, which would reanimate the currency competition in Europe. As currency competition was at the roots of high welfare gains previous to the introduction of the euro, Europe would face a brighter future.

---

21 Mayer, Thomas and Gunther Schnabl, "Post-Corona EMU: Economic Distancing by Parallel Currencies". *Intereconomics*, 55, 2020, pp. 387-391.

An International Role for the Euro?

Stefano Micossi[1]

1. Introduction

One proposition that commands universal agreement is that the euro deserves a greater international role, justified by the size of the European economy and the importance of its international trade and financial markets. And yet, as I will briefly summarise, the evidence is that nothing of the sort has been happening: after twenty years of existence, the euro's use as an international currency is more or less comparable, in its various dimensions of currency use, to the combined role of the franc français and Deutsche Mark before the euro's inception. The relative weight of the dollar, on the other hand, has increased on many accounts.

Two questions arise in this context: the first one is whether and to what extent policy can change this state of affairs; the second is whether we Europeans really want this greater international role for our common currency, given its broader implications for internal macro-economic and regulatory policies. In this article I will mainly dwell on the second question; however, some comments on the first one appear necessary to place the ensuing discussion in proper context.

Before addressing these issues, it is useful to quickly recall the benefits sought from an international reserve status. As long as the main currencies were linked to a fixed parity with gold, and financial markets were much less integrated than nowadays, the main advantage came from seigniorage and from the possibility to use one's own currency to finance external deficits – which were easily identified in the overall balance of payments accounts by drawing a line between the official balance (the amount to be settled with official reserves) on the one hand, and all remaining transactions on the other. This world ceased to exist with the transition to a floating exchange rate regime between the main world economic areas and the gigantic growth of financial markets since the 1970s – which made the creation of means of payments in different currencies, especially the dollar, essentially endogenous (demand driven).

---

1 Director General of Assonime, President of the Luiss School of European Political Economy and a member of the CEPS Board of Directors. The author is grateful to the editors for useful comments, while retaining full responsibility for the opinions expressed in this article.

Following the demise of the Bretton Woods system, in the main currency areas the exchange rate by and large ceased to be a policy target, but most other countries moved to a regime of managed float. Moreover, many emerging countries learnt from painful experiences that a cushion of reserve currencies and credit lines from private and official sources is required to meet 'sudden stops' of external finance. Therefore, the demand for foreign currency reserves has increased substantially.

Within this context, the main benefit from the reserve currency status may mainly lie in moderating exchange rate oscillations and dampening speculative capital flows. Private companies from reserve currency countries also have the advantage of conducting their international transactions in their own national currency with the important attendant benefits of trading with a stable means of invoicing, payment, and financial risk hedging. A related benefit may reside in a lower cost of funding – at least relative to financial markets of currencies traded in thin markets – especially in times of heightened risk aversion and flight to safety by international investors. However, these benefits are not a free good and must be conquered. I will discuss some key requirements for obtaining the reserve currency status which depend upon consequent political choices at EU level. Beyond this, the main question that cannot be eluded is whether the reserve currency status requires a worldwide geo-political projection, something the European Union is struggling to achieve.

2. *International currencies*

Almost fifty years have passed since the demise of the Bretton Woods exchange rate arrangements, and the dollar remains the dominant world reserve currency, with the euro finishing as a distant second in terms of global importance, and the yen playing a limited role in the Pacific area. China clearly nurtures the ambition of making its currency, the renmimbi, the third player worldwide, but it still has a long way to go to create the minimum market conditions for such a development.

The status of international currency has various dimensions, including its role in foreign currency reserves, trade invoicing and payment, debt and equity issues in financial markets, and the 'safe' store of value for international investors. Fig. 1 summarises the share of the main reserve currencies in the diverse functions they play. As can be seen, these shares are fairly stable across the different functions, with the US dollar hovering between 50 and 60 per cent and the euro between 15 and 20 per cent. The only exception to this stable pattern is in the euro share of global payments, around 37 per cent, which is a direct consequence of the weight of export and import transactions in the European economy.

An International Role for the Euro?

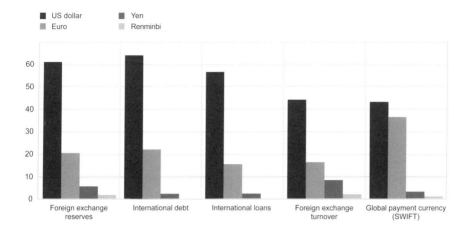

Fig 1. Global Reserve Currencies
Source: ECB (latest data are for the fourth quarter of 2019).

The global financial crisis has heightened the importance of the dollar also due to the role played by Federal Reserve swap lines in providing liquidity to the world financial system under stress – including very large lines with the ECB and through it to private financial institutions in Europe. Since all dollar liquidity transactions must be cleared through the US banking system, this has also given US regulators fresh leverage over world banking institutions, which have been obliged to comply with US rules in such areas as Anti Money Laundering or respecting political embargoes.

These trends are to an important extent influenced by the advent into the world economy of emerging Asian countries, which by and large have chosen the dollar and do not do full justice to the role of the euro in international reserves. Indeed, the shares of the main foreign exchange reserves look rather stable over the past thirty years, around 60 per cent for the dollar and 20 per cent for the euro. Since the absolute volume of foreign exchange reserves has in the meantime increased ten-fold to nearly 11 trillion dollars, the absolute volume of reserves held in euro has risen by a similar proportion – reaching about €2 trillion. An important observation is that some 50 per cent of the global foreign exchange turnover in euro was carried out in the United Kingdom, whose currency is not the euro, against only 13 per cent in euro area financial markets, something that raises questions about the attractiveness of euro area foreign exchange markets.

In a world in which political shocks play an increasing role in generating uncertainty, gold has also come back as a safe harbour for both official and private agents, as apparent from its high market price, but without any other reserve currency functions. According to the ECB,[2] gold holdings now represent 12 per cent of total foreign exchange reserves.

It is also useful to look at the evidence provided by the indicator of international reserve status developed by Ilzetzki et al.,[3] which assigns to each country an 'anchor' or 'reference' currency status and then aggregates the countries' GDP by reference currency. The main finding is that the US dollar has massively increased its reach, from some 45 per cent of world GDP in the 1980s to around 70 per cent nowadays; its weight as a reserve currency always was and is even more now well beyond the weight of the US economy in the world economy. The contrary has happened to the euro, which was used as a reference currency by 25 per cent of world GDP in 2000 and has now fallen to about 15 per cent. If eurozone countries are excluded from the calculation, this proportion falls to 3.5 per cent of world GDP. A closer look at the data indicates that the euro has been chosen by euro member countries and by European countries that have not joined the euro, but may do so in the future, and whose economies are closely integrated with those of the euro-countries.

The conclusion is straightforward. Over the past decades the dollar's reach has become truly global, with currencies from all over the world using the dollar as the anchor or reference currency in their exchange rate management, securities issuance, invoicing and means of payment, while the euro remains confined to a regional role for its members, its neighbouring countries and some former African colonies. Its limited role is compounded by the limited development of capital markets in continental Europe – whereby the capital market transactions are concentrated in the City of London, which belongs to a country that is leaving the EU.

Why this is the case is well explained by Ilzetzki et al.,[4] who also provide an overview on the literature on the subject. Their main conclusion is that many mutually-reinforcing factors combine in giving a global means of exchange, store of value and unit of account the nature of a natural monopoly – including the convenience of yield, of invoicing trade in a single currency (which the rise of global supply chains must have increased) and of holding wealth in instruments easily exchanged in deep and liquid financial markets. The currency denomination in trade of goods and services on the one hand, and exchange of financial assets on the other, may be closely complementary.

---

2   European Central Bank, *The international role of the euro*, Jun. 2020.
3   Ilzetzki Ethan, Carmen M. Reinhart and Kenneth S. Rogoff, 'Why Is the Euro Punching Below Its Weight?', *NBER Working Paper* No. 26760, May 2020.
4   Ilzetzki Ethan, Carmen M. Reinhart and Kenneth S. Rogoff, *op. cit.*

History seems to confirm the persistence of the global anchor currency.[5] The Spanish silver dollar persisted as a global currency well after the decline of the Spanish empire. The pound sterling acquired its reserve status after the Napoleonic wars and surrendered it to the dollar well after the US economy had surpassed the UK economy in size; similarly, today's share of the dollar in international reserve transactions is much larger than the weight of the US economy in the world economy. This development underlines the importance, in explaining the reserve currency status, of geo-political factors such as a dominating economic, trading and financial strength in the world economy, underpinned also by military might, which allows the issuing country to project its political influence globally.

Moreover, a global currency must be widely and easily available on demand. When this is the case, powerful network economies contribute to strengthening its attractiveness. Two ingredients are important in this regard: the first one is that the domestic markets for goods, services and capitals must be open to foreign supply and foreign investment; the second one is that the reserve currency must be underpinned by a large and liquid market for a safe asset guaranteed by the issuing country.

On these grounds, it is clear that the euro still has a long way to go before being able to aspire to a reserve currency status in the world economy. However, its international use may be enhanced by specific steps that can make the euro more attractive for international traders and investors. They involve the creation of a true Capital Markets Union and the establishment of a European safe asset guaranteed by the European budget and thus, ultimately, by its Member States.

3. Capital Markets Union

The Capital Markets Union (CMU) is a complex project entailing a host of markets, financial instruments, and legal and institutional dimensions.[6] While Article 63 of the Treaty on the Functioning of the European Union (TFEU) provides for the full freedom of capital movements between Member States, and between Member States and third countries, in practice this freedom is ensured more for portfolio

---

5   A somewhat different view is taken by Eichengreen, Barry, Arnaud Mehl and Livia Chitu, *How Global Currencies Work: Past, Present and Future*, Princeton University Press, 2018. Francesco Papadia and Konstantinos Efstathiou showed that there are changes in the usage of international currencies over time, in particular in the private functions. See Efstathiou, Konstantinos, and Francesco Papadia (2019), "The euro as an international currency", *LUISS-SEP Policy Brief*, Jan. 2019.

6   European Commission, 'Towards a stronger international role of the euro', COM (2018) 796/4, Brussels, 5 Dec. 2018.

investments and much less for real direct investment. In addition, regulatory standards for the implementation of European legislation differ considerably, due to the insufficient coordination of national regulatory agencies, with undesirable effects of market segmentation.

Indeed, the rationale underlying company law harmonisation directives was the fear that freedom of establishment could unleash an undesirable race to the bottom in corporate law and business arrangements. In this regard, most Member States hang on to a "real seat" legal doctrine implying that the applicable corporate law would be that of the location of the main center of the company's commercial and financial operations. Under this doctrine, the legal seat and the main operations of a company must coincide, potentially limiting company mobility and freedom of establishment.

Over time the Court of Justice of the European Union (ECJ) has opened ever-broader breaches into the closed walls of the real seat doctrine, de facto turning the European company law system into an "incorporation" system, whereby the applicable company law is determined by the place of legal incorporation. However, the tension between the two legal systems has not abated, reflecting continuing Member States' resistance to the real integration of capital markets. As a result, key capital market institutions continue to hinder effective integration of "real" capital markets, notably regarding the cross-border flows of direct investments. They include such aspects as: the freedom to choose the market where to issue shares; the market for corporate control and the takeover directive; golden shares, or public powers to limit private autonomy in the public interest; and the rules for cross-border company mobility.

The second necessary requirement for open and free capital markets is the establishment of a European single regulator with direct own regulatory powers. Here, progress has been remarkably slow; efforts have mostly been limited to ensuring the convergence of supervisory practices to achieve a gradual buildup of institutional procedures and cultural attitudes – under the constraints imposed by the EU Treaties on delegated powers. An improved convergence of regulatory standards was expected to come from the creation of the European Securities and Market Authority (ESMA), which was set up as an EU body with legal personality and was entrusted with binding powers to develop common implementing standards as the single rulebook for capital markets. Furthermore, ESMA was also identified as a single supervisor for a small set of market participants (credit rating agencies and trade repositories) – a potential harbinger of further transfers of powers. However, in practice these changes have not affected the very nature of ESMA as a network of national supervisory authorities due to the composition of its governing bodies and its decision-making procedures, which are still based on the principle of national representation.

A useful model for reform is provided by the European Central Bank, where a "management board" independent of national authorities and composed of independent and highly qualified individuals acts as an executive board, setting the agenda and preparing substantive decisions, while the representatives of national central banks only intervene in a broader "Governing Council" that is called upon to deliberate based on the proposals presented by the executive board.

4. Market fragmentation

The main requirement for the development of a global currency status is the existence of a large and liquid 'safe' government bond market. Although the debt ratios of the US and the EU are not, in the aggregate, very different, and indeed the US debt ratio has increased more rapidly than the average debt ratio of the euro (Fig. 2), investors see the US sovereign debt as not only a safe asset, but indeed the ultimate haven in case of instability in the world economy. This is not true for the euro area sovereign debts, which are of very different quality, as demonstrated by persistent financial fragmentation.

With financial fragmentation, the risks of similar financial instruments and financial intermediaries in different euro-area members are priced differently by market investors, limiting cross-border interbank and capital flows, which in turn act as a major limitation on the Capital Markets Union. The problem is aggravated by the incomplete architecture of the monetary union, which still lacks cross-border deposit insurance, a credible crisis resolution mechanism for banks, and a full public backstop in case of a systemic bank crisis, while banks continue to hold substantial amounts of national sovereign debt. Consequently, the 'doom loop' between a bank crisis and a sovereign crisis has not been vanquished and may still reappear following, for example, a rating downgrade of a highly indebted sovereign below investment grade.

The key factor behind financial market fragmentation is the threat of sovereign debt restructuring and, ultimately, of the exit of a country from the euro. Fig. 2 also shows sovereign-debt-to-GDP ratios for Germany and Italy, two euro-members that are widely divergent in this regard, as well as the whole euro-area and the United States.. In general, the average debt-ratio for the euro area results from widely varying debt ratios among its members. Thus, interest rate spreads between euro sovereigns remain sizeable even under the present ECB ultra-expansionary monetary policy. As a result, capital flows from international investors seeking safe havens concentrate on 'core' countries – Germany, the Netherlands, Luxembourg, even France and Belgium – while shunning Greece, Italy, Portugal, and Spain. Consequently, interest rates have fallen below zero in the former countries, while remaining well above in the latter.

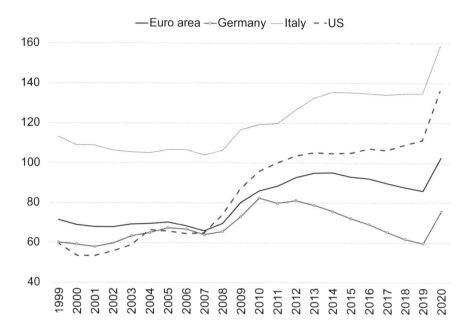

Fig. 2 Public debt in selected countries (% of GDP)
Source: AMECO.

As solid academic research has established, this happens because of a special externality created by the combination of a common currency managed by an independent central bank and fiscal and economic policies managed at national levels. When the latter diverge, doubts are likely to arise on the sustainability of the sovereign debts of some countries, since the liquidity for their orderly roll-over depends on the willingness of the ECB to intervene as lender of last resort for distressed sovereigns – an intervention that persistent divergence in economic fundamentals makes highly controversial within the ECB Governing Council and official policy circles.

In sum, the creation of a large and liquid market in the euro area for sovereign debt requires the existence of a common debt seen by international investors as absolutely safe from risk of default, which may only be possible if there was a joint and several guarantee against the risk of currency redenomination. Prima facie, this condition is not likely to be met without, if not a full fiscal union, at least credible governance mechanisms to ensure the convergence of fiscal policies in euro-countries.

As an intermediate step, one would also like to see a completion of the Banking Union, with the establishment of cross-border deposit insurance, a credible crisis management system (which present arrangements do not guarantee) and an adequate joint fiscal backstop for the resolution and deposit insurance funds (which are both under negotiation – the former almost ready to come into existence, though it is largely insufficient, the latter still nowhere in sight together with the cross-border deposit insurance). Various other regulatory improvements to foster the international role of the euro are presented in European Commission (2018).

5. A ready-made safe asset

Despite the difficulties generated by the incomplete monetary and fiscal union, various proposals have been advanced to build a European safe asset under existing circumstances. Brunnermeier et al.[7] made an influential proposal for developing sovereign bond-backed securities (SBBS) with varying seniority tranches, with the most senior tranche (European Safe Bonds, or ESBies) being as safe as the German "Bund". Being based on private contracts, their SBBS would not entail any risk sharing.

A High-Level Task Force on Safe Assets was established by the ESRB to assess the feasibility and impact on financial stability of creating a market for SBBS. They concluded that the development of a demand-led market for SBBS might be feasible 'under certain conditions', but could not agree either on its desirability (for the feared impact on sovereign debt markets) or its viability without regulatory support (including the introduction of concentration charges to penalise banks' holdings of national sovereigns, the usability of ESBies as collateral in ECB operations, and complex enabling product legislation). The Commission followed up in May 2018 with a proposal for a Regulation on SBBS, which Parliament and Council failed to approve before the end of the past legislature. All these proposals aim to create safety by combining diversification of the underlying sovereign risk with seniority over national debts; this last feature is most problematic due to its likely adverse impact on sovereign markets' spreads and liquidity.

More importantly, the very idea of building a safe asset without risk-sharing by euro-area members seems to be an artefact founded on a wrong premise: that the monetary union can survive indefinitely without any element of fiscal union, i.e., at least, some joint sharing of sovereign risks. Some sovereign risk sharing in the EMU is unavoidable precisely to conquer the externalities generated by the common currency that I have described.

---

7 Brunnermeier, Markus, Sam Langfield, Marco Pagano, Riccardo Reis, Stijn Van Nieuwerburgh and Dimitri Vayanos, "ESBies: safety in the tranches", *Economic Policy*, 32, issue 90, 2017, pp. 175-219.

Thus, the inevitable conclusion is that a European safe asset must be issued by an EU public entity – arguably, the ESM – and must enjoy a public guarantee against sovereign default. The simple scheme that I would like to propose consists in the ESM purchasing the sovereign bonds held by the European System of Central Banks (ESCB) as a result of the asset purchase programmes undertaken to enact its quantitative easing policies. The sovereign bonds would be purchased according to the proportions established in the asset purchase programmes, thus avoiding any undesirable differential impact on national sovereign bond markets. More importantly, the sovereign bonds purchased from the ESCB should continue to enjoy the guarantee against default de facto offered today by national central banks, so that no sovereign risk would be transferred to the ESM.

As a counterpart, the ESM would offer its own securities to banks and private investors in capital markets, in suitable maturities. These securities would be guaranteed by its sizeable (callable) capital; in addition, they would enjoy the guarantee of its Member States already in place for ESM liabilities, in proportions determined by the Member States shares in the ESM capital. This double guarantee, together with the guarantee maintained by national central banks on their sovereign paper, should be more than enough to ensure the Triple A rating for ESM securities without any special seniority privilege. A major drawback of the various proposals for a safe asset previously examined would thus be eliminated.

While of course these purchases by the ESM would develop gradually over time, they would eventually make available a total amount of over €2 trillion that would offer plenty of space for the diversification of banks' sovereign portfolios, as well as for large investments by international investors. A sizeable addition to these will be represented by the debt issued by the European Commission to fund its new programme, Next Generation EU. An adequate basis would thus be established for the development of a large, deep and liquid market for a European safe security, which would become the basis for a truly integrated Capital Markets Union and underpin the international role of the euro as a reserve currency and investment instrument. Over time, it would become clear that there is no need to reimburse these liabilities, but simply to roll them over, so that they become a stable component of the international monetary system.

This scheme has several other attractive properties that are worth mentioning. First, over time it would free the ESCB from the encumbrance of sovereigns in their balance sheets, thus creating suitable conditions for unwinding the large increase in their balance sheets after quantitative easing policies come to an end. As ESM purchases proceed, the liquidity created by the asset purchase programme would be reabsorbed, but the ECB would receive cash from the ESM. It could then decide to purchase other securities, to maintain an unchanged policy stance, or let its balance sheet shrink if it deemed that the existing degree of monetary stimulus was unwarranted. The time for such a decision will of course be determined well after the current coronavirus crisis ends.

Second, by bringing to the market a large supply of new high-quality assets, the scheme is likely to relieve the downward pressure on interest rates in the bond markets of 'safe' (low debt) euro-area countries, opening the way to interest rate increases in core countries even with present ECB policies. Moreover, these ESM securities would price counter-cyclically, as they would become a safe haven for investors fleeing instability; and they could become the principal instrument of monetary policy operations, as the ECB could purchase and sell them freely without effects on national budgetary policies.

6. A concluding remark

The foregoing analysis shows that creating the conditions for the euro to become an international reserve currency requires a complex policy set up that cannot bear fruit rapidly. However, if this is what is wanted, these policy requirements should be made explicit in the public debate before Parliaments and the public. They entail moving decisively to open capital markets by completing the Banking Union and the Capital Markets Union. They require a willingness to issue and jointly guarantee a very large common debt instrument, something that could be done by building the joint debt instrument on the ECB's sovereign debt purchases and the securities issued to finance Next Generation EU.

The fundamental question that remains to be answered, however, is the following: is the euro area, or perhaps the EU itself, ready to take up such responsibility in the world? Is it ready to project its economic power and influence worldwide, which would in turn entail a common foreign and defence policy and a willingness to deploy these tools to assert a larger political influence in the world?

My inability to answer this question justifies the question mark in the title of this paper.

The Necessity for a New International Role of the Euro

Sabine Seeger[1]

In the 1960s, Robert A. Mundell predicted that the Soviet Union would disintegrate, that Europe would adopt a single currency, and that the dollar would retain its status as number one in the international monetary system. All the predictions of the Canadian Nobel Prize winner hit the mark. Today, the Soviet Union is long gone, the euro is well established, and the greenback remains at the top. But changes are on the way. Wrong decisions by the US government and the COVID-19 crisis are eroding the value of the US currency. The exchange rate has been falling for months. Stephen S. Roach of Yale University considers the greenback "the most overvalued currency in the world".[2] He predicts a crash. Harold James even compares it to the former Soviet ruble: "The dollar will lose purchasing power internationally, it may even start to look like the old Soviet ruble, even if there is a dramatic change in leadership and strategy (in Washington)".[3] But what happens if the dollar declines further? "There will have to be an alternative ready to supplant it; you cannot replace something with nothing. And there is not yet a clear alternative available", says Nouriel Roubini.[4]

However, what could be the alternative? Could it be the euro? Europe's single currency seems to be stable. Despite its young age, the currency introduced in 1999 has done well and even survived its puberty crisis in 2011-2013. It is and will remain attractive: 19 EU countries with 340 million people are now members of the euro area, and two more – Croatia and Bulgaria – are sitting in the "waiting room". Their currencies must prove their worth in ERM II. Initial reservations have long since been overcome, especially in Germany, where people were skeptical about what they called "Teuro". However, after the reluctance of the first few years, the public's acceptance has increased steadily. The approval rate in the euro zone recently rose to 76 percent, 65 percent believe that the common currency is beneficial for their own country. These are record figures.[5]

---

1 Sabine Seeger founded the Euro Workshop at Villa Vigoni. She has served as correspondent for Italy, the European Union and South East Asia for the Neue Züricher Zeitungs Group, Rheinischer Merkur and VDI-Nachrichten. She now advises international companies on European affairs.
2 Roach, Stephen S., *The Vice Tightens on the Dollar*, Project Syndicate, 25 Sep. 2020.
3 James, Harold, *Late Soviet America*, Project Syndicate, 1 Jul. 2020.
4 Roubini, Nouriel, *Interview*, Project Syndicate, Oct. 2020.
5 European Commission, *Eurobarometer* 481, Nov. 2019.

Outside its borders, the euro has very quickly established itself as the second most important currency and has recovered rapidly after a period of weakness during the financial crisis ten years ago. Apart from the non-euro countries of the EU, such as Denmark, 60 countries with 175 million people have pegged their currencies to the euro in one way or another. Moreover, around 40 percent of global trade is invoiced in euros – about as much as in dollars. Additionally, the latest SWIFT data show that more than 30 percent of global payments are made in euros, while the dollar accounts for more than 40 percent. On top of this, more than 20 years after its introduction, it is fair to say that the euro has proven that it is anything but a soft currency. On the contrary, it is such a success story that it has led some politicians to speak of a currency that has what it takes to "become a big player in the international monetary world and, in the long term, to break the dominance of the US dollar as the leading currency".[6]

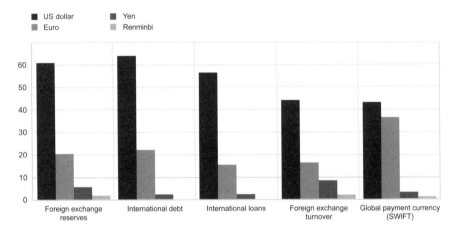

Fig. 1 The euro remains the second most important currency in the international monetary system. Source: ECB (latest data are for the fourth quarter of 2019).

When the mothers and fathers of the single currency enshrined the monetary union provisions in the Maastricht Treaty, they had the single market in mind and with it a common playing field for Europe's businesses. Few thought beyond that. "Maastricht was ultimately also a response by Europeans to globalisation", as Theo Waigel sums up in a book in honor of Horst Köhler.[7] Otmar Issing recalls: "Even before the euro saw the light of the day, there was speculation about its role as an international currency. It seemed as though a rival to the US dollar was emerging, and over and above the purely economic aspects, many saw the euro as a kind of European weapon against the super-

---

6   Oettinger, Günter, „Der Euro hat das Zeug zum Weltstar", *Tagesspiegel*, 18 Aug. 2020.
7   Waigel, Theo, *Der Euro – eine Karriere*, Freiburg im Breisgau, 2013, p. 240.

power USA".[8] Issing dismisses this as speculation, because the idea of a real use of the euro as a geopolitical instrument was considered surreal. Even the discussion was taboo for a long time. The ECB, which since 2001 has produced an annual report on the international role of the euro, took a more neutral stance, neither supporting nor opposing its internationalization. "From a policy point of view, the Eurosystem does not pursue the internationalization of the euro as an independent policy goal, which implies that it "neither fosters nor hinders this process".[9]

The Bundesbank also held back. For decades, it had resisted the international use of the D-Mark. The central bankers were driven by the concern that a greater role for the Deutsche Mark would constrain the room of manoeuvre for internal monetary policy as the Bundesbank would have to pay more attention to the sentiments of international investors. Even more Deutsche Mark assets in the hands of foreign investors could also more easily influence the exchange rate of the D-Mark. Until the 1980s, the German central bank slowed down any "globalisation" of the D-Mark, although international investors had increasingly taken a liking to the Mark. It remained faithful to its reservations even in the early stages of the euro, and thus clashed with the French, who were much more in favor of such aspirations.

Europe's early monetary policymakers did not believe in the usefulness of a stronger global role for the euro. What they saw was the absence of deeply developed financial markets and the incapacity to provide a deep and elastic supply of safe assets, not to mention an insufficient geopolitical weight or even military power. In their view, the euro did not meet the classical conditions for a major currency determined by economic size, credibility, trade relations, and financial depth.

The shortcomings were obvious and with the financial crisis it became clear that action was needed. Many measures were already taken in the aftermath of the financial crisis, some of them under pressure, and they pointed in the right direction. Nevertheless, much remained open. The "Five-Presidents-Report", which the Commission presented in June 2015, states that "Europe's Economic and Monetary Union currently offers the image of a house that has been built for decades but is only partially completed. In the midst of the storm, the walls and roof had to be quickly fixed". In order to reinforce it for the future (by consolidating the Economic and Monetary Union) the political quintet focused on completing the economic and institutional architecture. The aim was to deepen the internal market, increase competitiveness, reduce macroeconomic imbalances, coordinate economic policies more closely, unify the financial system by creating a banking union and, above all, establish a capital markets union thereby contributing to overcome the market fragmentation."[10]

---

8   Issing, Otman, *The Birth of the Euro*, Cambridge, 2008, p.176.
9   ECB, *Review of the international role of the euro*, 2001.
10 European Commission, *Five-Presidents-Report*, Jun. 2015.

The ECB also changed its stance. Under the impression of the financial crisis and the subsequent stabilization, which went hand in hand with growing attractiveness of the euro on the financial markets, it reversed course. The advantages were obvious. "It has become apparent that a stronger international role enhances monetary policy transmission, reduces the impact of exchange rate shocks and lowers financing costs" Johannes Gräb of the ECB noted when he explained the underlying motives years later.[11]

However, political reasons seemed to be decisive. The geopolitical order as we knew it until then changed radically. China's ambition of becoming a world power through expansive growth, its "Belt and Road Initiative" pushed further and further into Europe, at times threatenening to divide Europeans. The cooperative aspects of the bilateral relationship decreased, while the competitive aspects increased. The "strategic partner" turned into a "systemic rival". In the United States, Donald Trump, a man who had made "America First" his policy, took office as President. He instigated trade wars and refused to cooperate with international organizations such as the WTO – multilateralism deeply weakened. The president weaponized the dollar threatening the U.S.'s main trading partners with massive sanctions if they continued to do business with Iran. The EU's dependence on Russian gas was also a thorn in the President's side which he intended to stop by preventing the completion of the German-Russian North-Stream-2 gas pipeline – with sanctions. The dollar became a major tool of U.S. foreign policy at a time of deep and growing geopolitical rifts.

The old world power, the USA, threatened to collide with the newly emerging one, China. And in between stood Europe, which had to live with a deterioration in transatlantic relations on the one hand and the challenges of China on the other. The old continent was slipping into a dangerous sandwich position. How to assert itself was the question when Commission President Jean-Claude Juncker took the floor and promoted the "Hour of European Sovereignty" in his State of the Union address in autumn 2018. He claimed a "global political capability" for an EU as a "global player" that contributes to shaping the global way forward. Also, with the help of its currency. "The euro must become the face and the tool of the new European sovereignty", proclaimed the Luxembourger, referring to the fact that 80 percent of EU energy imports are paid for in dollars and that European airlines still handle the purchase of European aircrafts using the dollar.[12]

---

11 Gräb, Johannes, "The international role of the euro over the past two decades – developments, lessons and outlook", *Revue Bancaire et Financiere*, Forum Financier Belge, 2020, 1.

12 Juncker, Jean-Claude, *State of the Union 2018, The hour of European Sovereignty*, European Commission, Sep. 2018.

Shortly after Juncker's speech, euro area leaders encouraged the Commission to take steps to internationalize the euro. A public consultation showed that there was broad majority support for the project. Hence the Commission broadened its scope by reinforcing the euro area's internal strength. In order to do so the Commission thereby focused on completing the Economic and Monetary Union, the Banking Union, and the Capital Markets Union. This should also lead to deeper financial markets which should boost the euro as an international currency. However, a first attempt to establish a Capital Markets Union (CMU) remained elusive and forced the von-der-Leyen-Commission to launch CMU II – a crucial step in order to finally diminish the fragmentation of Europe's financial markets. The current Commission, which considers itself a "geopolitical" one, is looking at sectors that could further boost the international role of the euro, such as the use of the euro in the energy markets, in raw materials and food commodity trading, as well as in the transport sector (aviation or shipbuilders).

While a string of crucial proposals had been tabled, the specific aspect of a euro safe asset, which would attract international investors, had been overseen. The debate on this is almost as old as the euro itself and is highly controversial. Many proposals were made, none ever had a chance – until COVID-19 caught up with Europe and plunged the economy into the worst crisis since World War II. Following the pattern of "never miss a good crisis", which in the past often led to further steps towards integration, the EU leadership adopted an innovation that Council President Charles Michel celebrated as a "Copernican moment". On 21 July 2020 the 27 heads of state and government emerged from a European Council marathon with an agreement called Next Generation EU (NGEU) and a multi-year European Union budget through 2027. A compromise was reached after four days and four nights of bitter negotiations that would allow the European Commission to finance a € 750 billion fund – the Next Generation EU – through the financial markets for the first time in its history. This would result in the largest ever euro-denominated issuance at supranational level. The EU being allowed to borrow in order to finance expenditures as a collective body would break two main historical taboos: first and foremost the long time resistance to EU common issuance and, second, the fierce opposition to financial transfers within the euro zone, a "conditio sine qua non" for northern countries such as Germany to join the monetary union. The step represents a quantum leap that could lead to a certain degree of burden sharing on the one hand, and on the other hand form the core for a centralized fiscal capacity, thus filling a gap perceived by many in the construction of the Economic and Monetary Union. The agreement not only "signaled a political readiness to design a common fiscal tool when the need arises", the ECB stated, "it could, while a one-off, also imply lessons for Economic and Monetary Union, which still lacks a permanent fiscal capacity at supranational level for macroeconomic stabilization in deep crises.[13]

---

13 "The fiscal implications of the EU's recovery package", *ECB Economic Bulletin*, Issue 6/2020, Sep. 2020.

However, at the moment of writing, the agreement still has to overcome two major obstacles: on the one hand, it requires the approval of the European Parliament, which is still pending because of the hitherto very vague formulation of the commitment of the Fund's resources to the rule of law. On the other hand, it has to be ratified by the Member States, which is likely to be difficult, especially in countries such as Hungary and Poland, precisely because of this commitment. Even if these pitfalls are overcome, it is not yet clear whether the new package would prove effective. In order to do so disbursements have to fulfill the purposes of structural reform and the modalities be handled efficiently and flexibly. Finally, there is the issue of internal coherence, because what the Member States have to face now has very different effects and depends on how they entered the crisis.

Since the COVID-19 crisis has served as a catalyst to fill the remaining gaps within the preconditions for a stronger international role of the euro, many are now fulfilled, at least on the political and fiscal side. Yet if one follows the logic of Barry Eichengreen, Arnaud J. Mehl and Livia Chitu,[14] according to which an international currency must follow not only pecuniary motives, such as safety, liquidity, network effects, trade links etc. (also called the "Mercury hypothesis"), but also geopolitical ones, such as political and military strength and assertiveness ("Mars hypothesis"), then it must be concluded that the latter are missing. Too often the EU is divided on key issues and has difficulties reaching common decisions. In foreign policy, its influence falls far short of its economic size. Its security policy efforts are still in their infancy, despite all the pledges to build a security and defense union. Too often Europe follows the "small country syndrome", as observed by Marco Buti,[15] former director general for economic and financial affairs at the European Commission, by not playing a more important role in global matters. So there is still a long way to go.

Conclusion

Certainly, it was not only the greatly weakened projection of the US dollar that brought the euro into sharper focus, but also a lot of efforts done by European leadership. The efforts for a deeper and more complete European Monetary Union, by advancing the Banking Union and the Capital Markets Union in the context of the pursuit of sound economic policies in the euro area, made a difference. Despite international trade disputes and geopolitical tensions, the international role of the euro has stabilized. "The

---

14 Eichengreen, Barry, Arnaud J. Mehl and Livia Chitu, "Mars or Mercury? The geopolitics of international currency choice", *NBER Working Paper Series*, Working Paper 24145, Dec. 2017.
15 Marco Buti, "The international role of the euro", *SUERF Policy Note*, n. 174, Jun. 2020.

euro remained unchallenged as the second most important currency in the international monetary system", concludes the ECB.[16] However as long as the common currency still lacks real political power it will not develop to a "world star". If it really wants to emerge from the shadow of the dollar, Europe must be guided more by Mars and demonstrate geopolitical strategic capability. Hence it must gain credibility, and this requires first and foremost internal coherence in order to be effective and powerful externally. Member States will emerge from the crisis in varying degrees, which exacerbates the issue of further convergence. While the needs of the less strong are taken into account in the "Next Generation EU" package, it remains to be seen whether the strategic effects will be achieved. Cooperation on security is there, but it is still in its early stages. Only when it really stands, when firm structures are in place, will it shape the euro's global standing and provide an opportunity to break the dominance of the dollar.

---

16   European Central Bank, *The international role of the euro*, Jun. 2020.